Mrs. Lench 12-4-73

3.95

Talking Your Way Around the World

Books by Mario Pei

Published by Harper & Row

The *Holiday* Magazine Language Books for the Traveler:
  Getting Along in Spanish (with Eloy Vaquero)
  Getting Along in Italian
How to Learn Languages and What Languages to Learn
Talking Your Way Around the World

Published by J. B. Lippincott Co.

The Story of Language
All About Language
The Story of the English Language

Published by Doubleday & Co.

Invitation to Linguistics
A Glossary of Linguistic Terminology

Published by the Devin-Adair Co.

Language for Everybody
One Language for the World

Published by Holt, Rinehart & Winston

First-Year French (with E. Méras)

Published by Lothrop, Lee & Shepard Co., Inc.

The Book of Place Names (with E. Lambert)
Our Names (with E. Lambert)

Published by Vanni Publications

The Italian Language
The Language of the Eighth-Century Texts in Northern France
The World's Chief Languages

Published by Ams Press, Inc.

The Families of Words
Voices of Man

Published by Funk & Wagnalls

Language Today

Published by Alfred Knopf

The Many Hues of English

Published by Hawthorn Books

What's in a Word
Words in Sheep's Clothing

Talking Your Way Around the World

enlarged third edition

Mario Pei
Professor Emeritus of Romance Philology
Columbia University

Harper & Row, Publishers
New York · Evanston · San Francisco · London

413
P

ENLARGED THIRD EDITION PUBLISHED 1971

STANDARD BOOK NUMBER: 06-013327-9

LIBRARY OF CONGRESS CATALOG CARD NUMBER: 78-138755

contents

acknowledgments

The author gratefully acknowledges his indebtedness to the Curtis Publishing Company for permitting the use in this work of the material contained in the author's *Holiday* magazine articles, as follows: "Watch Your Language," January 1954; "Want to Speak French?" March 1955; "Italy: the Language," April 1955; "English for Americans," July 1955; "Spanish Is Easy," January 1956; "One World Language," March 1956; "Beginner's Portuguese," November 1956; "A Start in German," January 1957; "Want to Speak Russian?" October 1958; "Who Said Latin Is Dead?" November 1958; "Swahili," April 1959; "The Hebrew Language," December 1967.

The author is further indebted to the Curtis Publishing Company for permitting the use of material from an article on the Japanese language to appear prior to publication in *Holiday*.

The author also wishes gratefully to acknowledge his indebtedness to Hearst Magazines, Incorporated, for permission to use the material contained in his *Good Housekeeping* magazine article, "Would You Care to Say It in Chinese?" (December 1944).

Part of the material contained in the chapter "World Pidgins" appeared in an article entitled "Pidgin English Around the World," published by the monthly magazine *Tomorrow* in January 1950.

All of the original magazine articles have been suitably expanded, modified, and brought up to date to adapt them to present-day tourist needs.

The author further wishes to acknowledge with gratitude the assistance he received from various colleagues and friends in the compilation of this material, particularly from Professor Ichiro Shirato, of the Department of Japanese of Columbia University, who carefully examined and revised the Japanese article, and Dr. Pao-Ch'en Lee, chairman of the Department of Mandarin Chinese of the United States Army Language School, Presidio of Monterey, Cal., who examined and revised the Chinese article and supplied lists of phrases and expressions. Dr. Alphonse Chaurize, Semitic scholar and editor of the New York Arabic-language weekly *Al-Isla'ah*, supplied much of the material for the Arabic chapter that has been added to this edition.

chapter one
watch your language
the languages of europe

Once there was an American who went to Europe. Wherever he traveled, he sought one thing he couldn't find—American bread. In vain the Europeans paraded their choicest bread products before him—long French loaves, round, crusty Italian loaves, Spanish *bollos*, twisted Vienna bread, German dark rye and pumpernickel. He was unhappy. Finally, one day in Florence, he came upon a restaurant run by Americans for Americans, where good, tasteless, crustless American sandwich bread was on display. In his boundless joy, he gratefully inscribed on a souvenir paper fan over his signature: "At last —at long last—I have found, on European soil, a piece of American bread!"

The souvenir fan was left in the restaurant for all to see and admire. Before it came to my notice, it had gone through various hands. Another American tourist had added his comment in a bold hand: "Mister, if American bread means that much to you, why didn't you stay in Peoria, where all the bakeries carry it?"

What goes for bread goes for language. If you think the entire world should speak English (which it well may some day); if you bristle at the strange sound of foreign voices speaking foreign tongues; if you wonder, as did an old lady of my acquaintance, why foreigners utter such uncouth words as *pain* and *Brot* and *khljeb* when it would be ever so much simpler for them to say *bread*, this article is not for you, but this prophecy is: You will either remain in America, where

1

everyone says *bread*, or, if you travel abroad, you will spend your days touring the churches and museums under the watchful eye of an English-speaking guide, and your evenings in the hotel lobby writing home to the folks and insincerely telling them you wish they were there.

But if you are possessed of the bold, venturesome spirit that urges you to go forth into the highways and byways of a foreign land, explore its culinary marvels in the restaurants and inns where the natives gather, and listen for the musical cadences of their strange speech forms, then Europe is indeed your oyster.

The keynote of Europe is variety—variety of political institutions and mental processes, religions and beliefs, customs and habits, landscape and architecture, food, drink, and dress; but above all, variety of language. Where in America you travel for days by train or car and hear the same familiar speech, with only minor variations, in Europe an overnight journey is almost sure to take you into a land utterly different from the one you left; and the major factor in the difference is usually the language.

This can be either a source of annoyance bordering on torture, or a glorious adventure in the novel and the unforeseen. Which it is depends entirely on you and your outlook. You can feel bewildered, frustrated, resentful, isolated like a pariah— or intrigued, charmed, fascinated and athirst for knowledge. As you pass from a country whose language you handle reasonably well to one where you are linguistically a babe in arms, you can come close to unreasoning terror or bask in delightful anticipation. With the right spirit, you can view each new linguistic encounter as an absorbing quest; without it, as a devastating ordeal.

But let us get a few things straight. If you don't care for foreign languages, you can still get along, because catering to tourists is one of Europe's most ancient trades. Just stick to the beaten paths, the hotel clerks, and the guides, and you will find, as some tourists gleefully report, that "everybody in Europe speaks English."

Secondly, do not think that anyone, even among the most traveled Europeans, speaks all the languages of the Continent. There are far too many. If a man spent his life doing nothing but learning languages, he would die long before he reached the end of the European roster. This means that on your travels in any European country you will find many native Europeans in the same linguistic boat with you. And it is an interesting fact about languages that, no matter how many you know, when you come across an unfamiliar one you are just as helpless and ineffectual as the man who knows only his own.

You can't learn them all. But can you learn something about them, enough to react (not respond) intelligently to them, know what charms to look for in them, be able to identify them, so that you won't think you are in Finland when you are in Norway, or in Greece when you are in Yugoslavia? That you can do, and quite easily. Such knowledge may, on occasion, be of some practical help, and it also gives you a start, a jumping-off place, in case you want to investigate any one language more thoroughly.

Is there any basic language preparation that the tourist can make, any advice that the linguist can offer in this welter of tongues?

Brief, basic grammars, and particularly phrase books such as G.I.'s used in World War II, will help considerably. Don't think, by the way, that phrase books are a modern invention; one of the earliest known, the Glosses of Kassel, was compiled in the eighth century A.D. to help Germanic people going into Romance countries to speak a few useful sentences, such as: "Shave the back of my neck." Thoroughly up-to-date manuals of this sort, covering the main European languages, are the author's *The World's Chief Languages* and Archibald Lyall's *Guide to the Languages of Europe*.

One other piece of advice is of a more personal kind. Drop your inhibitions and start speaking, even if you have mastered only a few words of a language. The natives will almost invariably understand you, and they'll love you for making the try. Don't worry if you don't understand everything they say back to you. They will speak more slowly, use sign language, or switch to English, but it will give both them and you a glow of satisfaction to know that you're deferring to their language instead of imposing your own. I shall never forget how the elevator operator in a Budapest hotel beamed every time I called out my floor in his language.

What are the dozen or so most useful expressions to know in each language? Here they are:

"Good morning" (or "Good day," or "Good afternoon," or "Good evening").

"How are you?"

"Good-by."

"Thank you."

"You're welcome" (in the sense of "don't mention it"; our American expression often makes foreigners think we are more hospitable than is actually the case).

"Please."

"Give me." (Add "please" at every opportunity; a bald "Give me" is considered impolite in most languages.)

"How much?"

"Where is?" "Where are?"

"Do you speak English?" (or any other language you happen to know).

"I don't understand."

"Speak more slowly." (This is terribly important. Foreign languages are not spoken faster than English; you only think so because you are not used to them. Remind the foreigner to slow down, and you will understand him much better.)

"Glad to meet you."

"Come in!"

"Fine (or bad) weather." (Yes, they like to discuss the weather abroad too. If you join in, you will soon automatically learn the words for warm, hot, cold, wind, rain, and so on.)

Add to these the basic numerals—one to ten, then by tens to a hundred, and a thousand.

All this will take you only a couple of hours in each language, and you will be amazed at the magic effect it will produce.

With a few minor exceptions, all the languages of Europe belong to the same great language family, called Indo-European, because it includes most of Europe and stretches eastward all the way to India. It may surprise you to learn of this kinship between English, Welsh, French, German, Russian, Greek, and Hindustani, but it is easily provable. In fact, all these languages were originally one (not that this makes it easier to learn them).

The parent language, splitting up in the course of prehistoric migrations, gave rise to separate groups—Celtic, Teutonic, Italic, Slavic, Greek, Albanian, to name only the principal European members. Most of these subdivisions split in turn into separate languages. The chief representatives of Celtic today are Irish, Welsh, and Breton. Teutonic gave rise to English, German, Dutch, and the Scandinavian tongues (Swedish, Norwegian, Danish and Icelandic). Italic, through Latin, became the well-known Romance languages: French, Spanish, Portuguese, Italian, Rumanian. Slavic branched out into Russian, Ukrainian, Polish, Czech, Serbo-Croatian and Bulgarian. Greek and Albanian, however, still stand undivided.

Missing from the Indo-European roster, you will notice, are some well-publicized European languages: Finnish, Hungarian, and Turkish, all of which belong to a distinct family whose original homeland was Siberia; and the picturesque Basque of the Franco-Spanish Pyrenean border, which is thought to be the sole survivor of a large group of languages spoken in Europe before the arrival of Indo-European. Basque is extremely complicated; legend says that the devil spent seven years trying to learn it so that he might tempt its speakers, then gave up in disgust, having learned only how to say "yes" and "no."

Here is striking proof of the fundamental kinship of most European languages—the little numeral "three":

Dutch—*drie*	Russian, Serbo-Croatian,
German—*drei*	Bulgarian—*tri*
Swedish, Norwegian,	Polish—*trzy*
Danish—*tre*	Czech—*tři*
Icelandic—*thrír*	Greek—*treis*
French—*trois*	Albanian—*tre*
Spanish—*tres*	Lithuanian—*trỹs*
Portuguese—*três*	Irish—*trí*
Italian—*tre*	Welsh—*trī*
Rumanian—*trei*	Esperanto—*tri*

But look at the same numeral in the languages outside the Indo-European group:

Finnish—*kolme*	Turkish—*üç*
Hungarian—*három*	Basque—*hirur*

But you are not approaching these languages historically; you are coming to them geographically, by plane or steamer, in the twentieth century. Why tell you of their past history? Simply because it has a distinct bearing on their present-day relationships, and on the ease with which you may acquire them.

Your English is basically Teutonic, a legacy from the Anglo-Saxons who founded the language, and who were among the Teutonic or Germanic invaders who in the fifth century A.D. took over most of the Roman Empire. This means that the rock-bottom words of English have direct counterparts in the other Teutonic languages, German, Dutch and Scandinavian. But the Normans, who wrested England from the Anglo-Saxons in 1066, spoke French, and many of their words came into use in English. That is why an English speaker feels at home with a large part of the vocabulary of the Romance languages. As for our learned and scientific words, they come mainly from Latin and Greek, and since practically all other civilized languages have taken such words from the same sources, we find a common high-plane vocabulary with all of them.

This is of some help, but not too much. Each language has its own sound pattern, and even where words resemble each other in writing they may diverge widely in speech. Take the word *nation*, as pronounced in English and in French; the former says *NAY-shun*, the latter *nah-SYÕ*.

Sometimes this difference in sound pattern causes trouble within what is supposed to be a single language. When you go to Europe, the chances are you will first touch the British Isles, where the official language, save in Éire, is our own English. But what a difference between the pronunciation, enunciation, and pitch of our American language and those of the King's English! And the King's English is far from being the only speech form of Britain. There are local dialects and intonations—the brogues and burrs of Ireland and Scotland, the melodious singsong of Wales, the staccato of the London Cockney, the harsh vigor of the northern speech, the deliberate utterance of the Midlands—that make English practically a foreign tongue.

The struggle in the mind of the American in Britain is between his sense of the picturesque and his desire for understanding, for what is gain to the one is loss to the other. What is he to do with the "soft mornin' " of Ireland and the "butterfly day" of Sussex, the "lippen" (believe) of Scotland and the "shan" (shall) of Yorkshire, or even the "lay-by" (hidden driveway) and "aubergine" (eggplant) of official English?

But English, after all, is English, and even a mass of differences in pronunciation, spelling, and semantics can't change the fact. If the conversational going gets too tough in certain corners of Britain, the American can always fall back on the device used in China by persons from different parts of the country—he can hold out paper and pencil and say, "Please write it out."

But before you leave Britain for the Continent, you can make your first venture into a fully foreign tongue—the Welsh of Cardiff, or the Scots Gaelic of the Highlands, or the Irish of Éire. (Don't call the Irish language Erse, by the way; this is a name bestowed upon it by the English, and the Irish don't care for it.) Here we have three offshoots from the Celtic branch of Indo-European, whose only near relative on the Continent is the Breton of France. Celtic was at one time far more widespread, because it was spoken by the ancient Gauls described by Julius Caesar in his *Gallic Wars*. But the Gauls became Romanized, learned Latin, and eventually turned into French speakers, so that this largest branch of Celtic withered away. Irish and Welsh remained alive through conquests and vicissitudes. In prehistoric times, Irish invaders settled in Scotland, merged with the aboriginal Picts, and gave rise to the Scots Gaelic, which only a few Scots continue to speak today.

The Irish were conquered by the English in the Middle Ages, and the use of the ancient Irish language was, to put it mildly, discouraged, with the result that it tended to disappear save in a few sheltered spots—in the Galway region, for instance, called *Gaeltacht* or land of the Gaels. By the time Éire regained its independence, less than one quarter of its people spoke Irish. The rest used English with an Irish brogue, definitely a survival of Irish-language intonations and sounds, living on through the centuries in the mouths of people who no longer spoke the ancestral language.

The government of Éire has been making strong efforts to restore the Irish language, and with some success. But the going is hard, because English is a great world tongue of immense prestige and practical value. American travelers in Éire report that the country is plastered with signs urging the cutting of the last linguistic bond with England, and the use of Irish instead of English—but the signs are all in English.

Typical of Irish are the nasal twangs that are faithfully

carried over into the brogue still heard among first-generation
Irishmen in America. So is the beautiful but highly misleading
Irish alphabet, which comes straight down from the uncial
characters of the early Middle Ages. Written Irish is the only
language in the world that can vie with English for spelling
difficulties.

Welsh, too, has spelling and pronunciation troubles. The
Welsh use *w* and *y* as pure vowels, and their written *ll* represents a sound that most foreigners find it impossible to reproduce (Llewellyn, to an untrained ear, sounds somewhat
like Sheweshin); moreover, it is a current joke among linguists
and non-linguists alike that one of the longest word combinations to be found in any language is the Welsh place name
Llanfairpwllgwyngyllgogeryghwyrndrobwllllantysiliogogogoch,
meaning "the Church of St. Mary near the raging whirlpool
and the Church of St. Tysilio by the red cave."

Welsh was the tongue of the Britons who were driven westward by the Anglo-Saxons in one of the earliest historical
conquests of Britain (some preferred to sail for the Continent,
landed in northwestern France, and gave rise to Breton). The
name Welsh was bestowed upon them by their Saxon foes and
means "foreigners." Their own proud name for themselves is
Cymri, whence Cumberland. During the Middle Ages, Welsh
lost ground before English, but not to the same extent as
Irish. Out of nearly 2,600,000 people in Wales today, roughly
half speak Welsh, and perhaps a quarter million do not speak
English at all.

All considered, the American traveling in Britain will encounter quaintness and strangeness, but no real difficulties in
the way of language. His troubles begin when he touches the
Continent, say, in France. The French-speaking world stretches from Cherbourg or Le Havre almost to the Rhine, and from
the Belgian lowlands to the Swiss and Italian Alps, the
Spanish Pyrenees and the blue Mediterranean—a unified,
standardized world in which the numerous local *patois* seem to
be almost submerged by the refined Parisian tongue, regulated
and regimented since Richelieu's time by the dictates of the
French Academy. If one cares to delve into the nooks and
corners, of course, one finds that this unity of *la belle langue
française* is more apparent than real, and that the great
medieval dialects of Normandy, Picardy, Lorraine, and dozens
of other provinces live on, along with the Walloon of Belgium,

the Romand of western Switzerland, the rich, tangy Provençal and Languedocien of the *Midi*.

French is one of the great American high-school languages, and many Americans advance upon Europe with what they fondly believe is a smattering of the French speech. They are quickly undeceived. French is far more than an assortment of irregular verbs and a sprinkling of textbook sentences in which the hat of my grandmother lies on the chair in the room for dining. It is a rich, living tongue, full of the *argot* of the *banlieues* and the slang of Parisian taxi drivers. The language of restaurant menus approaches its essence, but you can't forever talk of *cuisine*. French is, above all, a matter of pronunciation—full-bodied nasals, well-rounded middle vowels in which the out-thrust lips play a prominent part, precisely uttered consonants, calculated tempo, and rhythmical modulation. Good French is a delight to the ear, but also a source of unending wonderment to the uninitiated. It is also the most rewarding of the continental tongues in terms of what it will bring you in the way of courtesy, friendliness, and service if you succeed in proving to the natives that you know how to use it. The French speaker, like the English speaker, thinks everyone ought to know his language.

Two of France's neighbors, Belgium and Switzerland, have French as one of their official languages. In Belgium, French is co-official with Flemish, a conservative form of Dutch. When the medieval Low Countries split into two separate and independent nations, they did so along religious rather than linguistic lines, the Catholic Flamands preferring the company of the French-speaking Walloons to that of the Protestant Dutch.

Flemish and Dutch constitute an excellent introduction to the Teutonic languages of the Continent. They are close to Anglo-Saxon English in sound scheme and vocabulary, and it is surprising how many words and expressions are identical or nearly so. *Water* and *over* and *nek* and *kat* need no translation. *Ziek* and *deur* and *boek* sound almost like their English counterparts, *sick, door, book*. Who could fail to understand *dank U wel, hier is, wat kost 't?, 'n kop koffie?*

Not all Dutch is quite so simple, particularly since the written tongue uses what the Dutch jocularly label *stadhuiswoorden* ("City Hall words"), which they avoid in speech. Yet to an American, even more than to a Britisher, there is something atavistically reminiscent about Dutch. It isn't merely that the old Anglo-Saxons and the ancestors of the present-day Hollanders used practically the same Low German speech; there is also the fact that the Dutch founders of Nieuw Amsterdam have left us Americans a heritage that comes to the surface in words like *boss*, *stoop* and *cole slaw* and names like Roosevelt, Schuyler, Schermerhorn and Van Cortlandt. It may be worth remarking that in Dutch *sch* is not pronounced *sh*, as in German, but *s* followed by a quick clearing of the throat, and that the Dutch make the same guttural sound when they pronounce their written *g; goed* means "good," but what you hear is *hood*.

Beyond the Dutch frontier lies another world, the German, which is numerically the strongest in continental Europe. Not only is German spoken in practically all of the former Reich, in Austria, in most of Switzerland, in corners of France and Belgium and Italy; it is also (or was, until the end of the last war) the common medium of exchange of central Europe and a large part of the Balkans. German can be used in Czechoslovakia, Hungary, and northern Yugoslavia, countries that once formed part of the Austro-Hungarian Empire, and to a slightly lesser degree in Holland, Denmark, Sweden, and Poland. Even today, with the German-speaking world split in two by the Iron Curtain, it is a safe guess that at least one hundred million Europeans can be reached with *die deutsche Sprache*. Like all languages, great and small, German is crisscrossed by dialect lines. The current speech of Bremen and Hamburg differs materially from that of Berlin, which, in turn, is almost a foreign tongue in Vienna. Three quarters of Switzerland speaks German, or rather what the Swiss fondly call *Schwyzer-Tütsch*, whose speech forms are so individualistic that some Swiss have seriously proposed that it be set up as a separate language.

Official, standard German, like official, standard French, is one of our favorite high-school tongues. Its forms were for the most part set by Martin Luther's translation of the Bible, and it is a compromise between the Low German dialects of the seacoast and the High German of the uplands, with an edge in favor of the latter, which means that official German is farther removed from English than is Dutch.

German preserves the old Teutonic cases—nominative, genitive, dative, accusative—which English had and lost. It also preserves an archaic Teutonic word order which once aroused Mark Twain to satire: "I know not, where you this book bought have." But languages don't have to apologize for their forms to foreign learners; it suffices that they serve the needs of their own speakers.

In the extreme north of Europe are the Scandinavian tongues, Danish, Norwegian, and Swedish, with an Atlantic spearhead in Icelandic, the language of less than 200,000 people, a tongue so archaic that it comes closer than modern English to the Anglo-Saxon of the days of King Alfred. (Finnish, it may be remarked at this point, is definitely *not* a Scandinavian language, nor even an Indo-European one.) The Scandinavian tongues are as Teutonic as English and German, but form part of a separate branch. In theory, English should be closer to German than to Scandinavian. But before the coming of the Normans, vast droves of Scandinavians occupied northeastern England, mingled with the Anglo-Saxons, and influenced the course of our language, with the result that many of our basic English words are not Saxon, but Scandinavian. When you say, "They are ill," for instance, you are using three Scandinavian words. When you say, "Take the knife and cut the steak," only *the* and *and* are Anglo-Saxon; the rest is Scandinavian.

The continental Scandinavian languages are so close that it is relatively easy for a Dane, a Norwegian, and a Swede to understand one another. At the same time, each is proud of his linguistic individuality. Once, when I used a Danish written form to a Norwegian, he haughtily replied: "That word is Danish, and the Danes can keep it!" The fact of the matter is, however, that for a long time the Norwegians used Danish as their written language, and only recently have they swung over to an official tongue based on their own *Landsmål*.

One of the charming features of Swedish and Norwegian is the lilt, or pitch accent, of the spoken tongues. When a Swede says *flicka* ("girl"), it comes out in a sort of three-syllable singsong—*fli-i-cka*—with the first and last syllables pitched a couple of notes higher than the middle one. Norwegians and Swedes in our midst almost invariably give themselves away by transferring this lilt to their acquired English. And their drinking *skoal* (*skål*), if you observe it carefully, is a full-fledged ritual inherited from the ancient Vikings.

Coming back from cold Scandinavia to the sunny Mediterranean southlands means only a twenty-four-hour train trip—
unless you tarry awhile on the linguistic borderline between
the Teutonic and the Romance areas. The best place to do
your tarrying is indisputably Switzerland, for here you have a
multilingual nation whose inhabitants like and respect one
another regardless of the tongue they speak. Switzerland is a
mighty monument to the proposition that people don't have
to speak the same language if their hearts are in the right
place. Most of Switzerland speaks German, or rather, *Schwyzer-Tütsch;* the western corners, around Geneva and Lausanne,
speak a variety of French; the extreme south speaks Italian.

One section of the country, the Engadine, in Graubünden,
uses a Romance language variously named Rhetian, Romansch
or Ladin, a survival of the Vulgar Latin of the legions that
Rome sent up into the mountains to guard her northern
frontier. Romansch may be described as a cross between
French and Italian, with a few harsh guttural sounds from the
nearby German speakers, and a wealth of strange vowel
sounds that charm the ear, even as the written form dazzles
the eye, because in the vicinity of St. Moritz all the houses
bear poetic Romansch inscriptions over their doorways. One
time in the Engadine, fascinated by the sound of Romansch
and urged on by professional curiosity, I walked about eaves-
dropping on conversations until I was almost arrested as a spy.

A short bus ride across the border lies Italy, land of *bel
canto* and the world's most diversified dialects. It is perfectly
possible for two Italians, each speaking his own local tongue,
not to understand each other at all. When they lapse into the
standard national tongue, based largely on Dante's Tuscan,
the effect pleases the ear and charms the spirit. Here is a
tongue of smooth sounds and pure vocalic endings, super-
latively suited for singing and declamation, the most direct
descendant, among all the Romance varieties, of the sonorous
Latin of the Roman orators and poets and the early Christian
writers. But even cultured Italians carry over into their national language the intonations of their local dialects—the
staccato, precise utterance of the north, or the mellow pitch
of Florence, the jocular grumble of Rome, the infinite modulation of Naples, the explosive puffs of Sicily. Sardinia, which is
a steppingstone to the Hispanic lands of the west, speaks
another tongue, one which the linguists have decided is not an

Italian dialect at all, but rather a petrified survival of the popular Latin of republican Rome.

Other steppingstones to Spain are the Balearic Islands, where the visitor will hear a language that is not Spanish, not French, yet close to each. It is called Catalan, and he will hear it again in Barcelona and the nearby Catalonian countryside. Catalan is a controversial tongue, claimed by the Spaniards as a Spanish dialect, by the French as an offshoot of Provençal, and by the Catalans as a proud separate Romance language. Its history goes back to the early Middle Ages, and there was a period when both Catalan and the Galician of northwestern Spain vied with Castilian for the post of official tongue of the Iberian Peninsula. Castilian ultimately won, turning into standard Spanish, while Galician, defeated on its own home ground, spread southward and gave rise to Portuguese.

Spanish is another of America's favorite high-school languages. With Portuguese, it moved on to the Western Hemisphere, and while both languages assumed various dialectal forms in the process, they are still fairly standardized. There are strong links between Spanish and Portuguese, but there are also essential differences, as Americans discover when they try their college Spanish in Portuguese-speaking Brazil. There is even a story to the effect that a Brazilian, incensed at a statement that anyone knowing Spanish could at least read Portuguese, composed a letter in which nothing but a few prepositions and conjunctions coincided in the two languages. A window is *ventana* in Spanish, *janela* in Portuguese. Monday is *lunes* in one language, *segunda féira* in the other. The Portuguese are fond of the diminutive suffix *-inho*, which the Spaniards deride.

The list of European lands that Americans normally visit now grows small. In the Balkans there are three—Turkey, Greece, and Yugoslavia. Turkey's European holdings, which once extended to the very gates of Vienna, are small, and Istanbul, astride the Bosphorus, is the only European city where Turkish is extensively used. The language is an Asiatic one, unconnected with the Indo-European tongues, and very remotely linked with Finnish and Hungarian. Its structure is agglutinative, which means that many of its words are extremely long; a single Turkish verb form means "to be impossible to be made to be loved." In the 1920's, Kemâl Atatürk gave Turkish a Roman alphabet in the place of the

Arabic, and at the same time purged the language of the numerous Arabic and Persian loan words it had acquired in the course of many years of cultural dependence.

Greek is a tongue with which most educated persons of former generations were somewhat familiar, for our colleges and high schools taught it extensively. It is perhaps a pity that this practice has been discontinued, because at no time has the Greek language made such extensive contributions to our own as in these days of scientific and technological advance, when every new electronic, atomic, or antibiotic gadget receives a name derived from Greek roots.

The spoken Athenian of today comes closer to the language of Aristotle and Sophocles than does any Romance tongue to Latin. A man trained in classical Greek can, with a moderate amount of effort, read a present-day Greek newspaper, and the tourist who chooses to inspect the Parthenon and the Acropolis can recognize in the language spoken around him many of his own more cultural roots. *Efkharistó* is the modern "thank you," and the mind goes back to the Eucharist, a thanksgiving offering. "*Kakos*," says the modern Greek, shaking his head, meaning that something or somebody is bad, and if you are linguistically minded you will think of *cacophony*, a bad sound. The Greek alphabet is still the same, and if you glance at the store signs in Athens or Patras you will see sigmas and deltas and pis and omegas that remind you of mathematical symbols or, if that is how your mind works, of American fraternities and sororities.

Yugoslavia, "land of the South Slavs," is the only Slavic land left on our side of the Iron Curtain. Here the tourist will hear the soft melody of Serbo-Croatian, a tongue as mellifluous as the music of the *tamburitsa* and the strains of the *kolo*, along with the closely allied Slovenian of the hilly country around Trieste. Serbs and Croats speak pretty much the same tongue, but the former, being affiliated with the Eastern Church, write in a Cyrillic alphabet that comes close to the Russian, while the Catholic Croatians use Roman letters. One by-product is that Yugoslav place names are spelled out in both alphabets at railroad stations.

Serbo-Croatian is a typically Slavic language, with many cases for the nouns and aspects for the verbs, and its structure comes close to that of original Indo-European. Despite its musicality, Serbo-Croatian presents some apparently un-pronounceable words, like *Trst*, the Yugoslav name of Trieste, and *Krk*, the name of an Adriatic island called Veglia by the Italians. The trick is to pronounce the trilled *r* as though it were accompanied by a vowel, somewhat like English *kirk* and *thirst*. Anyone who gains a knowledge of Serbo-Croatian will not find the other Slavic languages too difficult.

These differences in geographical names for the same locality have to be taken into account. Sometimes the name remains nearly the same in various languages: the Italian Venezia becomes Venice, Venise, Venedig to the Englishman, Frenchman, and German. But there are cases where the change is drastic. The German form of Alsace-Lorraine, for instance, is Elsass-Lothringen. The Danube is the Donau, Duna, Dunaj, Dunav and Dunarea, according to whose land it flows through. If you found yourself in a country that called itself Sverige or Hellas, perhaps you would know it was Sweden or Greece; but would names like Suomi or Magyarország help you realize that you were in Finland or Hungary?

What of those remote lands behind the great Curtain, and their languages—Polish and Czech and Slovak and Bulgarian, akin to the tongues of Yugoslavia and also to the Russian and Ukrainian of the Soviet Union? What of Hungarian, a strange, isolated Asiatic tongue transplanted to the very heart of Europe by Árpád's Magyars, a group closely related to Attila's Huns? What of Rumanian, which has come down from the Latin of Trajan's legions, and is now under subjection to the hated Slavs? What of Albanian, that mountain tongue of the Balkans that is neither Greek, nor Romance, nor Slavic? The list could continue with the Lithuanian and Lettish of the Baltic, close to Slavic and yet different, and their next-door neighbor Estonian, which is not at all like either but has links with Finnish and Hungarian; with the numerous non-Russian tongues of European Russia, the Armenian and Georgian and Lesghian of the Caucasus, the Karelian of the north, the Tatar of the Crimea. All these are languages with which immediate contact is improbable; they are lost to the curious traveler, at least until saner times dawn over the world.

One other language belongs in our survey—Esperanto, the "language of hope." It is an artificial tongue, deliberately constructed to serve international purposes, and while it has little currency in the United States, it is fairly widespread in Europe and other parts of the world. (You will know its speakers by the little green star they wear in the lapel.) When the Gallup Poll asked free Europeans in several countries what language they would like to see established as a universal tongue, they chose English first and Esperanto second. It is a language of simple rules and no exceptions, with a grammar that can be condensed to a single page and a vocabulary drawn mainly from Latin, Greek, English, German, and the Romance languages—with practically no Slavic elements, which is strange, considering that its inventor, Lazarus Ludwig Zamenhof, was a native of Poland.

Esperanto is relatively easy to learn, easy to speak, read, and write, and many western Europeans have succumbed to its spell. One day, perhaps, it will save you the trouble of learning many languages. Or perhaps English, mightiest of the Free World's tongues, will take over the task. But for the present, the Tower of Babel stands, and you can still tour its western European corner without exhausting yourself. After all, western Europe has no more than thirty of the world's 2,796 languages.

GOOD MORNING

Here is how you say "good morning" or "good day" in Europe. In the Germanic languages, your greeting takes in the morning; in the Romance and the Slavic-Lithuanian tongues, it covers the whole day. English *day*, German *Tag*, and similar Scandinavian and Dutch forms come from one Indo-European root; Russian *dyen'*, Spanish *día*, Rumanian *ziuă*, Albanian *dita*, Lithuanian *dienà*, Welsh *dydd* come from another. Esperanto, trying to be neutral, borrows "good" from Romance, "day" from German.

German—*guten Morgen*   (GOO-tuhn MAWR-guhn).
Dutch—*goeden morgen*   (HOO-yeh MOR-heh).
Swedish, Norwegian, Danish—*god morgon*   (GODE MAWR-guhn).
French—*bonjour*   (bŏ-ZHOOR).
Spanish—*buenos días*   (BWEH-nohs DEE-ahs).
Portuguese—*bons dias*   (BŌSH DEE-ahsh).
Italian—*buon giorno*   (BWAWN JOHR-noh).
Rumanian—*bună ziua*   (BOO-nuh ZEE-wah).
Russian—*dobry dyen'*   (DAW-bree D'EHN'; *n'* like *ny* in "canyon").

Polish—*dzień dobry* (JEHN' DAW-bry; *dz* like *j* in "John," *ń* like Russian *n'* above).
Czech—*dobrý den* (DAW-bree DEHN).
Serbo-Croatian—*dobar dan* (DAW-bahr DAHN).
Lithuanian—*laba dieną* (LAH-bah DYEH-nah).
Welsh—*dydd da* (DEETH DAH; *dd* like *th* in "this").
Greek—*kaliméra* (kah-lyee-MEH-rah).
Albanian—*mirë dita* (MEE-ruh DEE-tah).
Finnish—*hyvää huomenta* (HÜ-va HWO-men-tah).
Hungarian—*jó reggelt* (YOH REG-gelt).
Turkish—*gün aydın* (GÜN EYE-duhn).
Esperanto—*bonan tagon* (BOH-nahn TAH-gohn).

HOW MUCH?

Since you'll probably do some shopping in Europe, it's a good idea to equip yourself to ask, "How much does it cost?" The answer you get may be in English, in sign language, or in what sounds like gibberish, but the shopkeeper will pretty surely be flattered to hear you using his language. Of the twenty-one expressions below, eleven use some form of our word "cost."

German—*Wieviel kostet es?* (vee-FEEL KOST-et ES)?
Dutch—*Wat kost 't?* (VAHT KOST it)?
Swedish—*Hur mycket kostar det?* (HÜR MIK-et KOST-ar DET)?
Danish and Norwegian—*Hvor meget koster det?* (VAWR MAY-get KOST-uhr DET)?
French—*Combien coûte cela?* (kō-BYĒ KOOT suh-LAH)?
Spanish—*¿Cuánto cuesta?* (KWAHN-toh KWEHS-tah)?
Portuguese—*Quanto custa?* (KWAHN-too KOOSH-tuh)?
Italian—*Quanto costa?* (KWAHN-toh KAWS-tah)?
Rumanian—*Cât costă?* (cut KOST-uh)?
Russian—*Skol'ko eto stoit?* (SKUL'-kuh EH-tuh STAW-yit)?
Polish—*Ile to kosztuje?* (EE-leh TAW kush-TOO-yeh)?
Czech—*Kolik?* (KAW-lick)?
Serbo-Croatian—*Koliko ovo iznosi?* (koh-LEE-koh AW-voh EEZ-naw-see)?
Lithuanian—*Kiek?* (KYEK)?
Welsh—*Faint?* (FAH-eent)?
Greek—*Poso?* (PAW-soh)?

Albanian—*Sa?* (SAH)?
Finnish—*Kuinka paljon?* (KOO-in-kah PAH-lyon)?
Hungarian—*Mennyibe kerül?* (MANY-beh KEH-rül; *ü* like French *u*)?
Turkish—*Fiyatı kaça?* (fee-ya-TUH KAH-chah)?
Esperanto—*Kiom kostas?* (KEE-ohm KOHS-tahs)?

THANK YOU

Here is a sampling of the many ways to say "Thank you" to the kind Europeans who do you favors. The German and Dutch forms, as well as Esperanto, come close to our own ("to thank" was originally a variant of "to think"; you direct your thought with gratitude toward your benefactor). French *merci* is related to our "mercy"; Italian *grazie* and Spanish *gracias* to our "grace"; Portuguese *obrigado* to "obliged"; Greek *efkharistó* to "Eucharist."

German—*danke schön* (DAHN-kuh SHÖHN).
Dutch—*dank U wel* (DAHNK Ü VEL).
Swedish—*tack* (TAHK).
Danish and Norwegian—*takk* (TAHK).
French—*merci* or *merci bien* (mehr-SEE BYÊH).
Spanish—*gracias* (GRAH-thyahs).
Portuguese—*obrigado* (oo-bree-GAH-doo).
Italian—*grazie* (GRAH-tsyeh).
Rumanian—*mulţumesc* (mool-tsoo-MESK; *ţ* like *ts*).
Russian—*spasibo* (spuh-S'EE-buh).
Polish—*dziękuję* (jen-KOO-yen).
Czech—*děkuji* (DYE-koo-yee).
Serbo-Croatian—*hvala* (HVAH-lah).
Greek—*efkharistó* (ef-khah-rees-TAW).
Albanian—*ju falem nderit* (you FAH-lem NDEH-reet).
Lithuanian—*ačiu labai* (AH-chee-oo LAH-buy).
Welsh—*diolch* (DEE-awlkh).
Finnish—*kiitoksia* (KEE-tuck-see-ah).
Hungarian—*köszönöm* (KÖ-sö-nöm; *ö* like French *eu*).
Turkish—*teşekkür ederim* (teh-sheh-KÜR EH-deh-reem; *ü* like French *u*).
Esperanto—*dankon* (DAHN-kohn).

chapter two

english for americans

"Start your trip in Britain—where there is no language barrier," says a travel ad in *Holiday*.

The advice is good. The statement is in the main true. But is it 100 per cent accurate? Does it tell the entire story?

Regretfully, we must return a negative answer—with qualifications.

"England and America" said Bernard Shaw, "are two countries separated by the same language." This seems as paradoxical as to say that they are two countries separated by the same tradition, or by semi-identical democratic institutions. Yet there is some truth in paradoxes.

It depends on the point of view. Two people looking at the same object from different angles can get very different impressions. Do you recall the children's tale of the elephant and the six blind men, each of whom reported differently after feeling, respectively, the elephant's trunk, tusk, ear, leg, body, and tail?

Consider the wealth of psychological difference betrayed by an ad for raincoats in a British periodical: "Perhaps the finest made." What American advertiser would dare voice the doubt conveyed by that "perhaps"?

Or take the adventure in national customs reported by a friend of the writer who recently went to Britain. He entered a London bank to cash a check (or should we say cheque?). Through the teller's window he could see no typewriters or adding machines—only ledger upon ledger, and solid, substantial Englishmen busily inscribing them by hand. The teller who cashed his check made the entry in triplicate. turning the page each time.

"Pardon me, sir," said my friend, "I am an American, and I am interested in business methods. Wouldn't you find it handier to use carbon paper for your triplicate entry?"

The teller looked up in surprise. "Perhaps," he replied, "but we've always done it this way."

"Besides," pursued my friend, "would it not do away with the possibility of mistakes in copying the same set of figures three times?"

"Oh," came the answer quick as a flash, "we never make mistakes!"

With such differences in thought and point of view, is it surprising that there should be differences in language between Britain and America?

The English language serves roughly three hundred million people, or about one-tenth of the world's population, as a mother tongue. In addition, it is more or less correctly used by at least one hundred million more as a secondary language, ranging all the way from the Pidgin English of the islands of Melanesia to the almost flawless speech of cultured foreigners. It is the most widely distributed tongue on the face of the earth, appearing in each of the five major continents and on most of the islands, large and small, that dot the oceans. It is spoken not only by whites of Anglo-Saxon, Germanic, Celtic, Latin, Slavic, and Semitic ancestry, but also by American and African Negroes, brown East Indians and Hawaiians, red American Indians, yellow Chinese and Japanese. Under the circumstances, the wonder is that the dialectal divergences are not far deeper than they are.

Each section of the English-speaking world has its own speech peculiarities in pronunciation, vocabulary, word meanings, grammar. The two main varieties, however, are the British and the American, with the language of Canada approaching the latter, that of the other parts of the Commonwealth, especially Australia, New Zealand, and South Africa, coming closer to the British. This is roughly a two-and-a-half-to-one split, with the numerical odds favoring American English, but pride of origin and weight of historical and literary tradition on the British side.

The countries of continental Europe are well aware of the split. They humorously hang out signs saying: "English spoken here—American understood," or offer to teach "English in three months—American in two." One Italian guide to American English presents on its jacket a variety of expressions such as "skip it," "in the bag," "hiya, kid," "scram," "lousy," then asks: "What sort of language is this? It is American, a language that is not at all English!" The English themselves are not above such low forms of humor as putting on their cinema marquees: "American Western film—English subtitles."

Aside from slang (racier and more abundant in the United States) and local dialects (far more varied in Britain), there are certain fundamental divergences between the two English languages which the traveler should take into account for his own protection and comfort.

Some people think of the King's English as interchangeable with the semi-incomprehensible Oxford accent; others equate it with the Cockney of London's less educated sections. Both views are incorrect. The Oxford accent is a class slang, evolved in university circles; Cockney is a local dialect, or rather two local dialects, separated by the Thames; but the King's English is an aristocratic Londonese that has grown up in the capital since Chaucer's time out of a mixture of Southern and East Midlands dialects, and has been refined and purified by centuries of parliamentary and court usage. In these days of international radio broadcasts and spoken films we find it far less difficult to understand than we did formerly, and there is something vaguely soothing, even to the American ear, in its gentle but expressive modulation and its clipped, precise utterance.

Its most noteworthy phonetic features (and note that many of them appear in various American regions) are the broad *a* in words like *bath* and *ask;* the open *o* of *not* and *sorry* (practically an *aw*-sound cut short); an *ow*-like quality in the long *o* of words like *ghost* and *phone;* an explosive twist to final consonants, especially *t;* and, of course, the ubiquitous vanishing *r* before consonants and at the end of words.

In personal and place names, there is a British tendency to efface unaccented syllables, often with results that surprise the American ear, as when *Leicester* turns into *Lester* and *Auchinlek* is pronounced *Afleck.*

Then there is the well-known difference in the pronunciation of individual words: *clerk* pronounced *clark, been* pronounced with the *ee* of *meet, leisure* as *lesure, lieutenant* as *leftenant, schedule* as *shedule, figure* as *figger*. In a *Dictionary of English Pronunciation with American Variants*, 28 per cent of the words show a different pronunciation.

Many words are stressed differently in Britain: *laboratory* and *financier* take the stress on the second syllable; *necessary* and *primarily* have the stress on only the first, *papa* and *mamma* on the last. *Speciality*, with stress on the *a*, is the British version of *specialty*.

The written language shows such differences in spelling that a single printed paragraph normally suffices to tell the reader whether the item is British or American. The British regularly spell with *-our* nouns that we spell with *-or* (*savour, behaviour, favourite;* note also, in connection with some British films, "Colour by Technicolor"); *x* appears instead of *ct* in *connexion, inflexion* and similar words; double *l* is preferred to single *l* in *travelled, travelling*, etc.; nouns in *-ense*, like *defense*, normally take *-ence* in Britain (the legal document used for the wedding of Queen Elizabeth II is entitled *Licence for Marriage*); our words ending in *-er* usually have *-re* in Britain (*theatre, centre*). Then there are individual spellings used by the British, like *jewellery, tyre, kerb, programme, grey, cheque, gaol* and *waggon*.

But the real difference between the two English languages lies in words and word meanings. Here is where the tourist is likely to find himself suddenly at a loss in the midst of a perfectly satisfactory conversation. An unfamiliar word, a subtle semantic difference can give him the impression that his interlocutor has lapsed into double talk. The misunderstandings that sometimes result may have far-reaching, even serious, consequences.

Take the case of the American theatrical producer whose show had just opened in London. His British agent cabled him: "Show a success; am posting notices." This, in American theatrical parlance, means that the show is closing. The American frantically cabled back, trying to find out why in the world a successful play should close. It took another cable for him to discover that "post" is British for "mail" and "notices" is British for "reviews."

During the war, the British government urgently asked the Americans for some thousands of bushels of "corn" to feed liberated populations. The American government shipped what in America is "corn," but in Britain is "maize" or

"Indian corn." The British really wanted wheat. This linguistic blunder cost a few million dollars to repair.

The number of words that do not coincide in use or meaning in the two English languages is legion. Some are well known by now, like "petrol" and "lorry" vs. "gas" and "truck." Others are a bit strange, but still thoroughly comprehensible, particularly in context. Then there are the ones that are likely to leave you high and dry, and wishing you were speaking German or French.

In a single issue of the British magazine *Men Only*, an examination of a dozen pages of advertising matter brings to light the following facts: The British speak of "tubs" of hair cream where we would use "jars." The hair for which the cream is recommended is said to be "scruffy"; we would say it is affected by dandruff. A shaving cream is described as "superfatted." For a "dry shaver" (electric razor) there are "mains," "onlets," and "power points" rather than "sockets" or "outlets." Typewriters may be hired. We rent them, which indicates a subtle semantic distinction in the two verbs: we rent things and hire people or, at the most, conveyances; they rent real estate, and hire persons and all movable objects. A medical preparation is to be obtained "from all chemists" (at all drugstores) without medical "certificate" (prescription; a medical certificate would be a more serious document in America). "Weathercoats" are offered for sale, but the word "raincoats" is concurrently used. "Bespoke" (custom-made) footwear is obtainable from your local "stockist" (retailer). Pipe tobacco comes in "fob-pocket tins" (fob pockets are a thing of the past with us). "Screenwipers" are easily recognized as our "windshield wipers," but what are "trafficators"? A "carburetter" we can understand, but a "saloon" would hardly be conceived of as our "sedan" if a picture of the car were not there to help us out. The British seem to have given up their old "accumulator" in favor of our "car battery," but they speak of "separators," which Webster does not record in connection with a car. Our "demonstration" for prospective car buyers is their "trial run." A week-long "holiday" (we are getting around to that use of the word, but still prefer "vacation") is to be had from a travel bureau at an "all-in price" (all-inclusive) "from round about £20." "Be wise—fit the finest tyre made," says a tire manufacturer. British understatement appears again in, "Obviously, it's something rather better than usual," and we wonder whether there is a covert criticism of an old American drinking custom in "Try a Myers and Ginger Ale—with a few drops of lemon juice, and iced if you wish."

A page of letters from the public in the same issue reveals that the British use "type" in the same sense as the French (we would use "guy"), and a correspondent from Rhodesia says, "Get cracking, or I will come over." We would say "get a move on!"

H. W. Horwill, in his *Anglo-American Interpreter*, published in 1939, brought out a long list of outstanding divergences between British and American English. Here again, some of them are positively misleading. If you speak of a car's "hood" in Britain, it means the top of the car (what we call "hood" is their "bonnet"). Our porterhouse steak is their "sirloin." Our "potato chips" are their "crisps," while their "chips" are our "French fries." If you ask for a dessert in Britain, you will get fruit ("sweet" is the term to use), and if you ask for biscuits you will get crackers. If you want the "elevator" to stop at the "third floor," you had better ask the "lift" operator for the "second storey." A British "bureau" is a writing desk, and a British "dresser" is a sideboard. A British "billion" is a "trillion."

Other vocabulary differences, without being misleading, are confusing. You merely wonder what the word or expression means, if you are not helped out by the context or the situation. "Multiple shop," "kiosk," "draper's," "aubergine," "egg-whisk," "trunk call," "luggage van," "goods waggon," may or may not register, depending on circumstances, as "chain store," "newsstand," "dry goods store," "eggplant," "egg-beater," "long-distance call," "baggage car," "freight car."

Then there is a long series of words where the stress is on what the linguist would call frequency of occurrence. It isn't that the British would not know the favorite or customary American expression, using it themselves on occasion, or vice versa. It is simply the ratio in which the two expressions are used.

Let us suppose you are motoring in Britain. You are travel-ing on a "dual carriage-way" (two-lane highway); the stop signs at intersections, which in America almost invariably bear the word "stop," in Britain more often say "halt." "Lay-by 100 yards ahead" says a sign; this means you will find a safety island into which you can turn for emergency repairs. Another sign says: "No overtaking"; this is our "no passing." Then comes an interesting succession: "Road works ahead"; "Road diversion" (detour); "Dead slow"; lastly the ominous "You have been warned."

Every culture, no matter how similar it may be to another culture, has its own distinguishing characteristics and objects. In America, if you order a cup of coffee, you will be asked: "Sugar and cream?" In Britain it will be "Black or white?" The latter refers to the addition of milk. In an American cocktail lounge, a Britisher might be disturbed by such expressions as "on the rocks" or "pink lady"; in a British pub, you will run across "mild and bitter," "shandy," "stone ginger," which won't mean very much to you because the objects, mixtures of beer and ale and soft drinks, somewhat akin to ginger ale, are not in use in America. The "bob" (shilling), "quid" (pound or sovereign) and "guinea" (21 shillings), being monetary units, have to be translated into dollars and cents; but the British also speak colloquially of a "pony" (£25) and a "monkey" (£500), in much the same way we refer colloquially to $10 as a "sawbuck" or to $1,000 as a "grand."

Americans occasionally take into their general language localisms that originally appeared in only one section of the country. In Britain, where the local dialects are far more numerous and varied, the phenomenon is more common. Mr. Churchill once remarked, at the outset of a parliamentary debate, that he was feeling "cock-hoot." This is a dialectal expression meaning "jaunty," but all the M.P.'s understood it. Other similar expressions with an Elizabethan flavor are "dowly" (melancholy), "dayligone" (twilight), "mizzle" (vanish), "fettle" (repair). Sussex calls big clouds "Hastings ladies" and refers to sunny weather as "a butterfly day"; Ireland greets you with "a soft mornin' to ye" and says you "have a long finger" if you are slow getting things done; but the chances are that all Britishers would understand these expressions. All Britishers, however, might not understand East Anglian "bor" for "neighbor," or Cornish "frightened" for "surprised," or Scottish "lippen" for "believe" and "aboon" for "about," or Ulster "thon" for "those," or Yorkshire "han" for "have" and "till" for "while." The last expression, indeed, led to disastrous results when a Yorkshire foreman instructed his southern English helper not to build a fire under the boiler "till" it was empty!

The linguistic field most distressing to the foreigner is that of colloquialism and slang. Slang is so fast-changing that what constitutes "good" slang one year may be forgotten by the next. That slang lends itself to misinterpretation is proved by a British glossary of Americanisms, where "to crack wise" is defined as "to speak knowingly," "flivver" as "cheap motor-car of delicate build," "heck" as "familiar for Hecuba, a New England deity," and "roughneck" as "the antithesis of highbrow."

A British reviewer once criticized the writer for giving "hop it!" (pronounced, incidentally, " 'up it!") as the British equivalent of the American "scram!" Yet my source was unimpeachable: a British movie, made and produced in England, with an all-British cast. The same reviewer took exception to "jiggery-pokery" as the equivalent of the American "boloney," and suggested "humbug" as a more plausible rendering; yet "jiggery-pokery" had been reported in the British press as the derisive cry that greeted Churchill from Labour benches when the Prime Minister quoted certain dubious statistics. A few other controversial items of the same type are "turf accountant" (bookie), "hankie-hatter" (bobby-soxer), "sitter-in" (baby sitter), "to fob off" (get rid of), "route swine" (road hog), "tiggerty-boo" (O. K.; but the British more commonly use "righto," or adopt the now world-wide American expression).

Then there are "knitting" for the feminine sex taken collectively, "shaky-do" for a serious occurrence, "snake" for a lively party, "to flannel" for "to soft-soap," "poodle-faker" for gigolo, "chucker-out" for bouncer, "hodge" for rube or hick. All of these expressions may be nonce-words, or things of the past, like our "23-skiddoo" of the early 1900's.

Less open to such objection are the now-famous British black-market expressions, "spiv," "spove," "drone," "eel," "limpet," "butterfly," "wide boy," all referring to profiteers and their molls. "Spiv" was at one time thought to be "vips" in reverse, then a back-formation from "spiffy," then a police abbreviation for "suspected persons and itinerant vagrants," but finally it was traced back to a document of 1690, which mentions "gypsies and spivics." "Spove" was created for the feminine of the species. "To cheek" and "to chivvy" have the sanction of parliamentary debate (one comes close in meaning to our "to sass," the other to our "to chisel"). "Smashing" and

"wizard" are two British colloquial expressions of approval
that seem to have replaced the "ripping" of earlier days.

The British language, like the American, likes short cuts.
"Oppo" is used for "opposite number," "demob" for "de-
mobilization" (which reminds one of the earlier short cut, now
forgotten as such, "mob" for *mobile vulgus,* or "fickle crowd");
"nappies" (diapers) stands for a longer expression that the
British do not like to use in full.

Just as in the case of fully legitimate words ("homely,"
which is "not beautiful" to us, but "pleasant," "homelike" to
the British), so also in slang expressions there is the possibility
of linguistic misunderstanding. "Mug" is "easy mark" to the
British criminal classes; "dinkey" means "cute"; "dab" is
"shark" or "crackerjack." And again we have the incomprehensible, double-talk aspect in forms like "bear garden" (we
would say "roughhouse"), "beak" (magistrate or judge), "to
work the oracle" (to get results), "to cod" (to kid along), "to
box clever" (to use one's brains), "steam" (hard work),
"stiffener" (bore), "toffee-nosed" (stuck-up).

We should perhaps point out that slang, like legitimate
language, travels back and forth across the Atlantic. Our current "swank," "spoof," "click," "wind up," "tell off," are of
British origin, while "tough guy," "lay off," "cop," "oh.
yeah" and "bump off" are among the terms that an English
police official deplores as having gotten into the vocabulary of
British youth. The two slangs, like the two languages, get
around.

Newspaper accounts publicize the criminal doings of the
few and relegate to obscurity the everyday legitimate activities of the many, which are socially beneficial but not news-
worthy. In the same way, there is a tendency for people to
overemphasize the picturesque and sometimes startling differences between two branches of what is fundamentally one
language, and to assume that the King's English and the
American language are two separate tongues. Actually, they
are only two dialectal variants of the same spoken and written
language, with the majority of words, sounds, grammatical
forms, and spellings coinciding rather than diverging. The
areas of contact probably cover no less than 90 per cent of
both languages. The written language, despite minor spelling
divergences, is the same; the literature, of course, is common
to all lands that describe themselves as English-speaking; and

even the popular spoken tongue shows *relatively* few differences.

While the technical peculiarities of one language have been made known to the speakers of the other by books, newspapers, and magazines, the radio and the spoken films have brought each spoken language within ear range of the other. We can listen with pleasure to Britishers on the radio; we no longer mind sitting through an English film. And the success of the Hollywood product in Britain seems to indicate that the British have become similarly accustomed to the American spoken tongue.

Let us therefore stress the fundamental unity of the English language, that marvelously resilient instrument of communication that spans oceans and mountains and continents, carrying with it the gospel of individual initiative and individual rights, the spirit of fair play and the doctrine of respect for one's fellow man. Variety there is, and there always will be. But variety is the spice of life, and the English language is nothing if not alive.

chapter three

a start in german

In Europe, French and Italian serve the western and southern fringes; English is the vogue language; Spanish, outside of Spain, is practically unheard of. The really big, important language is German. It may surprise some to hear it, but German is *the* leading European tongue.

In part this is due to the fact that German is almost exclusively a European language. English covers the British Isles, but the real stamping grounds of English are America, the Commonwealth and the Crown possessions, where nearly 75 per cent of English speakers are located. French is a fairly widespread language (at least fifty million Europeans speak it as a native tongue), but French is widespread all over the globe. Spanish is primarily a Western Hemisphere tongue, and the European speakers of Spanish do not go beyond thirty million. Russian, the giant of eastern Europe, has an over-all speaking population that surpasses that of German, but Russian straddles the Urals and extends over the vast expanses of northern Asia. German, on the other hand, is concentrated in the heartland of the European continent. Its one hundred million speakers embrace not only the total populations of West and East Germany and of Austria, but also three-fourths of Switzerland. This would total up to only about eighty million, but it is far from telling the entire story. There are at least twenty million people who speak German as a second language in the countries at the periphery of the Teutonic homeland—Holland, Denmark, Sweden, Poland, Czechoslovakia, Hungary, Yugoslavia, northern Italy, eastern France. If you find yourself in any of these countries and your international English and French won't work, by all means try German.

For this state of affairs there are interesting historical reasons. In the days before 1914, the Kaiser's Imperial Germany was the leading nation on the European continent, and this gave German the position of predominant trade language in neighboring smaller countries, like Holland, Denmark, and Sweden. The old German Empire extended beyond the German ethnic border, into French Alsace-Lorraine, Danish Schleswig-Holstein, Polish Silesia, and the Masurian region. The non-Germans in the German Empire all went to German schools and learned German. South of Imperial Germany's sixty-five million people lay another great imperial population of fifty-five million souls, the Austro-Hungarian. The old Hapsburg monarchy has often been likened to a mosaic. Here lived the Germans of Upper and Lower Austria, Carinthia and the Tyrol, the Magyars of Hungary, the Czechs and Slovaks of Bohemia and Moravia, the Poles and Ruthenians of Galicia, the Rumanians of Transylvania, the Serbs and Croats of Bosnia, Herzegovina, Dalmatia and Croatia, the Slovenes of Istria, the Italians of Trieste, Gorizia and the Trento region, along with a liberal sprinkling of gypsies and Yiddish-speaking Jews. Practically all those people used German as a common medium of exchange.

After the First World War and Wilson's self-determination for small nations, the Hapsburg Empire was dismembered. Czechoslovakia and Yugoslavia and a greater Rumania, a reunited Poland and an aggrandized Italy, a small but independent Hungary and an Austrian Republic of eight million people were the heirs. Lovely, melancholy Vienna, a four-million capital of a shrunken nation, starved and begged like an expatriated nobleman, until, in 1938, it succumbed to Hitler's *Anschluss*.

But in all the fragments of the former mosaic the German habit remained. To the present day, nearly half the population of countries like Czechoslovakia and Hungary, that lie entirely within the boundaries of the old Austro-Hungarian Empire, speak and understand German. In the Croatian and Slovenian sections of Yugoslavia, the Galician section of Poland, the Transylvanian area of Rumania, the Venezia Tridentina of Italy, the eastern regions of France, millions of people speak German. There is a newspaper story that when Schuman, the Alsatian former Premier of France, and de Gasperi, the

Trentino-born Premier of Italy, came together to discuss European union, they vainly tried French and Italian, then smiled knowingly and fell back on their common "ancestral" tongue, German.

This is still not all. After the Second World War, Russia and Poland took over large areas of eastern Germany—Prussia and Pomerania and Silesia, turning Königsberg into Kaliningrad, Breslau into Wroclaw, and Stettin into Szczecin. But the people who didn't run away still speak German.

This great tongue of central Europe is, like our own English, a member of the Teutonic or Germanic branch of the great Indo-European family of languages. In basic respects, it comes closer to English than do the Romance languages, from which English has so extensively borrowed.

Like English and Dutch, German belongs to the West Germanic branch of Teutonic. This sets it apart from Scandinavian, or North Germanic. Unlike English and Dutch, literary German is based largely on the High German dialects of West Germanic. The terms "High" and "Low" applied to West Germanic languages and dialects refer not to a cultural hierarchy, but to altitude as measured from the sea level; in other words, the Low German dialects are the ones of the low-lying coastline, the High German those of the Bavarian, Austrian, and Swiss mountain regions. The difference between the two seems to have started around the sixth century A.D., but is fully attested in the eighth; its most striking feature is a shift in consonant sounds (Grimm's Law), whereby in certain positions a Germanic *d* (which remains a *d* in Low German, Dutch, and English) turns into a *t* in High German, a *th* becomes a *t*, a *t* becomes *ss* or *z*, a *p* becomes *pf* or *f*, a *k* becomes *kh*. The ultimate result is that we have *cold* and *good* in English, *koud* and *goed* in Dutch, but *kalt* and *gut* in German. Other examples are English *bath*, German *Bad*; English *two*, *water* (Dutch *twee*, *water*) vs. German *zwei*, *Wasser*; English *lope* (Dutch *lopen*) vs. German *laufen*; English *break* (Dutch *breken*) vs. German *brechen*. English *dapper*, with *d* and *p*, is German *tapfer*, with *t* and *pf*. This rule of shift applies even to words which the Germanic languages borrowed at that period from Latin, so that Latin *planta* and *piper* become English *plant* and *pepper*, but German *Pflanze* and *Pfeffer*.

English, stemming from Anglo-Saxon, a Low German dialect of the North Sea coast, retains the original Germanic consonants. The German mainland is about evenly divided between Low and High German dialects, but when a literary form for all of Germany was sought at the time of the Reformation, Luther's German translation of the Bible, in 1531, effected a compromise which leaned rather heavily in favor of High German.

This does not mean that all of the German-speaking world follows Luther's linguistic model. There are numerous and widely diverging dialects. In seaport towns like Hamburg and Bremen you will hear *stehen* and *sprechen* ("stand" and "speak") pronounced with the English *st, sp* sounds rather than the standard German *sht, shp*. In Bavaria, Austria, and particularly Switzerland are variants of High German that go far beyond the standard language in their consonant shifting. The Swiss, in fact, sometimes claim to have a separate language, which they call *Schwyzer-Tütsch* (Swiss German).

Two interesting varieties of German that have reached our shores are Pennsylvania "Dutch" and Yiddish. The former is the German originally spoken by immigrants from the Palatinate, in western Germany, and is not at all "Dutch"; "Pennsylvania German" would be a far better name for it. Yiddish is a medieval German that goes back largely to the fifteenth and sixteenth centuries, when large Jewish communities, in part consisting of Jews expelled from Spain, spread over Germany and to the east. Even when these northern Jewish, or Ashkenazic, groups went beyond the eastern German frontiers and settled in Poland, Lithuania, Hungary, Rumania, and Russia, they continued to use their antiquated German as a vernacular, though interspersing it with Hebrew, Slavic, and, more recently, English words. The writing is done with Hebrew characters.

Despite the dialectal divergences described above, standard German is understood and spoken by the overwhelming majority of the inhabitants of the German-speaking countries. If you are going to Europe, it is a most useful language to know something about.

Mark Twain once humorously undertook to demonstrate that any American can speak German if he wants to, and the reverse has been abundantly proved by Herr Heinrich Schnibble in the pages of the *Saturday Evening Post*. There is a fundamental similarity, derived from a common origin, in the basic, everyday, earthy vocabulary of the two languages.

A word of warning is in order, however. While practically

all the words we have inherited from Anglo-Saxon have in German not merely a counterpart, but a word that comes from the identical West Germanic root (in other words, a cognate), cognates have a strange way of being deceptive. For one thing, they may look identical and have very different meanings, like *Lust* and *Gift*, which in German mean, respectively, "pleasure" and "poison." Again, there may be a change in form accompanied by a change in meaning. German *Zeit* corresponds, with the consonant shifts that were indicated earlier, to "tide"; actually, it means "time." Of course there is a semantic connection between "tide" and "time," which wait for no man. But people who let themselves be hypnotized by the beautiful workings of Grimm's Law let themselves in for other strange surprises. Consider the common German endings *-heit, -schaft, -ung, -tum,* which etymologically correspond to English *-hood, -ship, -ing, -dom.* "Freedom" is not *Freitum,* but *Freiheit,* literally "freehood." *Knechtschaft* is not "knightship," or even "knighthood," but "slavery" (the knight in former days served the baron, but it was service of a highly honorable, military variety; in English this connotation remained, but in German it degenerated to the point where the service took on a menial, slavish aspect). *Altertum* would be "olderdom" if we had kept the word in English; we didn't, but replaced it with "antiquity," drawn from Latin.

Still, the basic relationship between the Anglo-Saxon part of our language and the German vocabulary cannot be rejected. Words like *Brot, Milch, Fleisch, Fisch, Vater, Mutter, Bruder, Sohn, Tochter, finden, fallen, gut, besser, und, für* and thousands of others are there to show the very intimate kinship between the two languages. So, face German not as an alien tongue, but as a long-lost relative whom you are glad to see again.

The sounds of German are relatively simple to an English speaker. Most of them appear in English, though often with a different spelling. Like English, German differentiates between long and short vowel sounds. As in English, a vowel usually has the short value when it is followed in writing by a double consonant, the long value when written double or followed in spelling by *h*.

(From here on, capitals will be used to indicate stressed syllables or words.)

There is an *ah*-sound, as in English *father*, which we shall represent by AH (*Vater* [FAH-tuhr], father; *aber* [AH-buhr], but); and there is a shorter *a*-sound, like the *o* in American *not*, which may be represented by A (*Wasser* [VAS-suhr], water; *als* [ALS], when).

There is a long *e*, which is like the *ay* of *lay*, but with the tail end cut off. Let us indicate it by AY (*sehr* [ZAYR], very; *zehn* [TSAYN], ten). There is also a short *e*-sound, like that of *met*, for which we can use E (*Welt* [VELT], world; *besser* [BES-suhr], better). Either of these sounds may be represented in writing not only by *e*, but also by *ä* (*spät* [SHPAYT], late; *Männer* [MEN-nuhr], men). There is also an unstressed *e*, usually final in the word, or followed by a single final consonant, which is like the *e* of *the* in *the man*, or the *e* of *taken*, and for this we shall use UH (*heute* [HOI-tuh], today; *fallen* [FAL-luhn], to fall).

Written *ie* and long *i* give the sound of *i* in *machine* or *ee* of *see;* for this we can use EE (*sie* [ZEE], she; *hier* [HEER], here; *ihn* [EEN], him). But a written *i*, when short, gives the sound of *pin*, and for this we can use I (*mit* [MIT], with; *immer* [IM-muhr], always).

Long *o* is like the *o* of *bore* or *oh*, short *o* like the *o* of *often*, or better yet, if you can imitate a Britisher, like British *o* in *pot*. We shall use OH and O for them (*wo* [VOH], where; *ohne* [OH-nuh], without; *voll* [FOL], full; *morgen* [MOR-guhn], tomorrow).

Long *u* is like the *u* of *rule* or the *oo* of *food*, short *u* like the *u* of *put* or *pull*. Let's use OO and U for these (*gut* [GOOT], good; *nur* [NOOR], only; *und* [UNT], and; *um* [UM], about).

There is also a written *ö*, which is halfway between the *o* of *bore* and the *e* of *there* (round the lips as if for *bore*, then try to say *bare*). It may be long or short, and we shall represent it by ÖH and Ö (*hören* [HÖH-ruhn], to hear; *öffnen* [ÖF-nuhn], to open). And there is a written *ü*, halfway between the *ee* of *see* and the *oo* of *food* (round lips for *food*, then try to say *feed*); let's indicate it by ÜH and Ü (*früh* [FRÜH], early; *für* [FÜHR], for; *fünf* [FÜNF], five).

Written *äu* and *eu* are pretty much like the OI of *oil* (*Häuser* [HOI-zuhr], houses; *treu* [TROI], loyal); while written *ei* is exactly like English so-called "long i" in "fine": *ein* (ĪN), one; *nein* (NĪN), no. Written *au* is always like OW in *how* (*Haus* [HOWS], house; *auf* [OWF], on).

Among the consonants, written *j* is always Y (*ja* [YAH], yes; *jetzt* [YETST], now); *s* before a vowel at the beginning of a word, or between vowels, is Z (*so* [ZOH], so; *sehen* [ZAYuhn], to see; *lesen* [LAY-zuhn], to read); *s* before *t* or *p*, and *sch* are SH (*stehen* [SHTAY-uhn], to stand; *spät* [SHPAYT], late; *schnell* [SHNEL], quickly). Written *v* is pronounced F (*Vogel* [FOH-guhl], bird; *von* [FON], of); written *w* as V (*wo* [VOH], where; *etwas* [ET-vas], something); written *z* as TS (*zu* [TSOO], to; *Herz* [HERTS], heart); *ti* before a vowel as TSY (*Nation* [na-TSYOHN], nation).

R and *l* differ considerably from their English counterparts, with *r* often pronounced as in French, with a trill of the uvula, the sort of gentle rasping sound one makes when he wants to clear the back of his palate (it is said that this pronunciation was imported into Germany by Frederick the Great, who greatly admired the French, and that it largely replaced an earlier tongue-trilled *r*, similar to that of Spanish or Italian, which is still heard on the stage, in the *Bühnenaussprache*, or theatrical pronunciation); while the *l*, particularly before consonants, is produced not in the back, but in the front of the mouth, as in English *million*. Try applying the *l*-sound of *million* to a word like *kalt*, and see how this sound differs from that of English *cold*.

Two German consonant sounds have no counterpart in English. They are both represented by the same written *ch* in German; but if the *ch* is preceded by *a, o* or *u*, it has the sound of Scottish *loch*, which we may represent by KH (*Buch* [BOOKH], book; *nach* [NAHKH], after); while if it is preceded by *e, i, ä, ö, ü, l, r* or *n*, the sound comes closer to English *h* in *huge*, being produced by forcing the breath through an opening between the tongue and the hard palate. For this sound the International Phonetic Alphabet uses the symbol ç, and we may well do the same (*ich* [IÇ], I; *Milch* [MILÇ], milk; *durch* [DURÇ], through; *natürlich* [na-TÜHR-liç], of course). Try the two sounds together in *noch nicht* (NOKH NIÇT), not yet. The Ç-sound is also occasionally heard in the ending *-ig*, which may, however, also sound -IG or -IK (*wenig* [VAY-niç, VAY-nig, VAY-nik], little).

Occasionally, in words borrowed from French, German has the sound of *s* in "pleasure." This sound will be represented by ZH: *Garage* (ga-RAH-zhuh), garage.

A written German final *-d, -b* or *-g* is usually heard as *-t, -p* or *-k*, respectively (*bald* [BALT], soon; *ab* [AP], from; *Tag* [TAHK], day).

Among German written-language conventions, it may be remarked that all nouns, both proper and common, are capitalized. So are polite *you* and *your* (*Sie, Ihr*); but not *I* (*ich*).

The common German greeting forms, which you will hear from Hamburg to Vienna and from the Saar to East Prussia, are:

Guten Morgen.   (GOOT-uhn MOR-guhn)   Good morning.
Guten Tag.   (GOOT-uhn TAHK)   Good day.
Guten Abend.   (GOOT-uhn AH-buhnt)   Good evening.
Gute Nacht.   (GOOT-uh NAKHT)   Good night.

There is a *Grüss' Gott* (literally "greet God") often heard in the mountain regions, but its use is not recommended to the tourist, save for recognition.

"Good-by" is *auf Wiedersehen* (OWF VEE-duhr-zayn); the form *adieu* (a-DYÖ) is an elegant borrowing from the French.

"How are you," "How are things," "How goes it," "How do you do," "Hello," are all best rendered by *Wie geht's?* (VEE GAYTS), to which you may add *Ihnen* (EEN-uhn), making it literally "How goes it to you?" The normal reply is *Danke, gut, und Ihnen?* (DAN-kuh, GOOT, unt EEN-uhn), which means "Well, thanks, and you?" The counter-reply is *Sehr* (or *ganz*) *gut* (ZAYR [GANTS] GOOT). "Very (quite) well." Note that *sehr*, the regular German word for "very," has as its cognate the English *sore;* do you remember how in medieval parlance "I am sore wroth" meant "I am very angry"? If English had stayed pure Anglo-Saxon, we would still be using *sore* in that sense; but the Normans came in with their *verai* ("true" or "truly," the same word that in French winds up as *vrai*), and that became our "very," displacing the old "sore."

The Germans are perhaps not quite so polite as the Latins. Some have accused them of being almost as abrupt as the Americans. This is largely a legend, built up on war experiences. What some (by no means all) Germans lack is tact. On arriving in a Munich hotel during the Hitler regime, I was given a circular which described the hotel's excellent dining-room service (it was truly excellent, by the way), and suggested that the guests should take as many meals as possible there. It went on to say: *"Das Frühstück ist obligatorisch—"* "Breakfast is compulsory, and will be reckoned on your bill whether you take it or not." I brought this little piece of literature back with me and showed it to an experienced traveler. "Tell me," I said, "how would the same idea have been gotten across by the French, or the Italians, or even the Swiss?" He laughed. "That's easy. They would have said: 'Breakfast, with the management's compliments, is included in the price of your room.' They would have soaked you just as much or more for it, but would have left you happy in the delusion that you were getting something free thrown in."

For uttered forms of politeness, however, German yields to no language. Here are a few of them:

Bitte. (BIT-tuh) Please.
Danke, or *danke schön.* (DAN-kuh SHÖHN) Thanks.
Bitte schön. (BIT-tuh SHÖHN) Don't mention it.
Verzeihen Sie. (fer-TSĪ-uhn ZEE) Excuse me (the French *pardon* may also be used).
Es tut mir leid. (ES TOOT MEER LĪT) I'm sorry.
Es macht nichts aus. (ES MAKHT NIÇTS OWS) It doesn't matter.

When you go shopping in a German city, some of these expressions will come in handy:

Geben Sie mir bitte. (GAY-buhn ZEE MEER BIT-tuh) Please give me.
Zeigen Sie mir. (TSĪ-guhn ZEE MEER) Show me.
Sagen Sie mir. (ZAH-guhn ZEE MEER) Tell me.

What you are likely to hear from salespeople is:

Womit kann ich dienen, gnädige Frau? (voh-MIT KAN IÇ DEE-nuhn, GNAY-di-guh FROW) What can I do for you, madam?
Noch etwas? (NOKH ET-vas) Anything else?
Was noch? (VAS NOKH) What else?

Some of your possible replies:

Das ist alles. (DAS IST AL-luhs) That's all.
Nichts mehr. (NIÇTS MAYR) Nothing else.
Wieviel? (VEE-FEEL) How much?
Zu viel! (TSOO FEEL) Too much!

Common ways of saying "sir," "madam," "miss" in polite address are: *mein Herr* (MĪN HER), *gnädige Frau* (GNAY-di-guh FROW), *mein Fräulein* (MĪN FROI-lĭn), or *gnädiges Fräulein* (GNAY-di-guhs FROI-lĭn). In addressing a mixed group, guides will sometimes say *meine Damen und Herren*

(MĪ-nuh DAH-muhn unt HER-ruhn), sometimes *meine Herrschaften* (MĪ-nuh HER-shaf-tuhn).

Let us try a few shopping phrases:

Geben Sie mir bitte ein Paket Zigaretten und zwei Zigarren! (GAY-buhn ZEE MEER BIT-tuh ĪN pa-KET tsi-ga-RET-tuhn unt TSVĪ tsi-GAR-ruhn) Please give me a pack of cigarettes and two cigars.

Wünschen Sie auch Streichhölzer, mein Herr? (VÜN-shuhn ZEE OWKH SHTRĪÇ-HÖL-tsuhr, MĪN HER) Do you want matches too, sir?

Wieviel kostet es? (VEE-FEEL KOS-tuht ES) How much is that?

Nur zwei Mark fünfzig. (NOOR TSVĪ MARK FÜNF-tsiç) Only two marks fifty.

Das ist nicht billig. (DAS IST NIÇT BIL-liç) That isn't cheap.

A few of the things you may want, arranged to follow "I want" or "Please give me":

ein Stück Brot (ĪN SHTÜK BROT) a piece of bread (German omits "of" in expressions of this kind.)

eine Flasche Wein (Ī-nuh FLAH-shuh VĪN) a bottle of wine

eine Tasse Kaffee (Ī-nuh TAS-suh ka-FAY) a cup of coffee

ein Paar Handschuhe (ĪN PAHR HANT-SHOO-uh) a pair of gloves

einen Hut (Ī-nuhn HOOT) a hat

ein Taschentuch (ĪN TASH-uhn-tookh) a handkerchief

drei Hemden (DRĪ HEM-duhn) three shirts

Sightseeing calls for a question-and-answer routine:

Wo ist, wo sind? (VOH IST, VOH ZINT) Where is, where are?

Hier ist, sind (HEER IST, ZINT) Here is, are.

Da ist, sind (DAH IST, ZINT) There is, are.

("There is" when you are not pointing out, but merely making a statement of existence, is *es gibt* (ES GIPT), which explains Mrs. Katzenjammer's "It giffs pie for supper.")

Wohin gehen Sie (wir)? (VOH-hin GAY-uhn ZEE [VEER]) Where are you (we) going?

In welcher Richtung?   (IN VEL-çuhr RIÇ-tung)   In which
direction?
In dieser (jener) Richtung.   (IN DEE-zuhr [YAY-nuhr]
RIÇ-tung)   In this (that) direction; this (that) way.
Nach rechts (links).   (NAKH REÇTS [LINKS])   To the
right (left).
Kommen Sie mit mir.   (KOM-muhn ZEE MIT MEER)
Come with me. (The *mir* may be omitted.)

A few of the places of interest to which you may wish to be
directed are:

die Kirche   (dee KEER-çuh)   the church
der Dom   (dayr DOHM)   the cathedral
das Hotel, der Gasthof   (das hoh-TEL, dayr GAST-hohf)
the hotel
die Brücke   (dee BRÜK-kuh)   the bridge
das Amt   (das AMT)   the office, bureau
das Postamt   (das POST-amt)   the post office
der Bahnhof   (dayr BAHN-hohf)   the railroad station
die Toilette, das Klosett   (dee to-a-LET-tuh, das klo-ZET)
the lavatory   (Do not confuse *Klosett* with English
"closet.")

Directional signs, which pertain to the written language,
are often of extreme importance:

Achtung!   (AKH-tung)   Attention!
Bekanntmachung.   (be-KANT-MAKH-ung)   Notice.
Rauchen verboten.   (ROW-khuhn   fer-BOH-tuhn)   No
smoking.
Eintritt verboten or *Kein Eingang.*   (ĪN-TRIT fer-BOH-
tuhn, KĪN ĪN-gang)   No admittance, Keep out.
Rechts (links) fahren.   (REÇTS [LINKS] FAHR-uhn)
Keep right (left).
Eingang, Ausgang.   (ĪN-gang, OWS-gang)   Entrance,
Exit.
Herren.   (HER-uhn)   Men.
Damen, Frauen.   (DAH-muhn, FROW-uhn)   Ladies,
Women.
Einbahnstrasse.   (ĪN-bahn-shtras-suh)   One-way street.

Here are a few "speaking" and "understanding" phrases:

Sprechen Sie Deutsch (Englisch, Französisch)?   (SHPRE-

çuhn ZEE DOITSH [ENG-lish, fran-TSÖ-zish]) Do
you speak German (English, French)?
Ein wenig. (ĪN VAY-niç) A little.
Sprechen Sie bitte langsamer. (SHPRE-çuhn ZEE BIT-
tuh LANG-za-muhr) Speak more slowly, please.
Verstehen Sie? (fer-SHTAY-uhn ZEE) Do you under-
stand?
Ich verstehe nicht. (IÇ fer-SHTAY-uh NIÇT) I don't
understand.
Wissen Sie? (VIS-suhn ZEE) Do you know?
Ich weiss nicht. (IÇ VĪS NIÇT) I don't know.
Wovon reden Sie? (voh-FON RAY-duhn ZEE) What are
you talking about?
Wie heisst das auf deutsch? (VEE HĪST DAS OWF
DOITSH) What do you call that in German?
Wie sagt man —— auf deutsch? (VEE ZAKT MAN ——
OWF DOITSH) How do you say —— in German?
Ich bin Amerikaner (Amerikanerin if you are a woman) (IÇ
BIN a-me-ri-KAH-nuhr [a-me-ri-KAH-nuh-rin]) I am an
American.

Germany, too, has weather, and it forms an important topic
of conversation:

Es regnet. (ES REG-nuht) It's raining.
Es schneit. (ES SHNĪT) It's snowing.
Es ist warm (kalt). (ES IST VARM [KALT]) It's warm
(cold).
Es ist schönes (schlechtes) Wetter. (ES IST SHÖH-nuhs
[SHLEÇ-tuhs] VET-tuhr) It's fine (bad) weather.
Mir ist warm (kalt). (MEER IST VARM [KALT]) I'm
warm (cold).

Here are a few people you might need, with the magic
phrase that will bring them to you:

Ich brauche (IÇ BROW-khuh) I need
einen Arzt (Ī-nuhn ARTST) a doctor
einen Schutzmann (Ī-nuhn SHUTS-man) a policeman
einen Gepäckträger (Ī-nuhn guh-PEK-TRAY-guhr) a
porter
eine Taxi (Ī-nuh TAK-si) a taxi
einen Dolmetscher (Ī-nuhn DOL-met-shuhr) an interpreter

Here are a few adjectives in common use. Remember that they may appear with various endings, according to their use in the sentence; *gut*, for example, may appear as *guter, gute, gutes, guten, gutem*. English adjectives once had similar endings, but English discarded them, and does not seem to miss them:

klein (KLĪN) small

erst (ERST) first

frei (FRĪ) free

rein (RĪN) clean

lang (LANG) long

müde (MÜH-duh) tired

schön (SHÖHN) beautiful, pretty

gross (GROHS) large

letzt (LETST) last

besetzt (be-ZETST) occupied, taken

schmutzig (SHMUT-siç) dirty

kurz (KURTS) short

leer (LAYR) empty

hässlich (HES-liç) ugly

It is well known that German grammar is difficult for English speakers, more so, perhaps, than the grammars of the Romance tongues. This is in part due to the fact that while English has discarded endings, German has kept them. An Anglo-Saxon of the days of King Alfred and a High German speaker from the court of Charlemagne's descendants would have understood each other with relative ease, but that no longer holds true today. In addition to the endings that German kept and English lost, there is also the matter of word order in a sentence. The German says "I know not, where you this book bought have," and "I want a gift to my brother to send."

Accordingly, as we offer you a few verbs in their infinitive forms, remember that the infinitive will often appear at the end of the German sentence. "I should like to speak to this gentleman" will come out as "I should like to this gentleman to speak," and "I shall see you tomorrow" as "I shall you tomorrow see":

ich möchte gern   (IÇ MÖÇ-tuh GERN)   I should like to

ich werde   (IÇ VER-duh)   I shall

kaufen   (KOWF-uhn)   to buy

verkaufen   (fer-KOWF-uhn)   to sell

besuchen   (be-ZOOKH-uhn)   to visit

fragen   (FRAH-guhn)   to ask

antworten   (AHNT-vor-tuhn)   to answer

bezahlen   (be-TSAH-luhn)   to pay (for)
mieten   (MEE-tuhn)   to rent, hire
essen   (ES-suhn)   to eat
trinken   (TRINK-uhn)   to drink
mich waschen   (MIÇ VASH-uhn)   to wash (myself)
mir die Hände waschen   (MEER DEE HEN-duh VASH-uhn)   to wash my hands
mich rasieren   (MIÇ ra-ZEE-ruhn)   to shave myself
fortgehen   (FORT-gay-uhn)   to go away
bleiben   (BLĪ-buhn)   to stay
ankommen   (AN-kom-muhn)   to arrive
warten   (VAR-tuhn)   to wait
machen   (MA-khuhn)   to make, do
nehmen   (NAY-muhn)   to take
schreiben   (SHRĪ-buhn)   to write

There is infinitely more to German than appears in these brief pages. But do not let that deter you. Remember that the speaker of a foreign tongue, even if he speaks English ten times more fluently than you speak his language, normally appreciates the gesture of friendliness and courtesy implicit in your attempt to say a few words his way instead of yours; so—

Wir werden ein wenig Deutsch sprechen, nicht wahr?   (VEER VER-duhn ĪN VAY-niç DOITSH SHPRE-çuhn, NIÇT VAHR?)

chapter four
let's speak french

In most European countries, the American tourist is not made aware of his linguistic insufficiency. The natives with whom he is likely to come in contact go out of their way to speak his language, understand his gestures, interpret his unspoken thought. If they speak English, they are proud of the fact and happy to practice, as indeed they should be, for three out of four of them confess to you, sooner or later, that they hope and intend to come to the United States. If they don't speak English, their attitude is: "Pray forgive me for not having yet learned your tongue! It is high on my agenda, and the next time we meet, I promise this deplorable situation will have been remedied!"

The one big exception is France. The average Frenchman, like the average American, thinks everybody should know *his* language. If there is no linguistic understanding between you, then, *parbleu*, it is your fault, not his, and he doesn't hesitate to let you know it. If he has to fall back on his own imperfect English, he will do so with a shrug of the shoulders which is condemnatory, not apologetic. If you essay your own imperfect French, he will view your attempts approvingly and give you "A" for effort, even while he smiles inwardly at your linguistic *gaucheries*. But if your French happens to be really satisfactory, he becomes your lifelong friend, and nothing he has to offer is too good for you.

For this spirit of linguistic condescension there are good and sufficient historical reasons. Ever since the time of the Crusades, French has been the international language of

Europe, the Near East, and North Africa, the tongue of di-
plomacy and culture, the language of refinement. From Portugal to Russia, from Norway to Sicily, what European, in the
centuries that preceded World War I, did not know *some*
French? Only the illiterate, the peasant, the boor.

Times, of course, have changed. Democracy in education
has relegated mere linguistic accomplishment to a secondary
role. Other languages, notably English, have come to the fore.
But it is difficult for the Frenchman to forget the once uncon-
tested predominance of his language on the international
scene—far harder than it is to resign himself to the loss of
overseas colonies and military prestige.

A tout seigneur, tout honneur, says the Frenchman, speaking
of his language: "To one who is every inch a gentleman, let
the full measure of honor be given!" French is indeed a
gentleman's (or a lady's) language. There is something in the
soft modulation of its tones, in the graceful construction of
its sentences, in the expressiveness of its every word, that suits
it supremely for the drawing room and the council table. When
good French is spoken, it evokes visions of eighteenth-century
noblemen in ruffles and knee breeches and powdered wigs,
bowing in stately grace to lovely ladies as they dance the
minuet or the pavane.

Contrary to popular belief, the Frenchman (at least in the
north of France) is sober in his gestures. His hands do not
move about wildly as he speaks, as is so often the case with
the Italian, the Spaniard, or the Provençal. If we may be
slightly paradoxical, he prefers to gesticulate with his voice.
The speaking of French calls for a tenseness and mobility of
the vocal organs without parallel in most other languages—
certainly not in American English, where the lips and tongue
and teeth are normally relaxed as you speak. The pitch-range
of the French voice is far greater than it is with us.

Still, there are a few French gestures that are typical. One,
which we have lately borrowed, is the circle composed of
thumb and forefinger, the other three fingers being raised,
which signifies perfection. Another, which the French share
with their southern European neighbors, is the characteristic
shoulder shrug that carries so many diverse meanings: "Don't
know"; "Don't care"; "Can't do a thing about it." And let us
not, of course, forget the two outstretched hands, palms up
and fingers spread, which betoken indignation, helplessness, or
a mixture of the two with other emotions, in infinite blends.

Of the major Romance languages, French is the one that has changed the most from the ancestral Latin. A word like the Latin *capra*, "goat," which continues to be *capra* in Italian, would still be easily recognized by an ancient Roman in its modern Spanish form, *cabra;* but would that same ancient Roman recognize the French offshoot, *chèvre?* For "horse," Cicero would have used the elegant *equus* ("equine" is still with us); Caesar, however, being used to the military slang of his legionaries, would have recognized the vulgar *caballus* used by Rome's lower classes. If he were to come back to life today, Italian *cavallo* and Spanish *caballo* would not stump him; but it is possible that French *cheval* would.

I once had a peculiar experience as I tutored in French a girl who had had in school both French and Latin. To make clear the meaning of a French word that seemed to baffle the victim, I brought in the original Latin form. "Do you mean to tell me," asked the startled student, "that there is a connection between French and Latin?"

What are the reasons for the extraordinary divergences between the parent and the daughter tongue? Many are alleged. Some say that the Gauls of Caesar's day, who spoke a Celtic tongue similar to Irish or Welsh, experienced difficulty in mastering the Latin sounds brought in by the Romans, and consequently distorted them almost beyond recognition in accordance with their own speech habits. If this is true, there certainly is no record of it in antiquity; quite the contrary. In the fourth century A.D., Symmachus, prefect of Rome, wrote to a friend that he was thinking of sending his son to the University of Lyon (at that time it was the Gallo-Roman town of Lugdunum), "because the Latin they speak there is purer than what we hear here in Rome."

Others say it was the Germanic invaders of Gaul, the Franks, who twisted the Latin speech of the Gallo-Romans until it turned into French. But Spain and Italy had Germanic invaders, too.

A third theory is that Charlemagne, the great medieval emperor, became distressed at the ungrammatical way his western subjects handled their Latin, and undertook to correct their speech by having the church sermons given in good classical Latin. But the people no longer really understood good classical Latin, and the net result was that their spoken language degenerated at a far faster clip than in Spain or Italy, where no reform movement was in progress. After about thirty years of the noble experiment, Charlemagne realized that he was doing more harm than good to the cause of linguistic purity and tried to reverse himself. But by that time the speech of the northern French provinces had changed so much that he discovered it was no longer Latin but something else. He actually made the distinction in his second edict, ordering that the "rustic Romance tongue," not the "Latin tongue" be henceforth used in the church sermons. This theory is borne out by the fact that a document unmistakably French first appears in 842, whereas Spanish and Italian don't begin to appear in written form until 950 and 960.

French between the ninth and the fourteenth centuries seems to have been a language as different in sound pattern and stress from the French of today as modern French is from English. Numerous French scholars have endeavored to translate the literary masterpiece of that era, the *Song of Roland*, into modern French. Their translations invariably fall flat, because the rhythm of the language is no longer the same. Down to the time of François Villon, French was a language of heavy stress and harsh sounds, like German or English. Beyond that point, it turns into a tongue of grace and refinement and clarity, the tongue we know today.

What is this modern spoken language, the possession of which, in greater or lesser measure, is an unfailing passport to the French heart?

The sound pattern of modern spoken French is dominated by the middle rounded vowels (represented in French spelling by *u* and *eu*, occasionally *oeu*) and the full-bodied nasals (*an, in, on, un*), both of which recur with striking frequency in French speech, and which are unlike anything we have in English. There is a theory to the effect that these sounds come from the original Celtic speech habits of the pre-Roman Gauls, but this is far from certain.

While these sounds are strange to us, they are not too difficult to reproduce. For both *u* and *eu*, protrude the lips as for English *oo*, or for a kiss; when the lips are firmly set in position, and *without moving them*, attempt to pronounce the *ee* of *meet* and the *a* of *gate*, respectively. The sounds that come out will be represented in our transcription by Ü and Ö, respectively. Try them out in a few simple words (note that henceforth large capitals will be used to indicate stressed words and syllables; the French word stress is light and some phoneticians advocate even stress on all syllables of a word; but since English has a strong *initial* stress, it may be well for the learner to stress [usually] his *final* French syllable):

lune (LÜN)   moon
tu (TÜ)   you (familiar)
butte (BÜT)   hillock
seul (SÖL)   alone
feu (FÖ)   fire
yeux (YÖ)   eyes

The four nasal sounds are most frequently represented in French writing by *a* or *e, i, o*, and *u*, followed by *n* or *m* in the same syllable; but many other spellings are possible. They are produced by partially blocking the passage between nose and throat as you pronounce, respectively, the *a* of *father*, the *e* of *met*, the *aw* of *law*, and the *u* of *cur*. This blocking effect can be fairly imitated by holding your nose with your fingers, but that is hardly necessary. Just pretend your nose is thoroughly stopped by a head cold. For the four sounds, we shall use in our transcription ÃH, ẼH, ÃW and ŨH:

an (ÃH)   year
anglais (ãh-GLEH)   English
fin (FẼH)   end
main (MẼH)   hand
on (ÃW)   someone
bon (BÃW)   good
un (ŨH)   one, a, an
lundi (lũh-DEE)   Monday

Another distinctive French sound is the uvular *r*, typical of good Parisian, and now current throughout all of France (other sections, notably the south, used a trilled *r* similar to that of Spanish or Italian, something like the *r* of *very* as pronounced by a Britisher). The Parisian uvular *r* is like a gentle rasping or clearing of the throat in its upper part, along the soft palate. Once heard it is never forgotten, and forms a stock part of all imitations on stage or screen of Frenchmen speaking English (it is not at all a bad idea to imitate in earnest what you sometimes imitate in fun).

Armed with these most unfamiliar of French sounds, we can now pass on to some common greetings:

Bonjour (bãw-ZHOOR)   Good day, Good morning, Good afternoon.
Bonsoir (bãw-SWAHR)   Good evening, Good night.
Au revoir (oh-ruh-VWAHR)   Good-by.
Comment vous portez-vous? (kaw-MÃH voo-pawr-TAY-VOO)   How do you do?
Comment allez-vous? (kaw-MÃH ta-LAY-VOO)   How are you?
Bien, merci, et vous-même? (BYÉH, mehr-SEE, ay voo-MEHM)   Well, thanks, and you?

French, like English, is a language of complicated spelling. But our main concern is the spoken, not the written, language. French vowel *sounds*, other than those already described, are, in our transcription:

A (a trifle more open than the *a* of *hat*).
AH (the *a* of *father*)
Both of these sounds usually appear in French spelling as *a;* AH sometimes appears as *â*:

là (LA)   there
pas (PAH)   not

EH (like the *e* of *met*); this may appear in French spelling as *e, è, ê, ai, ei,* etc.:

lettre (LEH-truh)   letter
père (PEHR)   father
fenêtre (fun-NEH-truh)   window (Don't be surprised if you hear, in rapid speech, FNEH-truh, or even FNEHT.)
j'ai (ZHEH)   I have
neige (NEHZH)   snow

AY (like the *a* of *gate*, but cut short). This may appear in French spelling as *e, é, ai,* etc.:

donner, donnez, donné (all pronounced daw-NAY)   to give, give, given
j'irai (zhee-RAY)   I shall go

UH (like *e* in *the man*). This sound is usually spelled *e*; in rapid speech, it is often skipped altogether, so don't worry if you don't hear it:

le livre (luh LEE-vruh)   the book
venir (vuh-NEER)   to come

EE (like *ee* in *meet*). It is usually spelled *i* or *î* (sometimes *ie*):

il (EEL) he
vie (VEE) life

AW (as in *law*, but cut short; the *o* of British *pot* will do, if you can talk like a Britisher). It is usually spelled *o*:

mode (MAWD) fashion
notre (NAW-truh, or NAWT) our

OH (like *o* in *go*, but cut short). It may appear in French spelling as *o, ô, au, eau,* etc.:

nos (NOH) our (with a plural noun)
nôtre (NOH-truh) ours
aussi (oh-SEE) also
eau (OH) water

OO (as in *food*). This appears in French spelling as *ou*:

où (OO) where
cou (KOO) neck

WAH (as in *watch*). Normally spelled *oi*:

voir (VWAHR) to see
avec moi (a-VEHK MWAH) with me

Consonant sounds, outside of *r*, calling for an extended description, are:

ZH (the *s* of *pleasure*), which may appear as *g* or *j*:

général (zhay-nay-RAL) general
jeune (ZHÖN) young

SH (which appears as *ch* in French spelling):

chat (SHA) cat
acheter (ash-TAY) to buy

NY (spelled *gn*):

campagne (kãh-PA-nyuh) country
agneau (a-NYOH) lamb

Y (spelled *i, y, ill, il,* etc.):

bien (BYẼH) well
il y a (ee-LYA) there is
fille (FEE-yuh) girl, daughter
travail (tra-VA-yuh) work

It may also be remarked that in pronouncing French *t, d, n, l,* the tip of the tongue strikes the back of the teeth rather than the gum ridge above the upper teeth, as it does in English. This makes a very slight difference in the pronunciation of those consonant sounds—not enough to cause you to be misunderstood, but enough to cause you to be taken for a foreigner if you do not conform. As a general rule, the tongue is curled downward when you speak French, whereas it curls upward when you speak English.

At this point, it is only right to come up for air. Let's do it with a bow, for the French are nothing if not polite. A few of the very many expressions of politeness in French are:

Monsieur (muh-SYÖ)   Mr., sir, gentleman; abbreviate in writing to *M*.

Madame (ma-DAM)   Mrs., madam, ma'am, lady (*Mme* is the abbreviation).

Mademoiselle (mad-mwah-ZEHL)   Miss, young lady (*Mlle* is the abbreviation).

These three expressions are used far more often than their English counterparts, and usually without the name; where the American says "Won't you come in, Mr. Jones?" the Frenchman puts it *"Voulez-vous entrer, Monsieur?"* (voo-LAY-VOO zäh-TRAY, muh-SYÖ).

S'il vous plaît. (seel voo PLEH)   Please.

Merci (beaucoup, infiniment). (mehr-SEE [boh-KOO, ĕh-fee-nee-MÃH])   Thanks (a lot, very much).

Il n'y a pas de quoi. (eel nya PAH duh KWAH)   Don't mention it. (This is often shortened to *pas de quoi*, which in rapid speech gets to sound like PAHT KWAH.)

Pardon. (par-DĀW)   Pardon me, excuse me.

Oui. (WEE)   Yes.

Non. (NÃW)   No.

Avec plaisir. (a-VEHK pleh-ZEER)   Gladly.

Permettez-moi de vous présenter mon ami. (pehr-meh-TAY-MWAH duh voo pray-zäh-TAY mäw-na-MEE)   May I introduce my friend?

Enchanté! (äh-shäh-TAY)   Delighted, pleased to meet you!

Now for a few practical hints about spoken French. The

French speaker tends to run his words together in such a way that the phrase or sentence, rather than the word, is the unit of speech, as well as of understanding, to the listener. The syllable is of paramount importance in the sound sequence, and the tendency is for the syllable to consist of consonant plus vowel. But this tendency, common to all the Romance languages, is opposed in French by another tendency, that of dropping *uh* sounds wherever possible, particularly at the end of words. This means that there are actually two French pronunciations—a dignified, highfalutin one, which is heard on the stage, or when poetry is declaimed, or when an orator makes a solemn commemoration speech; and another, rapid-fire one, used in ordinary conversation, where syllables are run together and weird consonant combinations result from the dropping of *uh* sounds. Compare, for instance:

notre maison (NAW-truh meh-ZÃW, in slow motion; NAWT meh-ZÃW in rapid speech)   our house; or
Je t'offre un bock. (zhuh TAW-fruh ûh BAWK, vs. ZHTAWF ûh BAWK, or better yet, SHTAWF ûh BAWK, because the ZH is turned into SH by the fact that a T follows)   I'll treat you to a beer.

Another peculiarity of French pronunciation is the linking process whereby the final written consonant of a word, normally silent, is often pronounced with the initial vowel of a closely connected following word. Compare:

ils font   (EEL FÃW)   they are doing (final -*s* of *ils* silent).
ils ont   (EEL-ZÃW)   they have (final -*s* of *ils* carried over to *ont* and pronounced as Z).

The fact that final written consonants are normally silent means that the distinction between singular and plural, which in writing is mostly carried, as in English, by a final *s* on the plural form, in speech appears only in the article, demonstrative adjective, or possessive adjective that precedes the noun:

le mur   (luh MÜR)   the wall
les murs   (lay MÜR)   the walls
ce billet   (suh bee-YEH)   this ticket
ces billets   (say bee-YEH)   these tickets
notre auto   (naw-troh-TOH)   our car
nos autos   (noh-zoh-TOH)   our cars

This makes spoken French a language of significant prefixes rather than of meaningful endings, and sets it apart from English, Spanish, Italian, German, Latin, or Russian, giving it a strange, but purely chance resemblance to the Bantu languages of central and southern Africa.

It may be stated at this point that by far the best way to acquire the spoken sounds of a language is to listen to and imitate a cultured native teacher (some people advocate the use of *any* native speaker, but that is an error; if a foreigner acquires American English with a southern hillbilly or Brooklyn Navy Yard pronunciation, is that any better than speaking it with a foreign accent?).

One of the troubles with cultured native teachers is that they are often too much concerned with teaching you, in their own imperfect English, minor points of grammar that seldom come up in real life, instead of hammering, as they should, on the pronunciation of high-frequency words and phrases in the tongue you want to learn. That is why some private language schools forbid all use of English in their classes. You can learn grammar from a book. What you can't learn from a book is the authentic pronunciation, and that should be the native teacher's main job.

If no native teacher is available, the next best thing is a set of good records. These give you words and phrases authentically pronounced by a cultured native; some even make provision for back-spacing, so that you can listen and repeat, listen and repeat, until you are satisfied that you sound something like your model.

Transcriptions such as the one we use are at best an unsatisfactory makeshift. The true sounds of one language very seldom have an exact counterpart in the writing system of another. Hence, in the absence of a native teacher or a good recording, do the best you can with our "kuh voo-LAY-VOO," and you'll manage to make yourself understood. But the first chance you get, as soon as you land in France, listen closely to a Frenchman saying *"Que voulez-vous?"* and notice the difference.

Now we come to that most important of topics, tourist wants.

The question, technically, is

Que voulez-vous? (kuh voo-LAY-VOO) What do you want? or

Que désirez-vous? (kuh day-zee-RAY-VOO) What do you wish?

but what you are more likely to hear is

Monsieur (or *Madame,* or *Mademoiselle*) *désire?* (muh-SYÖ [ma-DAM, mad-mwah-ZEHL] day-ZEER)

The answers:

Je désire (zhuh day-ZEER) I wish.
Je voudrais (zhuh voo-DREH) I should like.
Donnez-moi (daw-NAY-MWAH) Give me.
Apportez-moi (a-pawr-TAY-MWAH) Bring me.

The last two sound a little brutal to a French ear. They may be softened by a *s'il vous plaît* at the end of the sentence, or by turning them into a polite question:

Voulez-vous me donner? (voo-LAY-VOO muh daw-NAY)
   Will you give me?
Voulez-vous m'apporter? (voo-LAY-VOO ma-pawr-TAY)
   Will you bring me?

Here are a few samples of these expressions in combination:

Je voudrais un paquet de cigarettes. (zhuh voo-DREH ûh pa-KEH duh see-ga-REHT) I should like a package of cigarettes.
Voulez-vous me donner une boîte de bonbons au chocolat? (voo-LAY-VOO muh daw-NAY ün BWAHT duh bãw-BÃW zoh shaw-kaw-LA) Will you give me a box of chocolate candy?
Voulez-vous m'apporter une carafe de vin ordinaire? (voo-LAY-VOO ma-pawr-TAY ün ka-RAF duh VÊH awr-dee-NEHR) Will you bring me a pitcher of table wine?

Some specific shopping terms are:

Montrez-moi (or *Voulez-vous me montrer?*) (mãw-TRAY-MWAH, voo-LAY-VOO muh mãw-TRAY) Show me.
Combien? (or *Combien cela?*) (kãw-BYÊH, kãw-BYÊH suh-LA) How much?
C'est trop! (or *Ça coûte trop cher!*) (seh TROH, sa KOOT troh SHEHR) It's too much!

Encore quelque chose? (ăh-KAWR kehl-kuh-SHOHZ)   Anything else?
C'est tout! (seh-TOO)   That's all!

Here are a few often used requests for directions, and answers to them.

Voulez-vous me dire? (voo-LAY-VOO muh DEER)   Will you tell me?
Où est, où sont? (OO EH, OO SÃW)   Where is, Where are?
Où est-ce que nous allons? (OO EHS kuh noo-za-LÃW)   Where are we going?
De quel côté? (duh KEHL koh-TAY)   Which way?
Voici. (vwah-SEE)   Here is, Here are.
Voilà. (vwah-LA)   There is, There are.
Par ici. Par là. (pa-ree-SEE, par LA)   This way. That way.
Allez tout droit. (a-LAY too DRAWH)   Go straight ahead.
Accompagnez-moi. (a-kăw-pa-NYAY-MWAH)   Come with me.

Let's try a few of these in combination:

Pardon, voulez-vous me dire où se trouve l'église du Sacré-Coeur? (par-DÃW, voo-LAY-VOO muh DEER oo suh TROOV lay-GLEEZ dü sa-KRAY-KÖR)   Pardon me, can you tell me where the Church of the Sacred Heart is?
De quel côté est l'ascenseur? (duh KEHL koh-TAY EH la-săh-SÖR)   Which way is the elevator?
Où est-ce que je pourrais trouver une pharmacie? (OO EHS-kuh zhuh poo-REH troo-VAY ün far-ma-SEE)   Where can I find a drugstore?

Here are a few directional signs. They are more important in writing than in speech.

Défense de fumer. (day-FÃHS duh fü-MAY)   No smoking.
Défense d'entrer. (day-FÃHS dăh-TRAY)   No admittance.
Attention. (a-tăh-SYÃW)   Attention, Warning, Careful.
Tenez la droite (gauche). (tuh-NAY la DRWAHT, GOHSH)   Keep right (left).

Entrée, Sortie. (äh-TRAY, sawr-TEE) Entrance, Exit.
Messieurs, Dames. (meh-SYÖ, DAM) Gentlemen, Ladies (*Hommes, femmes,* "men," "women," are practically never used on rest-room doors).

"Speaking" terminology can serve, if nothing else, the purpose of pleasant conversation. Here are a few terms:

Parlez-vous français (anglais, allemand, espagnol)? (par-LAY-VOO fräh-SAY, äh-GLAY, al-MÄH, ehs-pa-NYAWL) Do you speak French (English, German, Spanish)?
Un peu. (ūh PÖ) A little.
Parlez plus lentement. (par-LAY PLÜ läht-MÄH) Speak more slowly.
Comprenez-vous? (käw-pruh-NAY-VOO) Do you understand?
Je ne comprends pas. (zhuh nuh käw-PRÄH PAH) I don't understand..
Que voulez-vous dire? (KUH voo-LAY-VOO DEER) What do you mean?
Comment s'appelle ceci en français? (kaw-MÄH sa-PEHL suh-SEE äh fräh-SAY) What do you call this in French?
Comment dit-on —— en français? (kaw-MÄH dee-TÄW —— äh fräh-SAY) How do you say —— in French?
Je suis Américain (Américaine if you are a woman). (zhuh SÜEE za-may-ree-KÊH, za-may-ree-KEHN) I am an American.

There are a few people you might need or want to send for:

J'ai besoin de—— (ZHEH buh-ZWÊH duh) I need——
Faites venir—— (FEHT vuh-NEER) Send for——
J'ai besoin d'un médecin (d'un interprète). (ZHEH buh-ZWÊH düh mayd-SÊH, düh nêh-tehr-PREHT) I need a doctor (an interpreter).
Faites venir le directeur (le consul américain)! (FEHT vuh-NEER luh dee-rehk-TÖR, luh käw-SÜL a-may-ree-KÊH) Send for the manager (the American consul)!

Perhaps no one can do anything about the weather, but the whole world likes to talk about it. The French are no exception:

Il pleut. (EEL PLÖ) It is raining.

Il fait beau (mauvais). (EEL FEH BOH, moh-VEH) It's
fine (bad) weather.
Il fait chaud (froid). (EEL FEH SHOH, FRWAH) It's
warm (cold).
Quel beau (mauvais) temps! (KEHL BOH, moh-VEH,
TÃH) What fine (awful) weather!
J'ai chaud (froid). (ZHEH SHOH, FRWAH) I'm warm
(cold).

Here are a few important verbs, given in the infinitive form.
With *je voudrais* (I should like), *je viens de* (I have just), *je
vais* (I am going to) or *je suis en train de* (I am in the act of,
I am —ing) before them, and an appropriate noun after them,
you can build complete, comprehensible, correct sentences:

je voudrais (zhuh voo-DREH) I should like to
je viens de (zhuh VYÊH duh) I have just
je vais (zhuh VEH) I am going to
je suis en train de (zhuh SÜEE zãh TRÊH duh) I am
—ing
acheter (ash-TAY) to buy
parler (par-LAY) to speak
visiter (vee-zee-TAY) to visit
demander (duh-mãh-DAY) to ask, ask for
manger (mãh-ZHAY) to eat
boire (BWAHR) to drink
aller (a-LAY) to go
chercher (shehr-SHAY) to look for
savoir (sa-VWAHR) to know (a fact), know how
connaître (kaw-NEH-truh) to know a person

In combination:

Je voudrais visiter l'église. (zhuh voo-DREH vee-zee-TAY
lay-GLEEZ) I should like to visit the church.
Je viens d'acheter une bouteille de champagne. (zhuh VYÊH
dash-TAY ün boo-TEH-yuh duh shãh-PA-nyuh) I have
just bought a bottle of champagne.
Je vais parler à l'agent de police. (zhuh VEH par-LAY a
la-ZHÃH duh paw-LEES) I'm going to speak to the
policeman.
Je suis en train de chercher un bon hôtel. (zhuh SÜEE zãh
TRÊH duh shehr-SHAY üh BÃW noh-TEHL) I'm
looking for a good hotel.

The verb *faire* (FEHR) means "to do," "to make"; *faire* followed by another verb means "to have something done": *faire repasser* (FEHR ruh-pa-SAY), to have pressed; *faire nettoyer* (FEHR neh-twah-YAY), to have cleaned; *faire laver* (FEHR la-VAY), to have washed; *faire réparer* (FEHR ray-pa-RAY), to have repaired.

Je voudrais faire repasser ce complet. (zhuh voo-DREH FEHR ruh-pa-SAY suh kãw-PLEH) I should like to have this suit pressed.

Je voudrais me faire couper les cheveux. (zhuh voo-DREH muh FEHR koo-PAY lay shuh-VÖ) I should like to get a haircut.

The present tense of *être* (EH-truh), to be, is as follows:

je suis (zhuh SÜEE) I am	*nous sommes* (noo SAWM) we are
tu es (tü EH) you are (familiar)	*vous êtes* (voo-ZEHT) you are
il est (ee-LEH) he is	*ils sont* (eel SÃW) they are
elle est (eh-LEH) she is	*elles sont* (ehl SÃW) they are (fem.)

The present tense of *avoir* (a-VWAHR), to have, runs:

j'ai (ZHEH) I have	*nous avons* (noo-za-VÃW) we have
tu as (tü A) you have (familiar)	*vous avez* (voo-za-VAY) you have
il a (ee-LA) he has	*ils ont* (eel-ZÃW) they have
elle a (eh-LA) she has	*elles ont* (ehl ZÃW) they have (fem.)

As anyone knows who has studied it in school, the French verb is a many-splendored thing, with innumerable forms. If one is to converse fluently, there is no substitute for learning these forms. But for practical tourist purposes, the forms we have given above cover a multitude of situations. Let the tourist's motto therefore be: *Je vais aller en France et je vais parler français un tout petit peu!* (zhuh VEH-za-LAY ãh frãhs ay zhuh VEH par-LAY frãh-SEH ũh too puh-TEE PÖ). Can you figure out what that means?

chapter five
spanish is easy!

Spanish, like English, is an imperial language. It extends over many widely scattered parts of the earth, and embraces a speaking population of over a hundred and fifty million, three fourths of whom are our neighbors in the Western Hemisphere.

But our interest in Spanish is recent. It began at the time of the First World War, when someone remarked that since we couldn't trade with Europe, we would have to trade with South America. We were so little prepared for this innovation that teachers of German, physics, and other subjects had to turn overnight into teachers of Spanish, keeping one lesson ahead of their classes.

Spanish is a language of wide distribution, and this leads, naturally enough, to a variety of dialectal forms. But the divergence is less than one would expect. The differences between the Spanish of Spain, that of Argentina, that of Mexico, that of Venezuela, and that of Cuba are, on the whole, less marked than those found among the dialects of the small Italian peninsula.

Furthermore, Spanish speakers don't worry about them. There is among them the same broad linguistic tolerance that prevails in the Anglo-Saxon world. They, too, know what it is to have their language spoken by people of widely different racial and cultural backgrounds—haughty Castilians and swarthy Moroccan Berbers, Peruvian Indians and Cuban Negroes, Filipinos and Aztecs, Mallorcans and Basques. But they are all bound together by a shadowy something of a

linguistic nature, very farfetchedly epitomized in New York City (one of the world's great Spanish-language centers, by virtue of a recent influx of nearly a million Puerto Ricans) by a festival known as *el Día de la Raza* ("the Day of the Race"), celebrated on Columbus Day. Actually, Spanish speakers are of all races under the sun; but they merge their backgrounds in an ideal of linguistic unity. They have even devised the term *Hispano*, which means not "Spanish" (which is *español*), but "pertaining to the great Spanish-speaking family."

No fewer than nineteen sovereign nations have Spanish as their official tongue. In addition to European Spain and its African possessions, there are North American Mexico; Central American Costa Rica, Guatemala, El Salvador, Honduras, Nicaragua, and Panama; Antillean Cuba and the Dominican Republic; South American Argentina, Chile, Uruguay, Peru, Bolivia, Paraguay, Ecuador, Colombia, and Venezuela. Then there are the Philippines, which were long a Spanish colony and where Spanish is still widely spoken, and American dependencies like Puerto Rico and the Canal Zone. There are millions of Spanish speakers in New York State, New Mexico, Texas, Arizona, and California (in New Mexico, Spanish is co-official with English in the state legislature).

It would be surprising indeed if this language did not have local varieties. The flora and fauna of Argentina are quite different from those of Colombia, and the nomenclature will vary accordingly. A farm hand will be a *peón* in Mexico, a *guaso* in Chile, a *guajiro* in Cuba. You will hear an automobile tire called *goma* in some countries, *llanta* in others. *Tabaco*, which is "tobacco" in Spain, becomes "cigar" in Cuba, where the Castilian *cigarro* ("cigar") is a cigarette. *Monte* can mean mountain or jungle, *manteca* can be grease or butter, according to your location. But, by and large, Spanish speakers manage to understand one another.

The variety of words is accompanied by a variety of gestures. If you are a beauteous young lady traveling in South America, do not be surprised if in one country the young men wolf-whistle at you by sticking their index finger into their cheek, while in another they use thumb and forefinger to open wide one of their eyes, as if preparing to receive an eye drop from an oculist. Both gestures are indicative of appreciation of feminine charm, but in Spain they are replaced by the *piropo*, a flowery spoken compliment, said to have been inherited from the poetry-loving Moors who held most

of Spain under their domination from the eighth to the fifteenth century. (*"¡Dichosa la madre que te parió!"* ["Happy the mother who bore you!"] is a sample of a briefer *piropo*.)

As to origin, Spanish is fundamentally Latin, the Latin of the legions that in a series of bloody Punic Wars wrested ancient Iberia from the Carthaginians. When Hannibal, the great Carthaginian general, opened his spectacular march on Rome that was to end in disaster and death, he began hostilities by attacking the Spanish city of Saguntum, an ally of Rome. Later, as the Romans took firm control of the Iberian Peninsula, they Romanized and Latinized most of the natives, to such an extent that in later centuries Spain furnished Rome with emperors, such as Hadrian, and with great orators, such as Seneca.

But a small die-hard band of native Iberians refused to submit to the Roman power. They went off into the mountain fastnesses of the northern Pyrenees, and there gave rise to the people of the Basques, who still today speak a strange, mysterious tongue utterly unlike those of their Spanish and French neighbors.

Roman Iberia lasted well over seven hundred years. Then Germanic invaders swarmed into the peninsula—Suevi and Vandals and Visigoths—founding a Visigothic dynasty that endured from the middle of the fifth to the beginning of the eighth century. It was during this time that most of the well-known Spanish family names were built up out of Visigothic roots—names like Ramírez, Hernández, Suárez, González. But, except for this, the reign of the Visigoths made relatively little impression on the Latin tongue of Spain.

It was the invasion of the African Moors in A.D. 711 that gave Spanish the indelible imprint that sets it off from its sister Romance tongues. The story (perhaps true, perhaps legendary) of that successful invasion is at least as dramatic as the Norman Conquest of England.

The Arabs, inspired by Mohammed's Koran, had swept with fire and sword across Christian North Africa, submerging the Cross and the vestiges of the Greco-Roman civilization that had thrived there since the fall of Carthage. Visigothic Spain, across the narrow strait that antiquity had dubbed the Pillars of Hercules, lay uneasy but secure, for the governor of the fortress that is now Ceuta was a Visigothic nobleman of proven prowess and loyalty. He made the mistake of sending

his daughter to be educated at the court of his king, in the capital city of Toledo, and the king, last of the Visigothic line, made the more fatal mistake of seducing her. When the father learned of this, he opened the gates of his fortress to the Moors, and hordes of fanatical Moslems poured into Spain across the Strait of Gibraltar (the modern name, by the way, is from the Arabic Jebel Tarik, "mountain of Tarik," leader of the invading forces). In less than fifty years the Moors had snatched all of Spain from the Visigoths, save for a narrow strip in the far north, where Galicia, Asturias, and the Basque Provinces stand today. One more victory in the field, and all of Spain would have been Moslem. But the victory never came. Instead, the entrenched Spanish Christians managed to repel the last furious attack of the Moors at Covadonga.

Then started that long, bitter border warfare known as the *Reconquista*—the retaking from the Moors, bit by bit, at the cost of infinite blood and sweat and tears, of what had been so swiftly lost to the Moors by the lust of one man and the treachery of another. The *Reconquista* went on from the end of the eighth century to the year 1492. Columbus' discovery of America coincided with the expulsion of the last Spanish Moors from Granada, and Spain was free and Christian once more.

But the seven centuries of Moorish domination had left their mark on the Spanish language, in the form of vast numbers of Arabic words, Arabic expressions, Arabic place names. It is primarily by these that Spanish and Portuguese differentiate themselves from other Romance tongues.

Run your eye over the *a*'s in a Spanish dictionary. You will find a seemingly endless array of words that start with *al-*, the Arabic article, and that have no counterpart, or only a borrowed one, in other Western tongues—*alhaja* for "jewel," *almeja* for "clam," *almacén* for "warehouse" (this one eventually turns into the French *magasin* and the English *magazine*), *alacrán* for "scorpion," *alcalde* for "mayor," *alguacil* for "bailiff" (this becomes *vizier* in another incarnation). Then look at the map of Spain, or any Spanish-speaking land, and observe the number of place names starting with *Guad-*, from the Arabic *wadi*, "river"—Guadalquivir, Guadalajara, Guadarrama, Guadalupe—and you will become acutely conscious of the impact of Arabic on Spanish. Even the Spanish exclamation of wishful thinking, *ojalá* ("would to God!"), is the Arabic *wa sha Allah!*

The other element in Spanish that sets it apart from Latin consists of the words that have either survived from the pre-Roman Iberians or have been brought in by the Basques, words like *vega*, "plain" (we get it in Las Vegas), *ascua*, "live coal," *gorra*, "cap," *izquierdo*, "left," *pizarra*, "slate," and the *bizarro* passed on to us as "bizarre."

One more fact about the Spanish vocabulary needs to be mentioned. Many of the American Indian words we have adopted into English came first into Spanish, which passed them on to us. This was natural, since the Spaniards preceded the English in discovering and exploring the New World. No English translation is therefore needed for such originally Indian words in Spanish as *chocolate*, *tomate*, *maíz*, *cacao*, *coyote*. But should we remind you that *huracán* gave us "hurricane," that *aguacate* gave us "avocado pear" and that *hamaca* became "hammock"?

Spanish is a good-neighbor language and a language of commercial, political, and cultural importance; but, in addition, it is the easiest of the major Western languages to learn, at least in its initial stages. This is due in part to the relative ease of pronunciation, in part to the Spanish Academy, which went out of its way to simplify grammatical rules and eliminate irregularities. In a beginner's three-month course, you can learn more Spanish than French, Italian, or German. The difficulties come later, when you tackle long-winded Spanish sentences with their loose word order.

But the tourist to Spain, Mexico, Cuba, or Argentina does not need to worry about the complicated arrangement of literary sentences. He has only to consider a few simple sounds and words.

The vowel sounds of Spanish are only five in number, and most simple:

AH (spelled *a*) is the *a* of *father*.

ama   (AH-mah)   he loves
altar   (ahl-TAHR)   altar

EH (spelled *e*) is halfway between the *e* of *met* and the *a* of *gate* cut short.

meses   (MEH-sehs)   months
este   (EHS-teh)   this

EE (spelled *i*) is the *ee* of *meet.*

sí (SEE)   yes
ir (EER)   to go

OH (spelled *o*) is the *o* of *go* cut short.

no (NOH)   no, not
pollo (POH-lyoh)   chicken

OO (spelled *u*) is the *oo* of *food.*

humo (OO-moh)   smoke
fumar (foo-MAHR) to smoke

The sound of *W* is indicated in Spanish spelling by *u* or *hu,* that of *Y* by *y, i* or *hi*:

bueno (BWEH-noh)   good
ya (YAH)   already, now
miedo (MYEH-doh)   fear
hueso (WEH-soh)   bone
muy (MOOY)   very
hierro (YEHR-roh)   iron

Spanish forms of greeting and leave-taking are uncomplicated but numerous:

Buenos días. (BWEH-nohs DEE-ahs)   Good day, Good morning.
Buenas tardes. (BWEH-nahs TAHR-dehs)   Good afternoon, Good evening.
Buenas noches. (BWEH-nahs NOH-chehs)   Good night.
Adiós. (ah-DYOHS)   Good-by.
Hasta la vista. (AHS-tah lah VEES-tah)   Good-by.
Hasta luego (mañana). (AHS-tah LWEH-goh [mah-NYAH-nah])   See you later (tomorrow).
¡Hola! (OH-lah)   Hello!
¿Cómo está usted? (KOH-moh ehs-TAH oos-TEHD)   How are you?
¿Qué tal? (KEH TAHL)   How's everything?
Muy bien, gracias, ¿y usted? (MOOY BYEHN, GRAH-thyas, ee oos-TEHD)   Very well, thank you, and you?

Note the curious inverted question and exclamation marks at the beginning of questions and exclamations. The Spanish Academy thoughtfully provided them, on the theory that one who is reading will often miss the point that he is up against a question until he gets to the end, whereupon he has to lift his voice suddenly if he is reading out loud. To make assurance doubly sure, the Academy also provided written accent marks to go over words used in a question, like *¿Dónde?* (where?) and *¿Cuándo?* (when?); if the word is not used in a question, the written accent does not appear. This is a little like wearing suspenders *and* a belt, but the Academy thought it would leave nothing to chance.

The following forms of address are used pretty much as in English, save that they are not generally used before a person's first name:

Señor   (seh-NYOHR)   Mr., sir, gentleman
Señora   (seh-NYOH-rah)   Mrs., madam, ma'am, lady
Señorita   (seh-nyoh-REE-tah)   Miss, young lady

The following, on the other hand, are used *only* before a person's first name. They do not at all imply undue familiarity, and it is perfectly all right to use them with anyone whose first name you know:

Don   (dohn)   Mr.
Doña   (DOH-nyah)   Mrs., miss

These are the polite ways of saying "you":

Usted   (oos-TEHD)   you
Ustedes   (oos-TEH-dehs)   you (plural)

They are usually abbreviated in writing to *Vd.*, *Vds.* (or *Ud.*, *Uds.*), respectively. They come originally from *Vuestra Merced*, *Vuestras Mercedes* ("Your Grace," "Your Graces"). In some countries, they are used even in familiar address, particularly in the plural. It is a little odd to hear a Spanish–American mother telling her children: "Your Graces have been naughty, and consequently Your Graces will go to bed without their suppers."

Spanish consonant sounds are almost as simple as the vowels.

Written *b* and *v* are both pronounced B if they come at the beginning of an utterance, or after a consonant; but if they appear between vowels, they are both sounded as a weak V, with the lower lip not touching the upper. This means that the Spanish speakers themselves may make spelling mistakes in words involving *b* and *v*. To distinguish them in spelling, they call *b* *"be de burro"* ("donkey *b*") and *v* *"ve de vaca"* ("cow *v*"), the idea being that anyone who is at all literate will know that *b* appears in the word for "donkey" and *v* in the word for "cow."

bien   (BYEHN)   well
enviar   (ehn-BYAHR)   to send
caballo   (kah-VAH-lyoh)   horse
bravo   (BRAH-voh)   brave

The letter *c* before *e* or *i*, and the letter *z*, used only before *a*, *o* or *u* in modern Spanish, have the sound of TH in "thing" in north Spanish Castilian, but are sounded like S in southern Spain and most of Spanish America. In this book, we shall follow the Castilian usage, but with the understanding that all *th* sounds may at will be replaced by *s* sounds.

cielo   (THYEH-loh or SYEH-loh)   sky, heaven
lazo   (LAH-thoh or LAH-soh)   loop, lasso

The letters *g*, before *e* or *i*, and *j*, in any position, represent an H sound which is stronger than in English (call it the *ch* of German *ach*, or of Scottish *loch* as pronounced by a Scotsman). If you use an English H sound, you will be understood:

general   (heh-neh-RAHL)   general
joven   (HOH-vehn)   young
giro   (HEE-roh)   money order
joya   (HOH-yah)   jewel

Spanish written *h*, on the other hand, is always silent:

hora   (OH-rah)   hour
hierro   (YEHR-roh)   iron

The written *ll* is LY in Castilian, a mere Y in most of Spanish America, while in Argentina and Chile it sometimes sounds like English J. (Here again, we shall follow Castilian usage.)

caballo   (kah-VAH-lyoh,   kah-VAH-yoh,   kah-VAH-joh)   horse

Written *ñ* is the NY of *canyon*:

año   (AH-nyoh)   year
señor   (seh-NYOHR)   sir

Written *s* is always hard, as in *this*, never soft, as in *these*:

rosa   (ROH-sah)   rose

The Spanish *r* is trilled; if initial or written double, it is trilled for a longer period of time:

caro   (KAH-roh)   dear
carro   (KAHR-roh)   cart

In the written groups *que, qui, gue, gui,* the *u* is silent:

que   (KEH)   which, that
guerra (GEHR-rah)   war
quien   (KYEHN)   who

For a language that is superpolite, Spanish distinguishes itself by having no real word for "please." You express it by a circumlocution: "Do me the favor of," "Have the kindness to":

Hágame usted el favor de darme.   (AH-gah-meh oos-TEHD ehl fah-VOHR deh DAHR-meh)   Please give me.
Tenga usted la bondad de decirme.   (TEHN-gah oos-TEHD lah bohn-DAHD deh deh-THEER-meh)   Please tell me.
(Mil) gracias.   ([MEEL] GRAH-thyahs)   Thank you (very much).
No hay de qué (or *De nada*).   (*noh* AHY *deh* KEH [deh NAH-dah])   Don't mention it.
Dispense usted.   (dees-PEHN-seh oos-TEHD)   Pardon me, Excuse me.
Lo siento (mucho).   (loh SYEHN-toh [MOO-choh])   I'm (very) sorry.
No importa (or *No es nada*).   (noh eem-POHR-tah [noh EHS NAH-dah])   It doesn't matter, It's nothing.
Sí.   (SEE)   Yes.
No.   (NOH)   No, not.
Con mucho gusto.   (kohn MOO-choh GOOS-toh)   With pleasure.
¿Permite que le presente a mi amigo?   (pehr-MEE-teh keh leh preh-SEHN-teh ah mee ah-MEE-goh)   May I introduce my friend?
¡Muchísimo gusto!   (moo-CHEE-see-moh GOOS-toh)   Delighted, pleased to meet you!

The question the tourist is most likely to hear is:

¿Qué quiere usted? (KEH KYEH-reh oos-TEHD) What do you want? or

¿Qué desea usted? (KEH deh-SEH-ah oos-TEHD) What do you wish?

Here are the formulas for answering:

(*Yo*) *quiero, deseo, quisiera* (YOH KYEH-roh, deh-SEH-oh, kee-SYEH-rah) I want, wish, should like (The use of *yo*, "I," is optional, since the ending of the verb indicates the subject.)

Déme usted. (DEH-meh oos-TEHD) Give me.

Tráigame usted. (TRAHY-gah-meh oos-TEHD) Bring me.

These may be softened by turning them into a question, or by using the "please" circumlocution:

¿Quiere usted darme (traerme)? (KYEH-reh oos-TEHD DAHR-meh [trah-EHR-meh]) Will you give me, bring me?

Haga usted el favor de darme (traerme). (AH-gah oos-TEHD ehl fah-VOHR deh DAHR-meh [trah-EHR-meh]) Please give me, (bring me).

Here are the names of some forms or containers:

un pedazo (oon peh-DAH-thoh) a piece
una tajada (OO-nah tah-HAH-dah) a slice
un paquete (oon pah-KEH-teh) a pack, package
una caja (OO-nah KAH-hah) a box
una botella (OO-nah boh-TEH-lyah) a bottle
un vaso (oon BAH-soh) a glass
una taza (OO-nah TAH-thah) a cup

The word for "of" is *de* (DEH).

Things you might want:

pan (PAHN) bread
jabón (hah-VOHN) soap
cigarrillos (thee-gahr-REE-lyohs) cigarettes
leche (LEH-cheh) milk
cerveza (thehr-BEH-thah) beer
agua (AH-gwah) water
té (TEH) tea
café (kah-FEH) coffee

vino (blanco, tinto)   (BEE-noh [BLAHN-koh, TEEN-toh])
wine (white, red)

Now let's try some of these:

Quisiera un paquete de cigarrillos.   (kee-SYEH-rah oon
pah-KEH-teh deh thee-gahr-REE-lyohs)   I should like a
package of cigarettes.

Tenga usted la bondad de darme una caja de cigarros.
(TEHN-gah oos-TEHD lah bohn-DAHD deh DAHR-meh
OO-nah KAH-hah deh thee-GAHR-rohs)   Please give
me a box of cigars.

¿Quiere usted darme una pastilla de jabón?   (KYEH-reh
oos-TEHD DAHR-meh OO-nah pahs-TEE-lyah deh
hah-VOHN)   Will you give me a cake of soap?

Mozo, tráigame usted una botella de agua mineral.   (MOH-
thoh, TRAHY-gah-meh oos-TEHD OO-nah boh-TEH-
lyah deh AH-gwah mee-neh-RAHL)   Waiter, bring me
a bottle of mineral water.

Here are additional shopping terms:

Muéstreme.   (MWEHS-treh-meh)   Show me.

¿Cuánto? (or *¿Cuánto cuesta?*)   (KWAHN-toh [KWAHN-
toh KWHES-tah])   How much?

Es demasiado.   (EHS deh-mah-SYAH-doh)   It's too
much.

¿Algo más? (or *¿Quiere más?*)   (AHL-goh MAHS [KYEH-
reh MAHS])   Anything else?

Nada más.   (NAH-dah MAHS)   Nothing else.

Ya basta (or *Es bastante*).   (YAH BAHS-tah [EHS bas-
TAHN-teh])   That's enough.

Here are a few directional expressions:

¿Puede usted decirme?   (PWEH-deh oos-TEHD deh-
THEER-meh)   Can you tell me?

¿Dónde está (están)?   (DOHN-deh ehs-TAH [ehs-TAHN])
Where is (are)?

¿Adónde vamos?   (ah-DOHN-deh VAH-mohs)   Where are
we going?

¿Por dónde?   (POHR DOHN-deh)   Which way?

Aquí está (están).   (ah-KEE ehs-TAH [ehs-TAHN)]   Here
is (are).

Por aquí.   (POHR ah-KEE)   This way.

Por allá.   (POHR ah-LYAH)   That way.

A la derecha (izquierda). (AH lah deh-REH-chah [ith-KYEHR-dah]) To the right (left).

Adelante. (ah-deh-LAHN-teh) Straight ahead.

Venga conmigo. (BEHN-gah kohn-MEE-goh) Come with me.

Try combining these with a few nouns:

la estación (lah ehs-tah-THYOHN) the station
el taxi (ehl TAHK-see) the taxi
el museo (ehl moo-SEH-oh) the museum
la ciudad (lah thyoo-DAHD) the city
la calle (lah KAH-lyeh) the street
la tienda (lah TYEHN-dah) the store
la farmacia (lah fahr-MAH-thyah) the drugstore
el correo (ehl kohr-REH-oh) the post office
el comedor (ehl koh-meh-DOHR) the dining room
el teléfono (ehl teh-LEH-foh-noh) the telephone
el cuarto de baño (ehl KWAHR-toh deh BAH-nyoh) the bathroom
el retrete (ehl reh-TREH-teh) the lavatory

Trying out a few combinations, this is what we get:

Dispense usted, ¿puede decirme donde está el museo? (dees-PEHN-seh oos-TEHD, PWEH-deh deh-THEER-meh DOHN-deh ehs-TAH ehl moo-SEH-oh) Pardon me, can you tell me where the museum is?

¿Quiere usted indicarme un cine? (KYEH-reh oos-TEHD een-dee-KAHR-meh oon THEE-neh) Would you show me a movie house?

¿Dónde puedo encontrar una farmacia? (DOHN-deh PWEH-doh ehn-kohn-TRAHR OO-nah fahr-MAH-thyah) Where can I find a drugstore?

Directional signs are important. They generally appear in written rather than spoken form.

Prohibido fumar. (proh-ee-VEE-doh foo-MAHR) No smoking.

¡Cuidado! (kwee-DAH-doh) Careful!

Aviso. (ah-VEE-soh) Notice.

Guardar la derecha (izquierda). (gwahr-DAHR la deh-REH-chah [eeth-KYEHR-dah]) Keep right (left).

Entrada, salida. (ehn-TRAH-dah, sah-LEE-dah) Entrance, Exit (used also for "arrival," "departure" in railroad stations).

Señores (or *caballeros*, or *hombres*).   (seh-NYOH-rehs [kah-vah-LYEH-rohs, OHM-brehs])   Gentlemen, Men.

Señoras (or *damas*, or *mujeres*).   (seh-NYOH-rahs [DAH-mahs, moo-HEH-rehs])   Ladies, Women.

Here are a few "speaking" terms:

¿Habla usted español (inglés, francés, alemán)?   (AH-vlah oos-TEHD ehs-pah-NYOHL [een-GLEHS, frahn-THEHS, ah-leh-MAHN])   Do you speak Spanish (English, French, German)?

Un poco.   (oon POH-koh)   A little.

Hable usted más despacio.   (AH-vleh oos-TEHD MAHS dehs-PAH-thyoh)   Speak more slowly.

¿Entiende usted?   (ehn-TYEHN-deh oos-TEHD)   Do you understand?

No entiendo.   (noh ehn-TYEHN-doh)   I don't understand.

¿Qué quiere usted decir?   (KEH KYEH-reh oos-TEHD deh-THEER)   What do you mean?

¿Cómo se llama esto en español?   (KOH-moh seh LYAH-mah EHS-toh ehn ehs-pah-NYOHL)   What do you call this in Spanish?

¿Cómo se dice —— en español?   (KOH-moh seh DEE-theh —— ehn ehs-pah-NYOHL)   How do you say —— in Spanish?

Soy norteamericano (norteamericana).   (soy NOHR-teh-ah-meh-ree-KAH-noh [-nah])   I'm an American. (Shift from *-o* to *-a* if you are a woman; and note that plain *americano* won't do, since the term applies to all inhabitants of Western Hemisphere nations.)

There are some people you may especially need:

Yo necesito (or *me hace falta*)   (YOH neh-theh-SEE-toh [meh AH-theh FAHL-tah])   I need

Mande usted venir (or *envíe usted por*)   (MAHN-deh oos-TEHD beh-NEER [ehn-BEE-eh oos-TEHD POHR])   Send for

el mozo   (ehl MOH-thoh)   the waiter

la criada   (lah kree-AH-dah)   the maid

un médico   (oon MEH-dee-koh)   a doctor

un intérprete   (oon een-TEHR-preh-teh)   an interpreter

The weather offers pleasant possibilities for elementary conversation. Here are a few weather terms:

Llueve. (LYWEH-veh) It is raining.

Hace buen (mal) tiempo. (AH-theh BWEHN [MAHL] TYEHM-poh) It is fine (bad) weather.

Hace calor (frío). (AH-theh kah-LOHR [FREE-oh]) It is warm (cold).

Tengo calor (frío). (TEHN-goh kah-LOHR [FREE-oh]) I am warm (cold).

¡Qué tiempo más hermoso (malo)! (KEH TYEHM-poh MAHS ehr-MOH-soh [MAH-loh]) What fine (bad) weather!

Adjectives ending in *-o* usually shift to *-a* in the feminine; those ending in *-e* or consonants remain unchanged. Those ending in vowels add *-s* in the plural; those ending in consonants add *-es*. They agree with the nouns they are used with in gender and number, but the chances are you will be understood even if your agreement is wrong.

hermoso (ehr-MOH-soh) beautiful, *hermosa, hermosos, hermosas*

libre (LEE-vreh) free, *libres*

azul (ah-THOOL) blue, *azules*

Lastly, a few important verbs, in the infinitive form. Use these with *quisiera* ("I should like"), *voy a* ("I am going to"), *acabo de* ("I have just"), *tengo que* ("I have to"), and you will be able to avoid some of the complicated Spanish verb tenses:

quisiera (kee-SYEH-rah) I should like to

voy a (BOY AH) I am going to

acabo de (ah-KAH-voh deh) I have just

tengo que (TEHN-goh keh) I have to

comprar (kohm-PRAHR) to buy

ver (BEHR) to see

hablar (ah-VLAHR) to speak

dar las gracias a (DAHR lahs GRAH-thyahs ah) to thank

preguntar (preh-goon-TAHR) to ask

comer (koh-MEHR) to eat, dine

ir (EER) to go (*ir a pie* [EER ah PYEH], "to go on foot"; for a conveyance use *en: ir en taxi* [EER ehn TAHK-see], "go by taxi")

entrar   (ehn-TRAHR)   to come in, go in
venir   (beh-NEER)   to come
saber   (sah-VEHR)   to know (a fact), know how
conocer   (koh-noh-THEHR)   to know, meet (a person)
hacer   (ah-THEHR)   to do, make
mandar   (mahn-DAHR)   to order (For "to have something done," Spanish generally uses *mandar* followed by
the infinitive: *mandar planchar* [mahn-DAHR plahn-
CHAHR], "to have pressed"; *mandar limpiar* [leem-
PYAHR], "to have cleaned"; *mandar lavar* [lah-VAHR],
"to have washed.")
quisiera afeitarme.   (ah-fey-TAHR-meh)   I should like to
shave, or get a shave.
quisiera cortarme el pelo.   (kohr-TAHR-meh ehl PEH-loh)
I should like to get a haircut.

In Spanish the forms of the verb *ser, estar* (SEHR, ehs-
TAHR), "to be," are:

soy, estoy (SOY, ehs-TOY) I   *somos, estamos* (SOH-mos,
am   ehs-TAH-mos) we are
es, está (EHS, ehs-TAH) he   *son, están* (SOHN, ehs-
is, she is, you are   TAHN) they are

Use *ser* when a noun follows: *soy médico* (SOY MEH-dee-
koh), "I am a doctor."
Use *estar* for location: *estoy aquí* (ehs-TOY ah-KEE), "I
am here."

The forms of the verb *tener* (teh-NEHR), "to have," are as
follows:

tengo (TEHN-goh) I have   *tenemos* (teh-NEH-mohs) we
tiene (TYEH-neh) he has,   have
she has, you have   *tienen* (TYEH-nehn) they
have

Not even the Spanish Academy, so successful in simplifying
the grammar of the language, has been able to simplify the
Spanish verb, which has many complications of tense, mood,
person, number, etc. But by using the infinitive forms given
above with the appropriate expressions, which call for the infinitive, the tourist can make himself generally understood.
Using a grammatical imperfection is invariably better than re-

maining tongue-tied. Let your motto therefore be: ¡*Voy a ir a España* (or *a la América española*) *y voy a hablar español* (BOY ah EER ah ehs-PAH-nyah [ah lah ah-MEH-ree-kah ehs-pah-NYOH-lah] ee BOY ah ah-VLAHR ehs-pah-NYOHL)!

chapter six

beginner's portuguese

A large prize once was won on a radio quiz program by a contestant who fortunately knew what language is spoken in Brazil. On another occasion, a businessman who had sent a letter in Spanish to a correspondent in Rio de Janeiro saw his letter returned with the annotation that if he could not communicate in the language of the country, his Brazilian opposite number would be happy to correspond in English, but not in a third language that was native to neither of them.

In spite of this, some North Americans continue to equate Latin America with Spanish America and to disregard the fact that in Brazil, a country larger than the continental United States, with a population that is almost half that of all South America, the official and popular tongue is Portuguese, not Spanish.

"Ah, but the two languages are very close, and anybody who understands one can understand the other!" That depends, as the Brazilian proved to his American colleague by composing a letter in Portuguese in which practically no word coincided with its Spanish counterpart. Consider this brief list of high-frequency words in the two languages:

	SPANISH	PORTUGUESE
window	*ventana*	*janela* (zhun-NEH-luh)
street	*calle*	*rua* (ROO-uh)
cigar	*cigarro, tabaco*	*charuto* (shuh-ROO-too; this is our "cheroot"; both words come from Tamil, a language of southern India)

hat	*sombrero*	*chapéu* (shuh-PEH-oo)
full	*lleno*	*cheio* (SHEH-yoo)
yesterday	*ayer*	*ontem* (ÕHN-tãy)
to speak	*hablar*	*falar* (fuh-LAHR)
to stay	*quedarse*	*ficar* (fee-KAHR)
to close	*cerrar*	*fechar* (fee-SHAHR)
to dine	*comer*	*jantar* (zhŭn-TAHR)
thank you	*gracias*	*obrigado* (oo-bree-GAH-doo)

Like Spanish, Portuguese grew up in the Iberian Peninsula. Iberians, Phoenicians, Greeks, Carthaginians, Romans, Germanic invaders, and Arabs contributed to the formation of both languages, but a Celtic element seems to have found its way into Portuguese and have given it a distinctive flavor, particularly for what regards the nasality in the pronunciation of vowels. Furthermore, the Germanic invaders who set up their rule in ancient Lusitania (roughly corresponding to modern Portugal) when the Roman Empire crumbled were the Suevi, while in Spain the Visigoths took charge. When Europe emerged from the welter of the early Middle Ages and the Moorish invasions that almost submerged the Iberian Peninsula, we find the Galicians and Portuguese united with the Asturians and Leonese of Spain, but in 1140 Portugal became independent, and has been independent ever since.

Galicia, the northwestern province of Spain that now extends north of Portugal, was the true birthplace of the Portuguese language, and even today, despite political accidents that placed it under Spanish rule, it speaks a popular language that is to all intents and purposes Portuguese.

In fact, Galician, or Gallego, was the first peninsular dialect to evolve a full-blown literary form, at a time when Castilian was still a rough-hewn military tongue. The courtly lyric poetry of Galicia held sway even at the Castilian court until the early fifteenth century.

As the Moors were slowly forced back, in the course of eight hundred years, out of a peninsula that they had completely subjugated in the early eighth century, the duality of Galician-Portuguese and Castilian became more pronounced. The two monarchies occasionally joined forces against their common Moslem foe. More often, they fought each other. Galician-Portuguese spread southward out of the northwest in a straight band resembling an unrolling carpet, while Castilian expanded not only to the south, but to the east and west, crowding out two older speech areas, the Leonese and the Aragonese, and ultimately covering the entire peninsula, save for the western strip of Portuguese and the eastern strip of Catalan.

In the days of discovery and exploration, the Portuguese almost outdid the Spaniards. Bartolomeu Dias and Vasco da Gama, who sailed around the Cape of Good Hope, and Magellan, who first circumnavigated the globe, were Portuguese. Even on United States soil, the expedition of De Soto (or should his name be spelled De Souto, Portuguese fashion?) was composed almost exclusively of Portuguese gentlemen, and the account of his travels in Florida and other states of the Deep South is written in Portuguese, not Spanish. At one time, the Pope divided up the newly discovered Western Hemisphere between Spain and Portugal, but both France and England objected on the ground that the will of father Adam had not been produced in evidence.

Today, as a result of the travels of those fearless men, Portuguese is a great imperial language, outstripping Italian in number of speakers and coming uncomfortably close to French. Nearly eighty million people speak it throughout the world, sixty million of whom are our own good Brazilian neighbors. The others include twelve million in Europe (Portugal, the Azores, and Madeira, with almost nine million inhabitants, plus three million Galicians whose official language is Spanish, but whose native dialect is the ancestor of Portuguese); at least six million of the twelve million inhabitants of Portugal's African possessions, Angola, Mozambique, Portuguese Guinea, and various islands (the Cape Verde among them); another million in the Indian coastal cities of Goa, Damão and Diu, the Chinese coast city of Macau, and the Portuguese section of Timor, in the vicinity of Indonesia; and last but not least, some three hundred thousand Portuguese who have settled in the United States, mostly on the New England and California coasts. Visitors to Martha's Vineyard are often regaled with excellent Portuguese radio programs from New Bedford on the mainland, and at least three very scholarly studies on the Portuguese language in North America have appeared in recent years, to this writer's knowledge. Famous American names like Cardozo, Dos Passos, and Davega are of Portuguese origin.

Then there are Portuguese Pidgins, or Creole languages,

planted by Portuguese traders all over the earth—in Zanzibar and Mombasa, Ceylon and Coromandel, Java and Singapore. The picturesque Papiamento of Curaçao, in the Dutch West Indies, was long thought to be of Spanish origin, but recent findings seem to point to Portuguese as its probable basic source.

One key to Portuguese success is tolerance. In Brazil are three racial strains, white, black, and red, but there is no color line of any sort. In the Portuguese Empire all people are granted full and complete citizenship and equal rights, so that when Nehru claims Goa, Damão and Diu for India the Portuguese are able to reply that these cities are not colonies, but integral parts of the Portuguese nation, and that all their inhabitants are full-fledged, single-class Portuguese citizens. In Portuguese Africa there is no racial discrimination; such facilities as exist are open to all.

Portugal and Brazil both suffer from a high rate of illiteracy. Yet, in the words of an impartial British observer, Aubrey Bell, "the illiterates are often the flower and cream of the nation. . . . The Portuguese people, for all its lack of letters, is one of the most civilised and intelligent in Europe." Bell wrote in 1915, and the situation has vastly improved since then. Both countries, Brazil and Portugal, have become tourists' paradises, as proved by the international colonies at Estoril and Rio.

Like all great languages, Portuguese has dialects. Linguists describe four main varieties in continental Portugal, plus two insular dialects, in the Azores and Madeira. The real split, however, is between the Portuguese of Portugal and that of Brazil, and it has striking points of similarity to the cleavage between the King's English of Britain and Mencken's American Language. Unlike English speakers, who go their own proud and separate ways, Portuguese speakers make use of a common language academy, which meets every ten years or so and tries to standardize usage for both countries. This works—sometimes. Upon completion of a Portuguese booklet done with the able collaboration of a Portuguese colleague, in which spelling and grammar were made to coincide with the prescriptions of the last meeting of the Academy, I was distressed to receive an urgent message just as the work was going to press; the Academy had changed the rules once more; could we catch the book in time to make the necessary changes?

As is the case with all languages that stray away from their homeland, Brazilian Portuguese is more archaic and conservative in pronunciation and grammar than the Portuguese of Portugal; but it is also strongly influenced by Indian and Negro admixtures, many of which have spread abroad. It is from the African element in Brazilian Portuguese that we get the names of such dances as *maxixe, samba, conga, mambo,* and a word like "zombie," which is the Afro-Brazilian *zumbi.* The Brazilians, on the other hand, have not hesitated to borrow from us. A streetcar, which is *carro elétrico* in Portugal, becomes *bonde* in Rio. The first streetcar line was financed by a North American issue of bonds, and the name of the financing device stuck to the product. Just as you have to watch dubious words like "bloody" in Britain, so you have to be careful with certain Lisbonese words in Brazil. *Rapariga* is just plain "girl" in Lisbon, but in Rio it's an insult.

This is not to say that all of Brazil speaks the identical language. The tongue of Rio, called Carioca (this, by the way, is an Indian name), is rivaled by the Paulista of the State of São Paulo in the south, by the dialect of Bahia in the north, and by a variety of other local speech forms, all of which are to varying degrees influenced by local native tongues. But what are dialects to a language that has over thirty terms for "calf," and calls a weasel by such poetic names as "little lady" (*doninha*) and "little girl" (*menina*)?

Portuguese is an expressive language, with a wealth of diminutives, compounded forms, and repetitions. If you want to say "real old," you use *velho e revelho,* "old and re-old." If you want to say "very pretty," use *lindo lindo,* "pretty pretty." You can turn any noun into an affectionate diminutive by adding to it the suffix *-inho,* loosely translated as "little." A Spanish correspondent, reporting to his Madrid paper from Lisbon, wondered at the Portuguese children feeding the hippo at the Lisbon zoo and yelling to it: "*Abre a boquinha!*" ("Open your dear little mouth!").

What the Portuguese speaker doesn't say with words, he says with gestures. "He speaks," says a Portuguese expert who has written a book-length article on "The Language of Gestures in Portugal," "with his whole body, using gestures unknown in other lands." And, he might have added, sometimes unknown in his own land. An American who spent long years in Brazil reports that the gestures he had learned in Rio were meaningless in Bahia.

The vowel sounds of Portuguese, particularly when un-
stressed, are a little on the indeterminate side, like those of
English and Russian, not clear-cut, like those of Spanish or
Italian.

A written *a* is AH when stressed, but something like *uh*
when unstressed. Thus *água*, "water," sounds like AH-gwuh.
If the stressed *a* is followed by an *n* or *m*, it sounds halfway
between English *a* in "grand" and English *u* in "grunt," and
is best transcribed by ŨH.

A stressed written *e* may have the open sound of EH (like *e*
in "met") or the closed sound of AY, but with the tail cut off.
Terra (TEHR-ruh) is "earth" or "land," but *mesa* (MAY-zuh)
is "table." If the *e* comes at the beginning of a word before *s*
plus consonant, it is barely heard: *está* ('SHTAH), "is"; at the
end of a word, even if followed by *s*, Portugal sounds it *uh*,
Brazil *ee*: *dente*, "tooth," is DĒHN-tuh in Lisbon, DĒHN-
chee in Rio.

Written *i* is invariably EE: *filho* (FEE-lyoo), son.

Stressed written *o* may be open, like AW cut short (or the
British sound of *o* in "pot"), or closed, like the *o* of "no" cut
short; *nove* (NAW-vuh) is "nine," and *novo* (NOH-voo) is
"new." Unstressed or at the end of a word, even if *s* follows,
written *o* sounds like the short *oo* of "good": *amigo* (uh-MEE-
goo), friend.

Written *u* is invariably the longer *oo* of "food": *muro* (MOO-
roo), wall.

Three diphthongs occur frequently in Portuguese, *ou, ei,*
and *oi*. The first two are exactly like English so-called long *o*
of "bone" and long *a* of "late," while *oi* is pronounced as in
English. In transcription, it will be best to leave *oi* in Portuguese spelling, which is not at all misleading, and to adopt
OH and AY for *ou* and *ei*, with the understanding that the tail
is *not* to be cut off the English sounds, as it is when OH stands
for Portuguese *o* and AY for Portuguese *e*: *touro* (TOH-roo),
bull; *dois* (DOISH), two; *leite* (LAY-tuh, or LAY-chee if you
prefer the Rio pronunciation), milk.

In Portuguese spelling, *ã* or *am, em, im, õ* or *om,* and *um*
represent nasal sounds which can be imitated by stopping the
nose as though you had a bad cold while you pronounce AH,
AY, EE, OH, and OO. They will be transcribed by ĀH, ĀY,
ĒĒ, ÕH and ÕŌ: *irmã* (eer-MĀH), sister; *bem* (BĀY),
well; *sim* (SĒĒ), yes; *bom* (BÕH), good; *um* (ÕŌ), one, a, an.

Written combinations like *ão, õe, ãe* nasalize both vowels;

for them, we may use ÕW (as in "how," but with nose
stopped); ÕY (as in "oink") and ẼYẼ (English "eye" with
stopped nose): *irmão* (eer-MÕW), brother; *botões* (boo-
TÕYSH), buttons; *pães* (PẼYẼSH), loaves.

Among the consonants, *c* before *a, o, u* or consonant is K,
but *c* before *e* or *i* (and *ç* in any position) is S: *casa* (KAH-
zuh) is "house"; *cidade* (see-DAH-duh or see-DAH-djee, according to whether you choose Lisbon or Rio) is "city"; *maçã*
(muh-SÃH) is "apple."

Ch and *x* are usually pronounced SH: *chamar* (shuh-
MAHR), to call; *peixe* (PAY-shuh), fish.

G before *a, o, u*, or consonant is the *g* of "good," but *g* before
e or *i* and *j* in any position is the *s* of "pleasure," transcribed
ZH: *largo* (LAHR-goo), wide; *geral* (zhuh-RAHL), general;
janela (zhuh-NEH-luh), window.

Written *lh* and *nh* give the sounds of LY and NY: *filho*
(FEE-lyoo), son; *senhor* (suh-NYOHR), sir.

Written *s* is sounded as *z* between vowels, and also at the
end of a word when the next word begins with a vowel:
presente (pruh-ZẼHN-tuh or pree-ZẼHN-chee), present; *as
águas* (uh-ZAH-gwuhsh), the waters. It has a more or less
pronounced SH sound, especially in Portugal, when final or
before another consonant: *dedos* (DAY-doosh), fingers; *está*
('SHTAH), is. Elsewhere, the sound is usually that of hard *s*:
sol (SOHL), sun.

Common greetings of both Portugal and Brazil are:

Bom dia (Bons dias).   (BÕH DEE-uh, BÕHSH DEE-uhsh;
    in Rio, *dia* will have rather the sound of DJEE-uh)
    Good day, Good morning.
Boa tarde (Boas tardes).   (BAW-uh TAHR-duh; TAHR-
    djee in Rio; BAW-uhsh TAHR-dush)   Good afternoon,
    Good evening.
Boa noite (Boas noites).   (BAW-uh NOI-tuh, BAW-uhsh
    NOI-tuhsh; in Rio, *noite* comes out as NOI-chee)   Good
    night.
Adeus. (uh-DEH-oosh) Good-by.
Até logo. (uh-TEH LAW-goo) See you later.
Como está? (KOH-moo 'SHTAH) How are you?
Como vai tudo? (KOH-moo VEYE TOO-doo) How's
    everything?
Bem, obrigado. (BÃY, oo-bree-GAH-doo)   Well, thanks.

It will have been noticed by now that the Rio pronunciation tends to give final *e*'s the sound of *ee* rather than *uh*, and that the groups *de, di, te, ti* tend to sound as *djee, chee*. This is one of the main Carioca features, but does not extend to all other parts of Brazil. Brazil will also often keep the final -*s* sound, which Portugal renders by *sh*. In Brazil more than in Portugal, a final -*l* turns into what is practically an *oo*-sound: *o Brasil* (oo bruh-ZEE-oo), Brazil.

One of the picturesque features of Portuguese is its favorite form of address when speaking politely. There exists a *Você* (voh-SAY) which has the same origin as Spanish *Usted*, but most Portuguese speakers prefer something that reminds one of our Congressional usage: *o senhor* (oo suh-NYOHR), *a senhora* (uh suh-NYOH-ruh), literally "the gentleman," "the lady," used as a substitute for "you" with the third person of the verb. Of course, these forms are a bit unwieldy, so, in the words of a Portuguese linguist, "Let us make use of an intermediate solution, which is one of the great triumphs of the Portuguese language, namely, to use no 'you' at all, but just the third person of the verb, which gives a neutral, anodyne tone to phrases and sentences."

But there is no neutrality in Portuguese politeness, which is second to none in the world. Here are some examples to illustrate its variety:

Faz o obséquio, por favor, tenha a bondade. (FAHZ oo oob-SEH-kee-oo, poor fuh-VOHR, TEH-nyuh uh bõhn-DAH-duh) Please.

Obrigado, muito agradecido. (oo-bree-GAH-doo, MWẼÉN-too uh-gruh-duh-SEE-doo) (note the strange nasalization of the *ui* in *muito*, "much" or "very," for which there is no written-language justification) Thanks a lot.

Não por isso. (NÕW poor EE-soo) Don't mention it (literally "Not for that").

Perdão. (puhr-DÕW) Pardon me, Excuse me.

Eu sinto muito, eu lamento muito. (EH-oo SÉÉN-too MWẼÉN-too, EH-oo luh-MÃYN-too MWẼÉN-too) I'm very sorry.

É nada, não faz diferença. (EH NAH-duh, NÕW FAHZ dee-fuh-REHN-suh) It's nothing, it doesn't matter.

Não se incomode. (NÕW suh ẽén-koo-MAW-duh) Don't bother.

Com sua licença. (kõhn SOO-uh lee-SĒHN-suh) By your leave.

Entre! (ĀYN-truh) Come in!

Com prazer. (kõhn pruh-ZAYR) Gladly.

Posso apresentar o meu amigo? (PAW-soo uh-pruh-zuhn-TAHR oo MEH-oo uh-MEE-goo) May I introduce my friend?

Muito prazer. (MWĒĒN-too pruh-ZAYR) Happy to meet you.

For the shopper, here is the customary list of useful expressions:

O que posso fazer para o senhor (a senhora)? (OO KUH PAW-soo fuh-ZAYR PUH-ruh oo suh-NYOHR, uh suh-NYOH-ruh) What can I do for you?

O que quer o senhor (a senhora)? (OO KUH KEHR oo suh-NYOHR, uh suh-NYOH-ruh) What do you want?

Eu quero, eu desejo. (EH-oo KEH-roo, EH-oo duh-ZEH-zhoo) I want, wish.

Eu quisera, eu desejaria. (EH-oo kee-ZEH-ruh, EH-oo duh-zuh-zhuh-REE-uh) I should like.

Quer me dar? (KEHR muh DAHR) Will you give me?

Mostre-me. (MAW-shtruh-muh) Show me.

Traga-me. (TRAH-guh-muh) Bring me.

Some of the things you might want:

um pedaço (õõ puh-DAH-soo) a piece
uma fatia (OO-muh fuh-TEE-uh) a slice
um pacote (õõ puh-KAW-tuh) a package
uma caixa (OO-muh KEYE-shuh) a box
uma garrafa (OO-muh guhr-RAH-fuh) a bottle
um copo (õõ KOH-poo) a glass
uma chícara (OO-muh SHEE-kuh-ruh) a cup
de (duh) of
pão (PÕW) bread
sabão (suh-BÕW) soap
cigarros (see-GAHR-roosh) cigarettes
cerveja (suhr-VAY-zhuh) beer
vinho (VEE-nyoo) wine
chá (SHAH) tea
café (kuh-FEH) coffee

Let's try out some of these in combination.

Eu desejaria um pacote de cigarros. (EH-oo duh-zuh-zhuh-REE-uh õõ puh-KAW-tuh duh see-GAHR-roosh) I should like a pack of cigarettes.

Quer me dar um pedaço de sabão? (KERH muh DAHR õõ puh-DAH-soo duh suh-BÕW) Will you give me a piece of soap?

Traga-me uma garrafa de cerveja. (TRAH-guh-muh OO-muh guhr-RAH-fuh duh suhr-VAY-zhuh) Bring me a bottle of beer.

There are also some necessary phrases and expressions:

Quanto custa? (KWŨHN-too KOOSH-tuh) How much is it?

É demasiado. (EH duh-muh-SYAH-doo) It's too much.

Veja! (VAY-zhuh) Look!

Mais alguma coisa? (MEYE-zuhl-GOO-muh KOI-zuh) Anything else?

Nada mais. (NAH-duh MEYESH) Nothing else.

Pode dizer-me? (PAW-duh dee-ZAYR-muh) Can you tell me?

Onde está? (ÕHN-duh 'SHTAH) Where is?

Onde estão? (ÕHN-duh 'SHTÕW) Where are?

Onde é que vai? (ÕHN-duh EH kuh VEYE) Where are you going?

Onde é que vamos? (ÕHN-duh EH kuh VUH-moosh) Where are we going?

Para que lado? (PUH-ruh kuh LAH-doo) Which way?

Eis aqui. (AY-zuh-KEE) Here is.

Eis ali. (AY-zuh-LEE) There is.

Por aqui. (poor uh-KEE) This way.

Por ali. (poor uh-LEE) That way.

Pela direita. (PEH-luh dee-RAY-tuh) To the right.

Pela esquerda. (PEH-luh 'SHKEHR-duh) To the left.

Vá todo direito. (VAH TOH-doo dee-RAY-too) Go straight ahead.

Venha comigo. (VÊH-nyuh koo-MEE-goo) Come with me.

Try combining these with a few places of interest:

a igreja (uh ee-GREH-zhuh) the church
o museu (oo moo-ZEH-oo) the museum

o ascensor   (oo uh-suhn-SOHR)   the elevator

o quarto de banho   (oo KWAHR-too duh BUH-nyoo)   the
bathroom

a retrete, o lavatório   (uh ruh-TRAY-tuh, oo luh-vuh-TOH-
ryoo)   the lavatory

a sala de jantar   (uh SAH-luh duh zhūhn-TAHR)   the
dining room

o hotel   (oo oh-TEHL)   the hotel

a esquadra (Portugal), *o posto de polícia* (Brazil)   (uh
'SHKWAH-druh, oo POHSH-too duh poo-LEE-syuh)
the police station

Let's combine a few of these:

Perdão, pode dizer-me onde está a igreja?   (puhr-DŌW,
PAW-duh dee-ZAYR-muh ŌHN-duh 'SHTAH uh ee-
GREH-zhuh)   Pardon me, can you tell me where the
church is?

Para que lado está a retrete?   (PUH-ruh kuh LAH-doo
'SHTAH uh ruh-TRAY-tuh)   Which way is the lavatory?

Onde é que posso achar um hotel?   (ŌHN-duh EH kuh
PAW-soo uh-SHAHR ōō oh-TEHL)   Where can I find
a hotel?

Here are a few directional signs, more likely to appear in
writing than in speech:

É proibido fumar.   (EH proo-ee-BEE-doo foo-MAHR)   No
smoking.

É proibido entrar.   (EH proo-ee-BEE-doo āyn-TRAHR)
No admittance.

Atenção   (uh-tūhn-SŌW)   Attention, Warning, Careful.

Siga pela direita (esquerda).   (SEE-guh PEH-luh dee-
RAY-tuh ['SHKEHR-duh])   Keep right (left).

Entrada, saída.   (āyn-TRAH-duh, suh-EE-duh)   Entrance, Exit.

Saída, chegada.   (suh-EE-duh, shuh-GAH-duh)   Departure, Arrival.

Senhores, homens.   (suh-NYOH-raysh, AW-māysh)   Men.

Senhoras, mulheres.   (suh-NYOH-ruhsh, moo-LYEH-
ruhsh)   Women.

In Brazil, you may find *Mictório* over railroad rest rooms.
An American flier, flying low over several Brazilian stations,

was surprised to find that all small Brazilian towns apparently had the same name.

Speaking is an important activity and one that pays dividends, for you can always talk about it:

Fala o senhor português (inglês, francês, espanhol, italiano)? (FAH-luh oo suh-NYOHR poor-too-GAYSH [ēēn-GLAYSH, frūhn-SAYSH, 'shpuh-NYOHL, ee-tuh-LYAH-noo]) Do you speak Portuguese (English, French, Spanish, Italian)?

Um pouco. (ōō POH-koo) A little.

Muito pouco. (MWĒĒN-too POH-koo) Very little.

Faça favor de falar mais devagar. (FAH-suh fuh-VOHR duh fuh-LAHR MEYESH duh-vuh-GAHR) Please speak more slowly.

Compreende? (kōōm-pree-ĒHN-duh) Do you understand?

Eu não compreendo. (EH-oo NŌW kōōm-pree-ĒHN-doo) I don't understand.

Em que está falando? (ĀY kuh 'SHTAH fuh-LŪHN-doo) What are you talking about?

O que quer dizer? (OO kuh KEHR dee-ZAYR) What do you mean?

Como se diz —— em português? (KOH-moo suh DEEZ —— ãy poor-too-GAYSH) How do you say —— in Portuguese?

Sou norte-americano. (SOH NAWR-tuh-muh-ree-KUH-noo) I'm an American. (Shift to *norte-americana* if you are a woman.)

Here are some people you may want to send for. But first, "I need" and "Send for":

Eu necessito (EH-oo nuh-suh-SEE-too) I need
Mande chamar (MŪHN-duh shuh-MAHR) Send for
o gerente (oo zhuh-RĒHN-tuh) the manager
um polícia (ōō poo-LEE-syuh) a policeman
um médico (ōō MEH-dee-koo) a doctor
um porteiro (ōō poor-TAY-roo) a porter
um intérprete (ōō ēēn-TEHR-pruh-tuh) an interpreter
o cônsul americano (oo KŌHN-sool uh-muh-ree-KUH-noo) the American consul

In combination, we might get sentences of this type:

Eu necessito um médico. (EH-oo nuh-suh-SEE-too õõ MEH-dee-koo)   I need a doctor.

Mande chamar um polícia. (MŨHN-duh shuh-MAHR õõ poo-LEE-syuh)   Send for a policeman.

The weather is something you can always discuss:

Chove. (SHAW-vuh)   It's raining.

Neva. (NEH-vuh)   It's snowing. (This is not too likely in Portuguese-speaking lands, but you might get into a mountain range.)

Faz sol. (FAHZ SOHL)   It's sunny.

Faz bom (mau) tempo. (FAHZ BÕH [MOW] TÃYM-poo)   It's fine (bad) weather.

Faz calor (frio). (FAHZ kuh-LOHR [FREE-oo])   It's warm (cold).

Tenho calor (frio). (TẼH-nyoo kuh-LOHR [FREE-oo])   I'm warm (cold).

Adjectives ending in *-o* change to *-a* if they are used with a feminine noun (as do the nouns themselves). The ending *-e* is common to both genders. In the plural, add *-s* if the noun or adjective ends in a vowel, *-es* if it ends in a consonant (with a few exceptions):

grande (GRŨHN-duh, GRŨHN-djee) large, big
pequeno (puh-KEH-noo)   small, little
quente (KẼHN-tuh)   hot, warm
frio (FREE-oo)   cold
bom, fem. *boa* (BÕH, BAW-uh)   good
mau, fem. *má* (MOW, MAH)   bad
primeiro (pree-MAY-roo)   first
último (OOL-tee-moo)   last
verdadeiro (vuhr-duh-DAY-roo)   true
livre (LEE-vruh)   free
ocupado (oo-koo-PAH-doo)   taken

Here are a few verbs of frequent occurrence in the infinitive form. Put *eu quisera* (EH-oo kee-ZEH-ruh) or *eu desejaria* (EH-oo duh-zuh-zhuh-REE-uh) before them (if you wish to be less grammatical and more colloquial, use *queria* [kuh-REE-uh] or *desejava* [duh-zuh-ZHAH-vuh]), an appropriate noun after them, and you will have a complete sentence meaning that you would like to do something. Put *vou* (VOH) before them, and you will have "I am going to" do something. Put *acabo de* (uh-KAH-boo duh) before them, and you will have "I have just done" something.

comprar (kŏhm-PRAHR) to buy
vender (vūhn-DAYR) to sell
ver (VAYR) to see
visitar (vuh-zee-TAHR) to visit
falar (fuh-LAHR) to speak
agradecer (uh-gruh-duh-SAYR) to thank
perguntar (puhr-gŏōn-TAHR) to ask
pedir (puh-DEER) to ask for
pagar (puh-GAHR) to pay, pay for
comer (koo-MAYR) to eat
beber (buh-BAYR) to drink
ir (EER) to go
entrar (ūhn-TRAHR) to go in
sair (suh-EER) to go out
descansar (duhsh-kūhn-SAHR) to rest
vir (VEER) to come
saber (suh-BAYR) to know (something)
conhecer (koo-nyuh-SAYR) to know (somebody or some place), to meet
achar (uh-SHAHR) to find
fumar (foo-MAHR) to smoke
fazer (fuh-ZAYR) to do, make
mandar fazer (mūhn-DAHR fuh-ZAYR) to have (something) done

Eu desejaria mandar limpar o meu fato. (EH-oo duh-zuh-zhuh-REE-uh mūhn-DAHR lēēm-PAHR oo MEH-oo FAH-too) I should like to have my suit cleaned.

The verb "to be" followed by a noun is usually *ser* (SAYR); but "to be" in a place, or a state of health, is usually *estar* ('SHTAHR):

sou, estou (SOH, 'SHTOH) I am
é, está (EH, 'SHTAH) he is, she is, you are
somos, estamos (SOH-moosh, 'SHTAH-moosh) we are
são, estão (SŌW, 'SHTŌW) they are

The verb *estar* can also be used with the present participle of another verb to mean "I am doing" something. To get the present participle of verbs in *-ar*, change to *-ando; -er* to *-endo; -ir* to *-indo*.

Estou falando. ('SHTOH fuh-LŬHN-doo)   I am speaking.

Estão saíndo: ('SHTŌW suh-ĒĒN-doo)   They are going out.

"To have" is commonly translated by *ter*, both to show ownership and in connection with past participles, which end in *-ado* for *-ar* verbs, in *-ido* for the others.

tenho (TĒH-nyoo)   I have
tem (TÃY)   he has, she has, you have
temos (TAY-moosh)   we have
têm (TÃY)   they have
Tenho ido ao Rio. (TĒH-nyoo EE-doo AH-oo REE-oo)   I have gone to Rio.
Temos falado aos nossos amigos. (TAY-moosh fuh-LAH-doo AH-oosh NOH-soo-zuh-MEE-goosh)   We have spoken to our friends.

The Portuguese verb is even more complex than the French or the Spanish, with numerous conjugations, tenses, and moods. Among its interesting peculiarities are a future subjunctive, a personalized infinitive (*Parti depois de terem falado*, "I left after to-have-they spoken," "I left after they had spoken"), and a split future, that permits the insertion of an object pronoun between its two constituent parts.

But if the tourist can make his wants known by the use of a few simple phrases, and understand part of what is said to him in return, he will not only make his own stay more pleasant, but also spread that international good will that is today such an integral part of good relations among the nations. So,

Vamos ao Brasil, e vamos falar um pouco em português!

chapter seven

italy: the language

The keynote to Italy is variety. You become aware of this the minute you set foot on Italian soil. There is variety of artistic and architectural forms, variety of landscape, variety of cuisine, variety of physical types, and, above all, variety of expression.

No world traveler who has seen Rome, Florence, Naples, Turin, and Bologna will ever be tempted to confuse them, as he might confuse Chicago, Philadelphia, Boston, Indianapolis, and Cincinnati. No gourmet who has tasted the *ossobuco con risotto* of Milan, the *polenta cogli osei* of Venice, and the *pasta con sarde* of Sicily will ever deny the infinite diversity of Italian gastronomy. No tourist who has listened to the multi-colored cadences and intonations of the North, Tuscany, Latium, and the South can really bring himself to believe that they are facets of the same tongue.

There are two things, however, that most Italian speakers hold in common. One is the gestural accompaniment that seems an idle redundancy when applied to a language so apparently endless in its forms of vocal expression. The other is the animation of the speakers, which foreigners often misinterpret as excitability.

Actually, the Italian is not *unduly* excitable; he does not speak *too* fast; he is not *overgenerous* with his gestures. All you have to do to prove this to yourself is to attend a typical sporting event in Italy (say the race of the *palio* in Siena) and compare the behavior of the spectators with that of a Yankee Stadium crowd in the Bronx.

But the Italian is normally more animated than his American opposite number, and he carries this animation into his everyday life, not just to the sports arena.

Watch two Italian businessmen taking a stroll through the *Galleria* in Naples and discussing their problems. Their voices rise to a higher, shriller pitch than would be normal in Rockefeller Plaza; but at times they sink to an almost inaudible whisper. One of the speakers suddenly stops, forcing the other to do likewise. He joins his hands, then throws them out wide, fingers apart. You don't have to hear what he says. His meaning is crystal clear: "How in the world could I accept a proposition like that?"

The other energetically nods assent as he cuts into his friend's rapid flow of talk. He raises his right hand, cupping thumb and fingers together, tips uppermost, and shakes it repeatedly up and down. "How in the world could he have expected you to accept it?" the gesture says just as clearly as if you could hear the words—which indeed you can, for they are loud enough even if you don't understand them.

After witnessing these scenes a few times, you begin to acquire a misplaced confidence. "After all," you say, "I don't really have to learn this language. I can get along with gestures!"

Undeceive yourself. The gesture language of Italy is fully as complicated as a spoken tongue with its grammar. Furthermore it, too, has dialectal varieties; the gestures used in Naples are not quite identical with those of Venice. And, in any case, they are misleading, since we, too, use gestures.

Try, for example, giving the American "come here" gesture: palm up, fingers crooked and moved back and forth with tips upward. The Italian will interpret that as "Good-by." Reverse your gesture, with palm and fingertips down. Now you have an American "Good-by" and an Italian "Come here." It can get to be very confusing.

So perhaps it is better to learn a few words of the spoken tongue, just to carry you through difficult spots. It is not too hard if you go about it the right way, for Italian is a tongue of smooth sounds and comparatively easy spelling, and of all the Romance languages it is the one that generally comes closest to its ancestral Latin, which has contributed so much to our own vocabulary.

To offset these advantages, Italian has a grammar that presents complications, at least at the outset. It also has more bewildering dialects than practically any other language on earth. The northern dialects, for instance, are distinguished by their lack of the characteristic Italian double consonant sounds and by the fall of many vowel endings (*fatto*, for example, may appear as *fato, fat, fait*). In the northwest, but not in the northeast, you will hear sounds that make you think you are listening to French (French *u* and *eu*, and French nasals). If you move just south of Rome, on the other hand, you will hear a heavy stress that is completely at variance with the clear, staccato pronunciation of the north, along with a prolongation of accented vowels and a general deadening of final vowels to the sound of *e* in *the*, with a singsong cadence that faintly reminds you of Chinese. In the toe of the Italian boot and in Sicily you become aware of a predominance of *ee* and *oo* sounds, along with a sharp, explosive pronunciation. It is only in the central part of Italy, from Florence to Rome, that you hear the beautiful, clear sounds of the literary tongue, at least in the mouths of the entire population.

But the tourist can bypass some of these difficulties. The dialects are taken care of by the fact that just about everybody with whom he is likely to have contact can speak the standard language. The grammar can be learned partly by indirection (that is, by learning phrases and expressions to the point where the grammatical pattern becomes natural), partly by concentrating on a few main points.

Take the matter of sounds and spellings first. There is no Italian sound that does not have a counterpart, identical or fairly close, in English. The *written* vowels are five: *a, e, i, o, u*. For three of them, there is no trouble whatsoever: whenever you see a written *a*, use the *ah*-sound of "father"; for the written Italian *i*, use the *ee* of "meet"; for the Italian *u*, use the *oo* of "food." The written Italian *e* is sometimes open (as in "met"; let us use *eh* to indicate this sound); sometimes closed, like the *ay* of "maybe," or better yet, our colloquial "mebbe"; we can use *ay* for this, but let us remember to make the *ay* short and clipped, not drawled. Italian written *o* sometimes has the sound of *aw* in "awful," but short and clipped (if you can imitate a Britisher, use the British *o* of "pot"); at other times it sounds like the initial part of our exclamation "oh!" but again short and clipped.

Let's train on the vowels, and at the same time learn a few easy, one-letter or one-syllable words:

a (AH) to
è (EH) is
e (AY) and
di (DEE) of
ho (AW) I have
o (OH) or
su (SOO) on

Italian does not use the written letters *y* and *w*, but replaces them with *i* and *u*:

piano (PYAH-noh)   piano, slowly, softly
qua   (KWAH)   here
buono (BWAW-noh)   good
guerra (GWEHR-rah)   war

At this point, we can leave off sounds for a while, and learn some common greetings.

buon giorno (BWAWN JOHR-noh)   Good day, Good morning, Good afternoon.
buona sera   (BWAW-nah SAY-rah)   Good evening.
buona notte (BWAW-nah NAWT-tay)   Good night.
arrivederci   (ahr-ree-vay-DAYR-chee)   Good-by (this means literally "to again seeing each other"; if you want to be more polite, shift to *arrivederla* [ahr-ree-vay-DAYR-lah], "to again seeing you"). *Addio* (ahd-DEE-oh) means literally "to God," and is more of a farewell. *Ciao* (CHAH-oh) is popular and familiar for both "Hello" and "Good-by." "Hello" on the phone is usually *pronto* (PROHN-toh), literally "Ready!"
Come sta? (KOH-may STAH) is "How are you?" Less formal is *Come va?* (KOH-may VAH), "How goes it?" The normal reply is:
Bene, grazie, e Lei? (BEH-nay, GRAH-tsyay, ay LEH-ee), "Well, thanks, and you?"

Most Italian consonant sounds are almost the same as in English. But there are a few spelling peculiarities. For instance, written Italian *ch* is *always* pronounced like a *k*:

chi (KEE) who, whom
che (KAY) what

C before *e* or *i* is *always* like English *ch* in "church":

cena (CHAY-nah) supper
amici (ah-MEE-chee) friends

G before *a*, *o*, *u* or a consonant is like the *g* of "God," but before *e* or *i* it is like English *j*:

largo (LAHR-goh) wide
gesto (JEHS-toh) gesture

Sc before *a*, *o*, or *u* is pronounced *sk*, but before *e* or *i* it is pronounced *sh*:

scala (SKAH-lah) stair, ladder
scuro (SKOO-roh) dark
pesce (PAY-shay) fish
sciopero (SHAW-pay-roh) strike

Sch (used only before *e* and *i*) is pronounced *sk*:

scherzo (SKAYR-tsoh) joke
schizzo (SKEE-tsoh) sketch

The only other sound-and-spelling combinations apt to give trouble are *gl* (usually like *lli* in "million"; we'll use LY for this); *gn* (like *ni* in "onion"; NY is our transcription); *h* (always silent); *r* (trilled as in British "very"); and *z* (sometimes TS, sometimes DZ):

meglio (MEH-lyoh) better
aglio (AH-lyoh) garlic
legno (LAY-nyoh) wood
agnello (ah-NYEHL-loh) lamb
ho (AW) I have
hanno (AHN-noh) they have
raro (RAH-roh) rare
roba (RAW-bah) stuff, things
grazie (GRAH-tsyay) thanks
zona (DZAW-nah) zone

Politeness plays a big role in Italian conversation. Here are a few of the many polite expressions in current use. A friendly smile helps, too.

Per favore, per piacere. (payr fah-VOH-ray, payr pyah-
   CHAY-ray) Please.
Grazie mille. (GRAH-tsyay MEEL-lay) Thanks a lot.
Prego. (PREH-goh) Don't mention it.

Scusi. (SKOO-see)   Excuse me, Pardon me, I beg your pardon.

Permesso? (payr-MAYS-soh)   May I come in? May I pass?

Avanti! (ah-VAHN-tee)   Come in!

Sì. (SEE)   Yes.

No. (NAW)   No.

Volentieri. (voh-layn-TYEH-ree)   Gladly.

The last important point in Italian pronunciation is the double consonant. In English, the fact that a consonant is written double usually makes no difference in the pronunciation. In Italian it does. A consonant that is written double is pronounced over a longer period of time than if it is written single. In the case of some consonants (particularly *t, d, c, g, p, b*) there is no way to lengthen the period of time when the consonant actually comes out; what you do instead is to stretch the holding period before you release the consonant. Take two words, *fato* (fate) and *fatto* (done). In *fato*, you pronounce FAH-, then go on to toh. In *fatto*, you pronounce FAHT- getting your tongue in position for *t*, but not releasing it; the release comes a fraction of a second later, when you say toh.

Try a few words where the single or double consonant makes a lot of difference in the meaning:

eco   (EH-koh)   echo
ecco   (EHK-koh)   here is, here are

ala   (AH-lah)   wing
alla   (AHL-lah)   to the

caro   (KAH-roh)   dear, expensive
carro   (KAHR-roh)   cart

nono   (NAW-noh)   ninth
nonno   (NAWN-noh)   grandfather

poso   (PAW-soh)   I lay down
posso   (PAWS-soh)   I can

cade   (KAH-day)   he falls
cadde   (KAHD-day)   he fell

The tourist almost invariably "wants" something. Here are a few useful "wanting" expressions, preceded by the questions that bring them on:

In che posso servirla? (een KAY PAWS-soh sayr-VEER-lah) May I help you?

che (or *cosa*, or *che cosa*) *vuole* (or *desidera*)? (KAY [KAW-sah, kay KAW-sah] VWAW-lay [day-SEE-day-rah]) What do you wish? (Often the entire expression is cut down to *desidera?*)

The answers:

Voglio (VAW-lyoh) I want.

Vorrei (vohr-REH-ee) I should like.

Mi dia (or *mi favorisca*) (mee DEE-ah, mee fah-voh-REES-kah) Give me.

Vuol darmi (or *vuol favorirmi*)? (VWAWL DAHR-mee, VWAWL fah-voh-REER-mee) Will you give me?

Mi porti (mee PAWR-tee) Bring me.

Now to try a few of these out:

Vorrei un pacchetto di sigarette. (vohr-REH-ee oon pahk-KAYT-toh dee see-gah-RAYT-tay) I should like to have a pack of cigarettes.

Vuol darmi un pezzo di sapone? (VWAWL DAHR-mee oon PEH-tsoh dee sah-POH-nay) Would you give me a piece of soap?

Mi porti una bottiglia di birra. (mee PAWR-tee OO-nah boht-TEE-lyah dee BEER-rah) Bring me a bottle of beer.

A few other shopping terms are:

Mi faccia vedere (mee FAH-chah vay-DAY-ray) Show me.

Quanto? (or *quanto costa?*) (KWAHN-toh, KWAHN-toh KAWS-tah) How much?

Troppo (TRAWP-poh) Too much.

Altro? (AHL-troh) Anything else?

Nient'altro (nyehn-TAHL-troh) Nothing else.

Numerals appear in price tags and on restaurant checks. Try a few of them with *lire*, the plural of *lira*, the Italian unit of currency. (You can't buy anything for one *lira*; it's less than two mills, and have you ever tried to spend a mill?) Here are a few samples of their use:

Questo vestito costa quindicimila cinquecento lire. (KWAYS-toh vays-TEE-toh KAWS-tah kween-dee-chee-MEE-lah

cheen-kway-CHEHN-toh LEE-ray) This suit costs
15,500 lire.

Quant'è il conto? Seimila quattrocento cinquanta lire. (kwahn-
TEH eel KOHN-toh? seh-ee-MEE-lah kwaht-troh-
CHEHN-toh cheen-KWAHN-tah LEE-ray) How
much is the bill? Six thousand four hundred fifty lire.

Finding one's way is important, too. Here are a few inquiries
and possible replies:

Sa dirmi? (SAH DEER-mee)   Can you tell me?
Dov'è? (doh-VEH)   Where is?
Dove va? (DOH-vay VAH)   Where are you going?
Dove andiamo? (DOH-vay ahn-DYAH-moh)   Where are
we going?
Da che parte si trova? (dah KAY PAHR-tay see TRAW-
vah)   Which way is?
Ecco. (EHK-koh)   Here is, Here are.
Di qua. (dee KWAH)   This way.
Di là. (dee LAH)   That way.
A destra. (ah DEHS-trah)   To the right.
A sinistra. (ah see-NEES-trah)   To the left.
Vada dritto. (VAH-dah DREET-toh)   Go straight ahead.
Venga con me. (VEHN-gah kohn MAY)   Come with me.

Let's try a few of these in combination:

Scusi, sa dirmi dov'è il Duomo? (SKOO-see, SAH DEER-
mee doh-VEH eel DWAW-moh)   Pardon me, can you
tell me where the cathedral is?
Da che parte si trova l'ascensore? (dah KAY PAHR-tay see
TRAW-vah lah-shayn-SOH-ray)   Which way is the
elevator?
Dove posso trovare un salone di bellezza? (DOH-vay PAWS-
soh troh-VAH-ray oon sah-LOH-nay dee bayl-LAY-
tsah)   Where can I find a beauty parlor?

Directional signs are of importance, even if they do come
only in written form. Here are a few samples:

Vietato fumare.   (vyay-TAH-toh foo-MAH-ray)   No
smoking.
Vietato l'ingresso.   (vyay-TAH-toh leen-GREHS-soh)   No
admittance.
Entrata, Uscita.   (ayn-TRAH-tah, oo-SHEE-tah)   Entrance, Exit.

Signori, or *uomini.* (see-NYOH-ree, WAW-mee-nee) Gentlemen, Men.

Signore, or *dame,* or *donne* (see-NYOH-ray, DAH-may, DAWN-nay) Ladies, Women. (Watch out for this, for it can be extremely embarrassing: *signore* is "gentleman," "sir," "Mr.," singular; it has a plural *signori.* But *signore* is also the plural of *signora,* "lady." If you, a male, see *signore* on a rest room door, don't figure it means "Mr." and go in. Watch for the telltale *-i.*)

Speaking is an important activity, even if you can't participate in it to the full. Here are a few phrases:

Parla italiano (inglese, francese, tedesco, spagnuolo)? (PAHR-lah ee-tah-LYAH-noh, een-GLAY-say, frahn-CHAY-say, tay-DAYS-koh, spah-NYWAW-loh) Do you speak Italian (English, French, German, Spanish)?

Un po'. (oon PAW) A little.

Molto poco. (MOHL-toh PAW-koh) Very little.

Parli più lentamente. (PAHR-lee PYOO layn-tah-MAYN-tay) Speak more slowly. (This is terribly important: the Italian is not speaking fast, by his standards; it only seems so to you, because you are not familiar with the language. If you can get him to do a slow-motion speech, you may be able to figure out his meaning.)

Capisce? (kah-PEE-shay) Do you understand?

Non capisco. (nawn kah-PEES-koh) I don't understand.

Cosa vuol dire? (KAW-sah VWAWL DEE-ray) What do you mean?

Come si chiama questo in italiano? (KOH-may see KYAH-mah KWAYS-toh een ee-tah-LYAH-noh) What do you call this in Italian?

Sono americano (americana if you are a woman). (SOH-noh ah-may-ree-KAH-noh, ah-may-ree-KAH-nah) I'm an American.

Siamo americani (americane if you are all women) (SYAH-moh ah-may-ree-KAH-nee, ah-may-ree-KAH-nay) We are Americans. (These expressions cover a multitude of sins, for the Italians generally like us.)

You may need or have to send for someone. Here is how to do it:

Ho bisogno di (AW bee-SAW-nyoh dee) I need

Faccia chiamare (FAH-chah kyah-MAH-ray) Send for

il direttore   (eel dee-rayt-TOH-ray)   the manager
un agente di polizia   (oon ah-JEHN-tay dee poh-lee-TSEE-ah)   a policeman
un medico   (oon MEH-dee-koh)   a doctor
un facchino   (oon fahk-KEE-noh)   a porter
un interprete   (oon een-TEHR-pray-tay)   an interpreter
il console americano   (eel KAWN-soh-lay ah-may-ree-KAH-noh)   the American consul

In combination:

Ho bisogno di un medico.   (AW bee-SAW-nyoh dee oon MEH-dee-koh)   I need a doctor.
Faccia chiamare un agente di polizia!   (FAH-chah kyah-MAH-ray oon ah-JEHN-tay dee poh-lee-TSEE-ah)   Send for a policeman!

The whole world, not Americans alone, likes to discuss the weather. It's the easiest way to strike up an acquaintance, both at home and abroad.

Piove.   (PYAW-vay)   It's raining.
Fa bel (cattivo) tempo.   (FAH BEHL, kaht-TEE-voh, TEHM-poh)   It's fine (bad) weather.
Fa caldo (freddo).   (FAH KAHL-doh, FRAYD-doh)   It's warm (cold).
Ho caldo (freddo).   (AW KAHL-doh, FRAYD-doh)   I'm warm (cold).

Here are a few important verbs. You can put *vorrei* (I should like) in front of most of them, an appropriate noun after them, and have a complete sentence:

Vorrei   (vohr-REH-ee)   I should like
comprare   (kohm-PRAH-ray)   to buy
vedere   (vay-DAY-ray)   to see
parlare   (pahr-LAH-ray)   to speak
visitare   (vee-see-TAH-ray)   to visit
domandare or *chiedere*   (doh-mahn-DAH-ray, KYEH-day-ray)   to ask, ask for
pagare   (pah-GAH-ray)   to pay, pay for
mangiare   (mahn-JAH-ray)   to eat
bere   (BAY-ray)   to drink
fare un bagno (una doccia)   (FAH-ray oon BAH-nyoh, oo-nah DOH-chah)   to take a bath (shower)

lavarmi le mani (lah-VAHR-mee lay MAH-nee) to wash my hands

andare (ahn-DAH-ray) to go

prendere (PREHN-day-ray) to take

sapere (sah-PAY-ray) to know (a fact), know how

conoscere (koh-NOH-shay-ray) to know (a fact or a person), to meet

trovare (troh-VAH-ray) to find

fare (FAH-ray) to do, make. (*Fare* followed by another verb means "to have something done": *far stirare* [FAHR stee-RAH-ray] to have pressed; *far pulire* [FAHR poo-LEE-ray] to have cleaned; *far riparare* [FAHR ree-pah-RAH-ray] to have repaired; *far lavare* [FAHR lah-VAH-ray] to have washed; *vorrei farmi fare la barba* [vohr-REH-ee FAHR-mee FAH-ray lah BAHR-bah] I should like to get a shave; *vorrei farmi tagliare i capelli* [vohr-REH-ee FAHR-mee tah-LYAH-ray ee kah-PAYL-lee] I should like to get a haircut.)

essere (EHS-say-ray) to be

avere (ah-VAY-ray) to have

Only a few points of grammar need be discussed here. If a noun or adjective ends in -*a* in the singular, it usually changes -*a* to -*e* in the plural (*la sigaretta, le sigarette*). If it ends in -*e* or -*o* in the singular, shift to -*i* in the plural (*il giornale, i giornali; il sigaro, i sigari*).

Verbs have mostly been given in the infinitive form (*parlare*, to speak), but they change the -*are*, -*ere*, -*ire* ending of the infinitive to a variety of other endings, according to person, number, tense, etc. During the war, the American G.I.'s used a Pidgin Italian in which all verbs appeared in the infinitive, and they discovered that they could be easily understood (*Noi parlare italiano*—We to speak Italian. *Voi dove andare?* —You where to go? for Where are you going?). This practice is not recommended by the schools of language, but it has been found to work in a number of instances.

To learn the full grammar of any foreign tongue so that you handle it with complete fluency and correctness requires years of study followed by years of practice. But why be tongue-tied in the name of perfectionism, when you can make yourself understood with a few hours' study? So, by all means, *andiamo in Italia e parliamo italiano!*

chapter eight

want to speak russian?

The Soviet Union covers one-sixth of the earth's land surface. It has a population estimated at well over two hundred million, of whom more than half speak Russian as a mother tongue, while the rest, having some 140 assorted languages of varied stocks, either have learned or are learning Russian, the predominant and official tongue. These facts alone place Russian among the leading world tongues.

But there is more. Russian is a language very much on the make. In all European countries with a Communist structure (Poland, Czechoslovakia, East Germany, Hungary, Rumania, Bulgaria, Albania), Russian is spreading fast. The governments of these countries have made it a compulsory subject of instruction in their schools, often at the expense of German, French, and English. There is little evidence that Russian has spread very far or very fast in Red China, but some increase undoubtedly exists. For military, diplomatic, and commercial purposes, the study of Russian has been spreading in various countries of the Western world, and here in the United States, where Russian was once practically unknown, there are flourishing Russian courses in most of our colleges and universities, and even in some of the more progressive high schools. It is quite likely that at least three hundred million persons throughout the world can be reached, directly or indirectly, with Russian. The fact that most of them are not accessible to most of us today does not necessarily mean that things will forever remain that way.

The Soviet Union has been making giant strides in science,

technology, and industrial production. The record and description of Soviet achievements lie largely in Russian-language books and periodicals. Self-interest dictates that more of us learn to read those records and descriptions with reasonable speed and accuracy. The Soviets have never made a pretense of liking our political ideas, but they have not scorned our language on that account. English is the foreign language most widely studied and read in the Soviet Union. Again as a matter of self-interest, not thousands, but millions of us should acquire some familiarity with the predominant language of the Soviet Union, Russian.

Russian is a language of the Slavic group of Indo-European. This means that it has a direct link with Ukrainian, Polish, Czech, Serbo-Croatian, Bulgarian, and other tongues of the Slavic family, so that a knowledge of Russian will be of great help in learning those tongues.

It also means that Russian bears a definite, though not immediate, relationship to English, which belongs to the Germanic branch of that same big Indo-European family of languages.

The Russians and we hold many word roots in common. Our "water" and their *voda* (vuh-DAH), our "ignite" and their *ogon'* (uh-GAWN') ("fire"), our "milk" and their *moloko* (muh-luh-KAW) were originally identical Indo-European words. Sometimes strange transmutations of form and meaning occurred as our Germanic, and their Slavic, branch of Indo-European speakers moved farther apart. Take the Russian word for "to see," *videt'* (V'EE-d'it'); many people will at once recognize its kinship with Latin *videre*, which also means "to see," and through the Latin, with our "video," "visible," etc. But are there native Anglo-Saxon words, not borrowed from Latin, that stem from the same root? Yes; words like "wit" and "wot." As in "water" and *voda*, Anglo-Saxon *w* corresponds to Slavic *v*, and Anglo-Saxon *t* to Slavic *d*. But what about the meaning? "Wit" and "wot" are connected with "knowing," not with "seeing." True; but after you "see" a thing, don't you "know" it? The same Indo-European root, by the way, developed in the ancient Sanskrit of India as *Veda*, "knowledge," and in ancient Greek as *voida* or *oida*, "to hear." ("Seeing" and "hearing" are the best ways to "know.")

Or take a very common Russian word, the word for "bread," which is *khleb* (khl'ehp). At first glance, you see no possible connection with any English word. But wait; if you trace our "loaf" back to Anglo-Saxon you find *hlāf*. Since Germanic or Anglo-Saxon *f* appears as *p* in most other Indo-European branches (consider "father," and "pater": or "foot" and "ped-"), you see at once that it's the same word. We got tired of sounding an *h* or *kh* before *l*, while the hardier Russians didn't.

This genetic relationship does not mean that you'll find Russian too easy—certainly not so easy as German, which belongs to the same branch as English, nor so easy as Latin and French, from which we have borrowed over half our words. The language is rich, beautiful, expressive, and rewarding, but also fraught with difficulties when you learn it at the adult stage.

To begin with, the Russians do not write with our Roman alphabet. They use instead an alphabet called Cyrillic after one of the two Greek bishops from Constantinople, Cyril and Methodius, who converted the Slavs to Christianity at the end of the ninth century and devised a written form for their language.

For our purpose it is not necessary to learn the Cyrillic alphabet. The transcription we shall use will approximate English as closely as possible, but it must be distinctly understood: (1) that it is only an approximation; (2) that it is definitely not the form in which the Russians write.

Russian has a good many sounds for which there is no real English counterpart. There are palatalized consonant sounds, transcribed by such devices as *t'*, *d'*, *l'*, *n'* (other works prefer *ty*, *dy*, *ly*, *ny*), which resemble English *t*, *d*, *l*, *n* pronounced in fast word combinations like "hit you," "did you," "will you," "seen you." There are other palatal sounds which we pronounce with the tongue lying flat and straight, while the Russians curl the tongue so that its tip touches the roof of the mouth (*ch*, *sh*, *zh*, *shch*). There is one vowel sound, usually transcribed by *y*, which approximates the English *y* of *rhythm* (another way of describing it is to say that you place your mouth organs in the position to say *ee*, then try to say *oo*). These are the main points to remember in connection with our transcription:

1. In words of more than one syllable, the stressed syllable is indicated as usual by capital letters.

2. Russian stressed vowels are clear and somewhat drawled; but unstressed vowels are short and dull, and often have the same *uh*-quality that they have in English "general" (JEHN-uhr-uhl). Thus, the word for "thank you," spelled *spasibo* in the Cyrillic equivalent of Roman characters, sounds like spuh-S'EE-buh.

3. In our transcription, AH is like the *a* of "father," which occurs only when stressed: MAHS-luh, "butter."

4. EH represents the sound of *e* in "met," prolonged if stressed, shorter if unstressed (in which case it will appear in small letters, eh): EH-tuh, "this"; guh-vuh-R'EE-t'eh, "(you) speak."

5. EE and I represent the same sound, that of *i* in "machine"; but EE is generally used when the stress falls on it, and the sound is prolonged; I (or i) when it is unstressed, and therefore shorter: V'EE-zhoo, "(I) see"; M'EE-n'i-moom, "minimum." (Note that any consonant preceding EE or I is palatalized; that is, pronounced as though it were going to be followed by a *y*.)

6. AW represents the sound of *aw* in "awful," which occurs only when stressed: MNAW-guh, "much."

7. OO is the *oo* of "soon" if stressed, that of "good" if unstressed (in which case it will appear in small letters): l'oo-BL'OO, "(I) love"; DOO-muh-yoo, "(I) think."

8. The combination uh (always unstressed) is to be sounded like *e* in "over," *a* in "general," or *o* in "forget": spuh-S'EE-buh, "thank you."

9. The symbol Y, preceded or followed by consonants, is to be sounded like the *y* of "rhythm" (byl, "was"; my, "we"; vy, "you").

10. The same symbol Y, preceded or followed by vowels in the same syllable, is to be sounded like the *y* of "yes" or "May" (yah, "I"; yook, "south"). Here is a word in which both values of Y appear: yuh-ZYK, "language."

11. Where the combination EYE appears in our transcription, pronounce it like English "eye": DEYE-t'eh mn'eh, "Give me." Pronounce OOY as in "phooey": ZDRAHF-stvooy-t'eh, "hello." Pronounce OI like the *oy* in "toy": suh mnoi, "with me." Pronounce EY as in "obey": suh-luh-V'EY, "nightingale."

12. Consonants followed by ' indicate that the consonant is to be palatalized, as happens in English "did you," "will you," etc. One might say that you utter the consonant as though it

were going to be followed by the *y* of "you," but the *y* itself never comes out: D'EH-luht', "to do"; t'i-P'EHR', "now."

13. The transcriptions CH, SH, ZH, SHCH are all to be pronounced with the tip of the tongue curled back to touch the hard palate: CHAWR-ny, "black"; shehst', "six"; oo-ZHEH, "already"; yish-CHAW, "yet." The symbol ZH represents the *s* of "measure."

14. Russian R is always trilled, as in Spanish or Italian. S is always unvoiced, as in "case." An L that is not palatalized (if it is palatalized it will appear as L') gets a pronunciation in the back of the mouth, as in English "milk." KH is like the German *ach* sound, or the Scottish *ch* of *loch*.

15. Some Russian consonant groups will at first glance seem unmanageable. This is only because they are unfamiliar to English speakers in the position in which they occur in Russian. Take, for instance, a combination like fshys-T'EE ("at six"). We do not have in English a combination like *fsh* at the beginning of a word or expression; but it occurs in "offshore." Try cutting out the initial vowel sound of the English word, and you will have a reasonable approximation of the Russian combination. In a word like NRAH-v'it'-suh ("to please"), try "in Russia," cutting out the *i* of *in*. In a word like s-chawt ("reckoning," "bill"), try "this child," cutting out the *thi-* of *this*. You will ultimately find that all Russian sounds and combinations are fully pronounceable with a little practice.

With this, we can proceed to a few phrases of everyday common politeness; and remember that the Russians, for all their communism, are very polite. A rude person is described as n'i-kool-TOOR-ny, which looks and sounds like "uncultured," but actually means "impolite," "boorish"; and such a person is socially shunned by his Communist comrades (a far worse insult is *khahm*, "Ham," the name of the son of Noah who mocked his father; *khahm* is one who scoffs at all traditional cultural values).

> ZDRAHF-stvooy-t'eh: this is the commonest Russian form of greeting; actually, it is an imperative and means "Be healthy"; it regularly does service for our "Good morning," "Good afternoon," "Good evening," "Hello," "Hi."
> If you find it too difficult to pronounce, use the abbreviated form ZDRAH-st'eh; but you may also use:
> DAW-bruh-yeh OO-truh, "Good morning."
> DAW-bry d'ehn', "Good day."

DAW-bry V'EH-chuhr, "Good evening."

spuh-KOI-noi NAW-chee, "Good night."

duh sv'i-DAH-n'uh, "Good-by."

duh SKAW-ruh-vuh sv'i-DAH-n'uh, "See you soon."

duh ZAHF-truh, "See you tomorrow."

duh V'EH-chuh-ruh, "See you tonight."

SLOO-shuh-yoo, "Hello!" (on the phone; it means literally "I'm listening").

kahk vy puh-zhy-VAH-yi-t'eh? "How are you?" "How do you do?"

spuh-S'EE-buh, khuh-ruh-SHAW, uh vy? "Well, thank you, and you?" (As in many other languages, "thank you" comes first.)

kahk d'i-LAH? "How are things?" (To this query, the humor-loving Russians often reply with a rhyme, kahk SAH-zhuh b'i-LAH, "as soot is white"; in other words, "awful!")

puh-ZHAHL-stuh, "Please."

bluh-guh-duh-R'OO (vahs), "Thank you" (less commonly used than the spuh-S'EE-buh mentioned above. For a godless society, the Russians have strangely retained two religious words to express gratitude; while bluh-guh-duh-R'OO is "I give blessings," spuh-S'EE-buh means literally "God save)".

N'EH zuh shtuh, "You're welcome," "Don't mention it"; literally, "not for what."

eez-v'i-N'EE-t'eh, or pruh-ST'EE-t'eh, "Pardon me."

v'i-nuh-VAHT, "I'm sorry."

EH-tuh n'i-chi-VAW, "It's nothing." (The expression n'i-chi-VAW, which you have probably seen in the spelling *nichevo*, carries to the Russian all sorts of subtle meanings, like the shrug of the shoulders to the Frenchman: "Can't help it," "So sorry," "Nothing we can do about it," "Doesn't matter," "Don't worry," etc.)

AW-chin' pr'i-YAHT-nuh, "Glad to meet you."

By most accounts, shopping in the Soviet Union is apt to be a slightly drab affair, with consumer goods in what government gobbledygook euphemistically terms "short supply" and ruble prices quite high. But it may not always be so. Here, accordingly, are a few shopping terms, with capitalistic freedom of choice thrown in:

pr'i-n'i-S'EE-t'eh mn'eh, "Bring me."

puh-kuh-ZHY-t'eh mn'eh, "Show me."
DEYE-t'eh mn'eh, "Give me."
shtaw yah muh-GOO dl'uh vahs SD'EH-luht'? "What can
I do for you?"
shtaw vy khuh-T'EE-t'eh? "What do you want?"
yah khuh-CHOO, "I want."
mn'eh NOOZH-nuh, "I need."
SKAWL'kuh? (EH-tuh STAW-yit)? "How much?" (does
this cost)?
SL'EESH-kuhm MNAW-guh, "Too much."
shtaw yish-CHAW? "What else?"
BAWL'-sheh n'i-chi-VAW, "Nothing else."

Here are a few of the things you might want; use these
expressions after yah khuh-CHOO, "I want":

koo-SAWK MY-luh, "a piece of soap"
LAWM-t'ik KHL'EH-buh, "a slice of bread"
foont M'AH-suh, "a pound of meat"
puh-K'EHT puh-p'i-RAWS, "a package of cigarettes"
kuh-RAWP-koo SP'EE-chuhk, "a box of matches"
boo-TYL-koo v'i-NAH, "a bottle of wine"
CHAHSH-koo CHAH-yoo, " a cup of tea"

The matter of directions is important:

skuh-ZHY-t'eh mn'eh, "Tell me."
gd'eh? "Where is, Where are?"
vawt, "Here is, Here are."
tahm, "There is, There are."
puh kuh-KOI duh-RAW-g'eh? "Which way?"
puh EH-toi stuh-ruh-N'EH, "This way."
nuh-PRAH-vuh, "To the right."
nuh-L'EH-vuh, "To the left."
PR'AH-muh, "Straight ahead."
ee-D'EE-t'eh suh-MNOI, "Come (or go) with me."

Here are a few nouns that you can use with some of the
above expressions (note that "is," "are" do not appear in
Russian; neither do "the," "a," "an"):

GAW-ruht, (the, a) "city"
OO-l'i-tsuh, (the, a) "street"
TS'EHR-kuhv', (the, a) "church"
guh-ST'EEN-n'i-tsuh, (the, a) "hotel"
duh-RAW-guh, (the, a) "road"

dawm, (the, a) "house"
KAWM-nuh-tuh, (the, a) "room"
oo-BAWR-nuh-yuh, (the, a) "lavatory," "toilet"
PAW-yist, (the, a) "train"
vuh-GAWN, (the, a) "railway coach"
stuh-LAW-vuh-yuh, (the, a) "dining room"
r'is-tuh-RAHN, (the, a) "restaurant"

Here are some useful expressions about speaking and understanding:

guh-vuh-R'EE-t'eh l'i vy puh-ROOS-k'ee (puh-uhn-GL'EE-sk'ee, puh-fruhn-TSOO-sk'ee, puh-n'i-M'EHTS-k'ee)? "Do you speak Russian (English, French, German)?"

yah guh-vuh-R'OO TAWL'-kuh n'i-MNAWZH-kuh, "I speak only a little."

guh-vuh-R'EE-t'eh M'EHD-l'in-n'i-yeh, "Speak more slowly."

puh-n'i-MAH-yi-t'eh l'i vy? "Do you understand?"
yah n'i puh-n'i-MAH-yoo, "I don't understand."
ZNAH-yi-t'eh l'i vy? "Do you know?"
yah n'i ZNAH-yoo, "I don't know."
MAW-zhy-t'eh l'i vy? "Can you?"
yah n'i muh-GOO, "I can't."
shtaw EH-tuh ZNAH-chit? "What does this mean?"
uh-CHAWM vy guh-vuh-R'EE-t'eh? "What are you talking about?"
kahk EH-tuh nuh-zy-VAH-yit-suh puh-ROOS-k'ee? "What do you call this in Russian?"
kahk guh-vuh-R'EET-suh —— puh-ROOS-k'ee? "How do you say —— in Russian?"
yah uh-m'i-r'i-KAH-n'its (yah uh-m'i-r'i-KAHN-kuh if you are a woman), "I'm an American."

The weather invariably lends itself to pleasant conversation, wherever you may be:

KHAW-luhd-nuh s'i-VAWD-n'uh, "It's cold today."
ZHAHR-kuh, "It's warm."
mn'eh KHAW-luhd-nuh, "I'm cold."
mn'eh t'i-PLAW, "I'm warm."
V'EH-tr'i-nuh, "It's windy."
SAWL-n'ich-nuh, "It's sunny."
khuh-RAW-shuh-yuh puh-GAW-duh, "It's nice weather."

pluh-KHAH-yuh puh-GAW-duh, "It's bad weather."
dawzhd' ee-D'AWT, "It's raining."
sn'ehk ee-D'AWT, "It's snowing."

There are a few people whose services you may need. If the person you need is a male, the formula is mn'eh NOO-zhyn, "to me is necessary"; follow it up with:

m'i-l'i-tsyuh-N'EHR, "a policeman"
vrahch, "a doctor"
nuh-S'EEL'-shchik, "a porter"
shuh-F'AWR, "a driver"
p'i-r'i-VAWT-chik, "an interpreter"
d'i-R'EHK-tuhr, "the manager"
tukh-S'EE, "a taxi" (use mn'eh NOOZH-nuh for this one)

Russian grammar is about as "complicated" as Latin grammar. We put "complicated" in quotes because to its own native speakers no language is complicated. It only seems so to foreigners because it diverges from their own habits of thought and expression.

Russian adheres to the ancient Indo-European structure far more than English (though English, too, had most of the trappings when it was still Anglo-Saxon). Russian is a language of prefixes, roots and, particularly, endings, the last of which English largely got rid of in the course of its history.

Russian nouns and adjectives show by their endings gender (masculine, feminine, or neuter), number (singular or plural) and case. There are seven cases: nominative for the subject, genitive for possession, dative for the indirect object, accusative for the direct object, vocative for direct address, instrumental for "by," "with," etc., and locative for use with various other prepositions. The vocative usually falls in with the nominative, but this still leaves 2 × 6 separate forms or uses for what English renders by "boy," "boy's," "boys," "boys'," and 3 × 2 × 6 for what English renders simply by "good" or "white." How do the Russians learn all this? Simply by force of habit, hearing each form of the noun or adjective used in certain contexts until it becomes second nature to use them in those connections. Where the young Russians have to get accustomed to many endings on their words, our own growing generations have to get used to certain word combinations which would (and do) bewilder adult Russian learners—the delicate use of "a," "the," or nothing at all before nouns, the use of "shall," "will," "have," "may," "might," "would," and other auxiliaries with our simple verb forms.

A typewriter is a slow and cumbersome replacement for ordinary handwriting until you have mastered the touch system. You can learn to manipulate complicated machinery with ease by acquiring a series of reflexes, but you will have to spend time and effort on acquiring the reflexes. Spoken language is nothing but a lengthy series of reflexes, but the growing child has years in which to acquire them, which the adult has not. That is why grammars are written. The grammatical rule is a generalization which it is hoped you may learn quickly and then apply in individual instances. It acts as a quick substitute for infinite repetitions of examples that would ultimately, but unconsciously, lead you to the same generalization. The child gets these examples over a long period of years, and eventually knows "instinctively" which form to use to express a certain meaning (actually, there is nothing "instinctive" about it; he has learned the hard, long way, by trial and error and infinite repetition). What a grammar hopes to do is to provide you with a short cut, whereby you may use your adult faculty of abstraction and generalization, and be able to say, "I know that in this particular situation I must use the instrumental case, which for this particular class of nouns happens to end in -uhm." But this does not mean that you don't have to go through a number of repetitions before you have it firmly fixed in your mind that the instrumental is the proper way to express "by means of," and that most masculine nouns end in -uhm in the instrumental singular. In other words, try to use a combination of the adult rule of grammar and the child's process of repetition.

Let us try going through a Russian noun and seeing how it operates. Here is MAHL'-chik, "boy." This is the nominative and also the vocative case in the singular. You can use it as the subject (MAHL'-chik zd'ehs, "The boy is here"), as a predicate noun (awn MAHL'-chik, "He is a boy"), or to call out (MAHL'-chik! "Boy!"). The genitive singular is MAHL'-chi-kuh, "boy's," "of a boy," "of the boy." By special arrangement applicable to nouns that denote males, this form is used also as the direct object or accusative (yah V'EE-zhoo MAHL'-chi-kuh, "I see the boy"). The dative, "to the boy," is MAHL'-chi-koo (yah dahl MAHL'-chi-koo khl'ehp, "I gave the boy the bread"). The instrumental, which denotes "with," "by means of," is MAHL'-chi-kuhm (yah byl s MAHL'-chi-kuhm, "I was with the boy"). The locative or prepositional case is used with a number of prepositions, among them aw or uh, "about" (yah guh-vuh-R'OO uh MAHL'-chi-k'eh, "I am speaking about the boy").

In the plural, MAHL'-chi-k'ee is the nominative or vocative (MAHL'-chi-k'ee zd'ehs', "The boys are here"; uh-N'EE MAHL'-chi-k'ee, "They are boys"; MAHL'-chi-k'ee! "Boys!"). MAHL'-chi-kuhf is the genitive or, again by special arrangement for nouns denoting males, the accusative (KN'EE-g'ee MAHL'-chi-kuhf, "the boys' books"; yah V'EE-zhoo MAHL'-chi-kuhf, "I see the boys"). The dative, "to the boys," is MAHL'-chi-kuhm. The instrumental ("by means of the boys") is MAHL'-chi-kuh-m'ee. The locative or preposi-tional ("about the boys") is uh MAHL'-chi-kuhkh.

The point is that after you have heard uh MAHL'-chi-kuhkh a few thousand times with the meaning of "about the boys," it won't occur to you to say uh MAHL'-chi-kuh-m'ee, and if anyone says it in your presence, you will laugh. If they ask you why you laugh, either you'll know the grammatical answer, in which case you'll tell them: "You never use the instrumental case with the preposition uh; you use the locative case"; or you won't know the grammatical answer, and then you'll say: "Nobody but you ever says it that way; everybody else says uh MAHL'-chi-kuhkh."

Put this philosophy into reverse. A Russian learning English says to you: "I see book on table." You correct him: "I see *the* book on *the* table." He says: "What is this thing 'the' that you use? I never use it or feel the need of it in my language." At this point, if you are an expert on English grammar, you go into a disquisition on the nature of the definite article, where to use it and where to omit it. (Why "I go to Belgium," "I love liberty," and not "I go to the Belgium," "I love the lib-erty"? After all, some languages say it that way.) If you don't know the grammatical answer, you give the really basic, fundamental reply: "Look, brother, every English speaker says 'I put the book on the table.' Don't ask me why. If you don't want people to laugh at you, you had better put in 'the,' too!"

The Russian noun is tough to an outside learner; the Rus-sian adjective is even tougher. If you use it to modify a noun directly, it will have 2 × 3 × 6 possible endings, according to number, gender, and case, and the endings will not be at all identical with those of the noun (khuh-RAW-shy MAHL'-chik, "good boy," subject; khuh-RAW-shuh-vuh MAHL'-chi-kuh, "of the good boy," or "good boy" as direct object; khuh-RAW-shuh-moo MAHL'-chi-koo, "to the good boy"; s khuh-RAW-shym MAHL'-chi-kuhm, "with the good boy"; uh khuh-RAW-shehm MAHL'-chi-k'eh, "about the good boy"). These complexities have their counterpart in the plural, and are multiplied in each gender, and in each of the numerous classes of nouns and adjectives.

If the adjective is used as a predicate adjective, where English would have the verb "to be," which the Russians omit in the present (but not in the past or future), there is, luckily, only one case, but in the singular there are three gender forms; in the plural, again fortunately, only one:

MAHL'-chik khuh-RAWSH, "The boy is good."
D'EH-voosh-kuh khuh-ruh-SHAH, "The girl is good."
v'i-NAW khuh-ruh-SHAW, "The wine is good."
MAHL'-chi-k'ee (D'EH-voosh-k'ee, V'EE-nuh) khuh-ruh-SHY, "The boys (girls, wines) are good."

The Russian verb would be simple, were it not that most verbs lead a double life, appearing in one form to indicate an action that is recurrent or habitual, in another to indicate what happens just once. D'EH-luht', for instance, means "to do," "to be doing," but only habitually, repeatedly, or in a continued sense. If you "do" just once and then are through, you use SD'EH-luht'.

Infinitives usually end in -t'. The present tense, as you may have noted, generally has the endings -oo for "I," -t for "he" or "she," -m for "we," -t'eh for "you," but they are complicated by what precedes them. As a sample, here is the present of guh-vuh-R'EET', to speak:

yah guh-vuh-R'OO, "I speak"
ty guh-vuh-R'EESH', "you (familiar singular) speak"
awn (uh-NAH) guh-vuh-R'EET, "he (she) speaks"
my guh-vuh-R'EEM, "we speak"
vy guh-vuh-R'EE-t'eh, "you (plural or polite singular) speak"
uh-N'EE guh-vuh-R'AHT, "they speak"

A good deal can be accomplished conversationally with the

verb khuh-T'EHT', "to want," followed by the infinitive. The present of khuh-T'EHT' is:

yah khuh-CHOO, "I want"
ty KHAW-chish', "you want"
awn (uh-NAH) KHAW-chit, "he (she) wants"
my khuh-T'EEM, "we want"
vy khuh-T'EE-t'eh, "you want"
uh-N'EE khuh-T'AHT, "they want"

To this, you may add the very easy Russian past tense, which is really a participle used like a predicate adjective. It agrees with the subject in gender and number, ending in -l for the masculine, -luh for the feminine, -l'ee for the plural of both genders, so that you have yah guh-vuh-R'EEL if a man says "I spoke," yah guh-vuh-R'EE-luh if a wóman says it, my guh-vuh-R'EE-l'ee for "We spoke," whether men or women.

Following is a brief list of infinitives, which you may use after "want," and of past forms, for which all you need to do is put a subject pronoun in front and shift from -l to -luh if the subject is feminine, to -l'ee if it is plural:

yah khuh-CHOO, "I want"	yah, "I"
koo-P'EET', "to buy"	koo-P'EEL, "bought"
zuh-pluh-T'EET', "to pay"	zuh-pluh-T'EEL, "paid"
oo-V'EE-d'eht', "to see"	oo-V'EE-d'ehl, "saw"
puh-bluh-guh-duh-R'EET', "to thank"	puh-bluh-guh-duh-R'EEL, "thanked"
skuh-ZAHT', "to say"	skuh-ZAHL, "said"
puh-pruh-S'EET', "to ask for"	puh-pruh-S'EEL, "asked for"
yehst', "to eat"	yehl, "ate"
p'eet', "to drink"	p'eel, "drank"
poi-T'EE, "to go"	puh-SHAWL (puh-SHLAH, puh-SHL'EE), "went"
neye-T'EE, "to find"	nuh-SHAWL (nuh-SHLAH, nuh-SHL'EE), "found"
SD'EH-luht', "to do"	SD'EH-luhl, "did"
byt', "to be"	byl (by-LAH, BY-l'ee), "was," "were"

Such is the language of our major competitor. But it may also be the language of our potential friends, for the Americans who have visited the Soviet Union in recent times are all agreed that, whatever their government may be thinking or planning, the Russian people as individuals are most anxious to be on friendly terms with us. Let us therefore reply in kind, and if we ever visit their land, let us tell them, in all sincerity:

my n'i VAH-shy vruh-G'EE; my VAH-shy droo-Z'AH!
("We are not your enemies; we are your friends!")

chapter nine
one world language
esperanto

As you travel about in the countries of Europe, particularly the smaller ones, in the lands of Latin America, in the more progressive countries of the Far East, you will occasionally encounter men wearing a button with a little green star in their coat lapels, and women displaying the same green star symbol on their dresses or blouses. The chances are you will pay the green star very little attention, because practically everyone abroad displays some symbol or other, political, religious, or social. But if you are in the know, you will recognize the green star as the mark of identification of those who are able to speak and understand the world's only full-blown international language in actual spoken use—Esperanto.

The name means "hope," or, more precisely, "one who hopes," and the green star symbolizes the firm hope of its wearers in a better future for mankind—a future in which all men, regardless of race, color, nationality, or religion, will be able to speak to and understand one another and so consider themselves as being members of the same world community.

If you happen to speak the language of the Green Star of Hope, you will find its wearers to be friendly, civilized, cultured, and ready to help you. They will greet you as a *samideano,* "one who shares the same idea," of a friendly world speaking the same tongue, and will place themselves at your disposal for whatever you may need in their country. Since there are several millions of them scattered all over the world, and they are particularly numerous in the smaller countries, whose languages are seldom studied by outsiders, the practical value of Esperanto is large—out of proportion, perhaps, to the number of people who speak it.

In Europe one frequently hears Esperanto on the radio. If you have never heard it before, it will sound like a smooth Romance tongue with which you happen to be unfamiliar. Its use is permissible, along with Latin, in international telegrams and cables. It has been successfully used at many international gatherings, including a recent convention of European Esperantists held in the Netherlands, where Prime Minister Willem Drees addressed the delighted audience in fluent Esperanto. About a hundred newspapers, magazines, and periodicals in Esperanto are published all over the world, from Brazil to Japan and from Norway to South Africa. Numerous important works of literature have been translated into Esperanto, and many original works have been composed in it. American popular songs sound good in their Esperanto translations. Have you ever heard "Home on the Range" sung in Esperanto by a male chorus? It is an experience.

Yet Esperanto, the favorite of believers in an international language the world over, has comparatively few adherents in the United States. This, despite the fact that it is taught in several schools in western states and has even been tried with considerable success in New York City's high schools.

A few years ago George Gallup ran a poll in the United States, Canada, Norway, and Holland. The questions were: (1) Would you like to see a language designed for international use taught in all the elementary schools throughout the world, so that children would grow up speaking it along with their own national tongue? (2) Outside of your own national language, what language would you like to see adopted as the international tongue for world-wide use?

Amazingly, the reply to the first question was between 70 and 80 per cent affirmative in all four countries polled. The United States, supposed to be traditionally isolationist and opposed to the study of foreign languages, made as good a showing as did Canada, Norway, and Holland.

On the second question, there was a wide rift. In the United States, where English was out of the running, about 25 per cent of the voters favored French, another 25 per cent preferred Spanish, 16 per cent voted for German, and the others chose a sprinkling of other languages (Italian, Russian, Latin, Greek). In Canada, where English was likewise out of the running, over 50 per cent voted for French. That could have been predicted easily, since French is native to almost one-fourth of Canada's population. Actually, French should have been excluded from the voting in Canada, since it is co-official with English.

The surprise came in the answers from Norway and Holland. Here English won an easy victory, getting 50 to 70 per cent of the vote in both countries. The runner-up, however, was neither French, nor German, nor Russian, nor even Spanish or Italian. It was Esperanto, which polled more than 25 per cent of the votes.

What is this Esperanto that is almost unknown in North America, yet is so popular in Europe?

It is a constructed, artificial language, deliberately designed to serve international purposes—one of at least six hundred such languages that have been presented to the world since the seventeenth century, when the idea of a "neutral," constructed tongue first took hold. Its inventor, Dr. Lazarus Ludwig Zamenhof, of Poland, grew up in Bialystok, a border town where Polish, Russian, Lithuanian, German, and Yiddish were all spoken. Noticing that language differences lent themselves to racial antipathies and hatreds, he resolved to seek a way to lead the world's peoples out of the mazes of the Tower of Babel. The result of his labors first appeared in 1887. Since he wished to remain anonymous, he signed himself Doktoro Esperanto, "Doctor who hopes" or "Doctor Hopeful." The name stuck to his product.

Many attempts had been made before his time. The French philosopher Descartes, in the seventeenth century, was the first to propose an artificial language for international scholarship. Before his time, in the Middle Ages and Renaissance, Latin had served that purpose, and it was common for students to wander from one to another of the great European universities (Bologna, Salerno, the Sorbonne, Oxford, Cambridge, Salamanca, Heidelberg, Prague, and Cracow) encountering no language difficulties, since all university work was carried on in Latin. But the fifteenth and sixteenth centuries saw the birth of European nationalisms and the rejection of Latin in favor of the national tongues. Descartes was therefore justified in suggesting that since no nation would use another nation's language, and all had discarded Latin, the only way out of the resulting confusion was to create a new language acceptable to all.

Actually, Descartes' language, which he barely outlined, was acceptable to no one. It was far too difficult and complicated, and completely unlike any of the languages in spoken use. The same fate befell some of his contemporaries, Urquhart, Dalgarno, Cave Beck, and Bishop Wilkins of England, all of whom tried to build languages out of logic and thin air.

Many attempts were made to create a suitable language for world use in the centuries that followed. About 1885 a German cleric, Monsignor Schleyer, came out with a language called Volapük, which enjoyed considerable vogue. But Volapük faded away at the appearance of Esperanto, a language that combined logic, ease of pronunciation, simple grammar, and a vocabulary that was drawn from the leading languages of the Western world—Latin, Greek, the Romance tongues, English, and German. Surprisingly, Zamenhof, who was a Pole, put very little Slavic into his creation, and practically no words from non-European languages. This feature, which may have had some merit in the 1890's and early 1900's, can hardly be said to be of advantage today.

Yet Esperanto quickly found its way into the most remote countries, Eastern as well as Western. Within a few years, Esperanto societies were formed in practically every country of Europe, as well as a great many Asiatic, African, and American nations. Canada seems to have enjoyed the distinction of the first Esperanto group and the first Esperanto periodical in the Western Hemisphere, but it was quickly followed by the United States, Mexico, Brazil, and Argentina. In some countries, the fortunes of Esperanto varied with the political situation. Tsarist Russia, which had at first welcomed it, later banned it because of the liberal implications of its linguistic philosophy. The Soviet regime, which had at first favored it, discarded it in the 1930's. Esperanto's doctrine of brotherly love among all peoples and races does not jibe well with any form of imperialism, nationalistic or Communistic.

The linguistic principles that inspired Dr. Zamenhof were: (1) absolute simplicity of sound and grammatical structure, so Esperanto would be easy to learn and to speak; (2) absolute correspondence between spoken sound and written symbol, to avoid spelling difficulties; (3) internationality and neutrality of vocabulary, so that no nation or language would be favored over another.

He was successful only in part, and the measure of his success with internationality was far greater in 1887 than it is today. In 1887, the only languages that had to be considered to achieve "internationality" and "neutrality" were the great Western tongues—Latin and Greek, English, German, French, Spanish, Italian. Today, Russian, Chinese, Japanese, Hindustani, and Arabic are among the great world languages. And fifty years from now, others, like Indonesian, may be knocking at the gate.

For the rest, the phonetic and grammatical simplicity of Esperanto is such that with an hour's study you can learn to pronounce it reasonably well, spell it correctly, and master its few rules of grammar, which have no exceptions. Of course, you will still have to learn words—perhaps as many as 10,000 of them—to achieve fluent control over the language.

Consider first Esperanto's sound-and-spelling scheme.

Written *a* is invariably pronounced as *ah;* written *e* is always *eh;* written *i* always *ee;* written *o* always *oh;* written *u* always *oo.*

Written *j,* wherever it occurs, is pronounced like English *y* in "boy," and written *ŭ* like English *w.*

Most consonants are pronounced as in English. Note, however, that written *c* is always sounded *ts;* *ĉ* is *ch;* while *g* is always as in "good," *ĝ* is like English *j* in "journal"; *ĵ* is like the *s* of "pleasure" (this we shall transcribe as *zh*); while *s* is always as in "sun," *ŝ* is like English *sh.* Each vowel forms a separate syllable, and the stress is always on the next to the last syllable.

All this sounds simple, but it is here that difficulties begin. Printers, particularly in English-speaking countries, object strenuously to letters written with suprascript symbols (*ĉ, ĝ, ĵ, ŝ, ŭ*). Since Esperanto makes no use of the English letters *q, w, x* and *y,* many of them ask why these unused letters couldn't be substituted for the suprascript symbols (*w* for *ŭ, q* for *ĉ, x* for *ŝ, y* for Esperanto *j,* and *j* for Esperanto *ĝ* or *ĵ,* or even for both). To this plea for typographical simplification, Esperantists so far have turned a deaf ear.

Accepting the Esperanto alphabet as it is, let us examine a few greetings and polite expressions in this simple language.

The phrase "I wish you" is understood to precede each of them, therefore the accusative ending is used:

Bonan matenon.   (BOH-nahn mah-TEH-nohn)   Good morning.

Bonan tagon.   (BOH-nahn TAH-gohn)   Good day, Good afternoon.

Bonan vesperon.   (BOH-nahn veh-SPEH-rohn)   Good evening.

Bonan nokton.   (BOH-nahn NOHK-tohn)   Good night.

Adiaŭ.   (ah-DEE-ow)   Good-by.

Ĝis revido.   (JEES reh-VEE-doh)   See you later, *au revoir.*

Ĝis morgaŭ.   (JEES MOHR-gow)   See you tomorrow.

Saluton.   (sah-LOO-tohn)   Hello! (greeting or phone call).

Kiel vi fartas?   (KEE-ehl VEE FAHR-tahs)   How are you?

Kiel aferoj iras?   (KEE-ehl ah-FEH-roy EE-rahs)   How are things?

Tre bone.   (TREH BOH-neh)   Very well.

Dankon, or *Mi dankas.*   (DAHN-kohn, MEE DAHN-kahs)   Thank you.

Tute ne.   (TOO-teh NEH)   Don't mention it.

Mi petas, or *Bonvolu.*   (MEE PEH-tahs, bohn-VOH-loo)   Please.

Pardonu.   (pahr-DOH-noo)   Pardon me, Excuse me.

Ne gravas.   (NEH GRAH-vahs)   It doesn't matter, Never mind.

Mi bedaŭras.   (MEE beh-DOW-rahs)   I'm sorry.

Estas nenio.   (EHS-tahs neh-NEE-oh)   It's nothing.

The international, but strongly occidental nature of Esperanto is clearly revealed by these expressions, which show the basic compromise between Romance and Germanic. *Bonan, matenon, vesperon, adiaŭ, revido, iras, gravas, tre, pardonu, estas* are clearly Latin-Romance. *Tagon, morgaŭ, fartas, dankon, bedaŭras* are as clearly Germanic. Slavic or oriental? There just isn't any, at least in these basic terms.

Among individual Romance and Germanic languages, Esperanto rather haphazardly or arbitrarily favors sometimes one, sometimes another. *Knabo,* meaning "boy," is definitely German, not English; *birdo,* "bird," is just as definitely English, not German. *Krajono,* "pencil," and *tranĉajo,* "slice" are definitely French; *skatolo,* "box" and *dogano,* "customs," are clearly Italian; *viro,* "man," and *peti,* "to ask for," are Latin; *veneno,* "poison," is perhaps Latin, perhaps Spanish. But the specifically Spanish–Portuguese element, as apart from the general Romance, is largely absent from Esperanto. It is possible that the Hispanic languages were not among those firmly possessed by Dr. Zamenhof. This makes no difference to Spanish and Portuguese Esperantists, who enthusiastically fasten onto the sounds of Esperanto, so similar to their own.

One question frequently asked in connection with any constructed language is: "Won't everybody pronounce it with his own national accent, so that in time you will get a series of dialects that may eventually become new languages?"
There is some truth to this. No matter how much you stress the simple Esperanto rules of pronunciation, it is difficult to keep the English speaker from pronouncing the very name of the language es-purr-AN-to, while the Frenchman says eh-spay-räh-TOH, and the Italian or Spaniard says ehs-peh-RAHN-toh. If you listen, as I once did, sitting just within ear range, to German and Chinese speakers of Esperanto, you would almost swear they were speaking German or Chinese.
But this need not worry us unduly. People who learn a foreign language after they have become adults almost invariably speak it with an accent, and this does not prevent understanding. The foreign accents vanish with second-generation speakers, and this would be true of Esperanto if it became truly universal. With radio, TV, and spoken films, not to mention speech work in the schools, the danger of new languages arising out of a universal Esperanto is remote.

If you are caught in Oslo, Rotterdam, Buenos Aires, or Tokyo with a shopkeeper or restaurant waiter who knows no English but wears the green star, this is what he and you can use:
Kiel mi povas vin servi?   (KEE-ehl MEE POH-vahs VEEN SEHR-vee)   What can I do for you?
Kion vi deziras?   (KEE-ohn VEE deh-ZEE-rahs)   What do you wish?
Mi deziras.   (MEE deh-ZEE-rahs)   I should like.
Ĉu vi bonvole donos al mi?   (CHOO VEE bohn-VOH-leh DOH-nohs ahl MEE)   Will you please give me?
Montru al mi.   (MOHN-troo ahl MEE)   Show me.
Portu al mi.   (POHR-too ahl MEE)   Bring me.

To complete these phrases, choose any of the following words, which are given here with the accusative ending:

Pecon (PEH-tsohn) a piece
Trançajon (trahn-CHAH-zhohn) a slice
Pakajon (pah-KAH-zhohn) a pack, package
Skatolon (skah-TOH-lohn) a box
Botelon (boh-TEH-lohn) a bottle
Glason (GLAH-sohn) a glass
Tason (TAH-sohn) a cup
De (deh) of
Da (dah) of (quantity)
Pano (PAH-noh) bread
Sapo (SAH-poh) soap
Cigaredoj (tsee-gah-REH-doy) cigarettes
Cigaroj (tsee-GAH-roy) cigars
Lakto (LAHK-toh) milk
Biero (bee-EH-roh) beer
Vino (VEE-noh) wine
Teo (TEH-oh) tea
Kafo (KAH-foh) coffee

In combination:

Mi deziras paketon da cigaredoj. (MEE deh-ZEE-rahs pah-KEH-tohn dah tsee-gah-REH-doy) I should like a pack of cigarettes.

Mi petas, montru al mi kelkajn kravatojn. (MEE PEH-tahs, MOHN-troo ahl MEE KEHL-kine krah-VAH-toyn) Please show me some neckties.

Bonvolu porti al mi tason da teo. (bohn-VOH-loo POHR-tee ahl MEE TAH-sohn dah TEH-oh) Please bring me a cup of tea.

And let us not forget these shopping expressions:

Kiom kostas? (KEE-ohm KOHS-tahs) How much is it?
Tro multe. (TROH MOOL-teh) Too much.
Rigardu! (ree-GAHR-doo) Look!
Ion pli? (EE-ohn PLEE) Anything else?
Nenion pli. (neh-NEE-ohn PLEE) Nothing else.

Esperanto grammar is simple, and can be given here in its practical entirety. There is no indefinite article, so that *libro* means "book" or "a book." The definite article is *la*, and, like the English "the," it never changes (*la libro*, "the book"; *la libroj*, "the books"). All nouns end in *-o*, and form the plural by adding *-j*, which is pronounced as a *-y*. If the noun is used as the object of a verb (but not of a preposition), add *-n*: *Mi havas la krajonojn.* (MEE HAH-vahs lah krah-YOH-noyn) I have the pencils.

All adjectives end in *-a*. They, too, add *-j* for the plural and *-n* if they are used with nouns that are verb-objects: *Mi deziras bonajn librojn.* (MEE deh-ZEE-rahs BOH-nine LEE-broyn) I want good books.

To make an adverb from an adjective, change the *-a* of the adjective to *-e* (*bona*, "good," *bone*, "well"; *simpla*, "simple," *simple*, "simply"). This also applies to nouns that are used as adverbs: *Mi parolas Esperante.* (MEE pah-ROH-lahs ehs-peh-RAHN-teh) I speak Esperanto (fashion).

Feminine nouns are formed from masculine ones by adding the suffix *-in:* *viroj, sinjoroj* (VEE-roy, see-NYOH-roy), "men," "gentlemen"; *virinoj, sinjorinoj* (vee-REE-noy, see-nyoh-REE-noy), "women," "ladies." For "Miss," use the word *fraŭlino.*

All verb-infinitives end in *-i*. Change the *-i* to *-as* for the present, to *-is* for the past, to *-os* for the future, to *-u* for the imperative. Use, as in English, with personal pronoun subjects: *mi*, "I"; *vi*, "you"; *li*, "he"; *ŝi*, "she"; *ĝi*, "it"; *ni*, "we"; *ili*, "they." These pronouns, too, add *-n* if they are verb-objects, and are placed, as in English, after the verb:

> *Kompreni* (kohm-PREH-nee) to understand
> *Mi komprenas vin.* (MEE kohm-PREH-nahs VEEN) I understand you.
> *Vi ne komprenas min.* (VEE NEH kohm-PREH-nahs MEEN) You don't understand me.
> *Ĉu li komprenas?* (CHOO LEE kohm-PREH-nahs) Does he understand? (*Ĉu* is an interrogative particle, used in questions that do not start with a specific interrogative word such as "when," "why," "who"; it works somewhat like the English "do" or "does" in similar sentences.)
> *Ŝi komprenis ilin.* (SHEE kohm-PREH-nees EE-leen) She understood them.
> *Ni ne komprenos ĝin.* (NEE NEH kohm-PREH-nohs JEEN) We shall not understand it.
> *Komprenu tion!* (kohm-PREH-noo TEE-ohn) Understand this!

Directions are important. Look for someone wearing the green star; then ask your question:

Ĉu vi povas diri al mi? (CHOO VEE POH-vahs DEE-ree ahl MEE) Can you tell me?
Kie estas? (KEE-eh EHS-tahs) Where is? Where are?
Kien vi (ni) iras? (KEE-ehn VEE (NEE) EE-rahs) Where are you (we) going?
En kiu direkto? (EHN KEE-oo dee-REHK-toh) Which way?
Jen (tie) estas. (YEHN (TEE-eh) EHS-tahs) Here is, Here are.
Ĉi tien. (CHEE TEE-ehn) This way.
Tien. (TEE-ehn) That way.
Dekstren, maldekstren. (DEHK-strehn, mahl-DEHK-strehn) To the right, To the left.
Rekte antaŭen. (REHK-teh ahn-TOW-ehn) Straight ahead.
Venu kun mi. (VEH-noo koon MEE) Come with me.

Combine these with a few places, such as:

la preĝejo (lah preh-JEH-yoh) the church
la katedralo (lah kah-teh-DRAH-loh) the cathedral
la hotelo (lah hoh-TEH-loh) the hotel
la necesejo (lah neh-tseh-SEH-yoh) the lavatory
la manĝejo (lah mahn-JEH-yoh) the dining room
la stacio (lah stah-TSEE-oh) the station
la dogano (lah doh-GAH-noh) the customs
Pardonu, ĉu vi povas diri al mi kie estas la stacio? (pahr-DOH-noo, CHOO VEE POH-vahs DEE-ree ahl MEE KEE-eh EHS-tahs lah stah-TSEE-oh) Pardon me, can you tell me where the station is?
En kiu direkto estas la manĝejo? (ehn KEE-oo dee-REHK-toh EHS-tahs lah mahn-JEH-yoh) Which way is the dining room?
Kie mi povas trovi bonan hotelon? (KEE-eh MEE POH-vahs TROH-vee BOH-nahn hoh-TEH-lohn) Where can I find a good hotel?

In some countries you may occasionally find directional signs in Esperanto:

Ne fumu, or, Malpermesite fumi. (NEH FOO-moo, mahl-pehr-meh-SEE-teh FOO-mee) No smoking.

Ne eniru, or, *Malpermesite eniri.* (NEH eh-NEE-roo, mahl-pehr-meh-SEE-teh eh-NEE-ree)   No admittance.

Atentu, or, *zorgu.* (ah-TEHN-too, ZOHR-goo)   Careful! Attention! Warning!

Avizo. (ah-VEE-zoh)   Notice.

Iru dekstren (maldekstren). (EE-roo DEHK-strehn, mahl-DEHK-strehn)   Keep right, Keep left.

Enirejo, elirejo. (eh-nee-REH-yoh, eh-lee-REH-yoh)   Entrance, Exit.

Viroj, sinjoroj. (VEE-roy, see-NYOH-roy)   Men, Gentlemen.

Virinoj, sinjorinoj. (vee-REE-noy, see-nyoh-REE-noy)   Women, Ladies.

Speaking terminology always comes in handy:

Ĉu vi parolas esperante? *(angle, france, germane, hispane, itale)?* (CHOO VEE pah-ROH-lahs ehs-peh-RAHN-teh, AHN-gleh, FRAHN-tseh, gehr-MAH-neh, hees-PAH-neh, ee-TAH-leh)   Do you speak Esperanto (English, French, German, Spanish, Italian)?

(Tre) iomete. (TREH ee-oh-MEH-teh)   (Very) little.

Mi petas, parolu pli malrapide. (MEE PEH-tahs, pah-ROH-loo PLEE mahl-rah-PEE-deh)   Please speak more slowly.

Ĉu vi komprenas (scias)? (CHOO VEE kohm-PREH-nahs, STSEE-ahs)   Do you understand (know)?

Mi ne komprenas (scias). (MEE NEH kohm-PREH-nahs, STSEE-ahs)   I don't understand (know).

Pri kio vi parolas? (PŘEE KEE-oh VEE pah-ROH-lahs)   What are you talking about?

Kion vi volas diri? (KEE-ohn VEE VOH-lahs DEE-ree)   What do you mean?

Kiel vi diras —— esperante? (KEE-ehl VEE DEE-rahs —— ehs-peh-RAHN-teh)   How do you say —— in Esperanto?

Mi estas Usonano. (MEE EHS-tahs oo-soh-NAH-noh)   I'm an American (this noun is formed from the initials of United States of North America; *Amerikano* would mean any North, South, or Central American).

Here are the words for a few people you may need:

Mi deziras (MEE deh-ZEE-rahs)   I wish
la direktoron (lah dee-rek-TOH-rohn)   the manager

policanon (poh-lee-TSAH-nohn)   a policeman
kuraciston (koo-rah-TSEES-tohn)   a doctor
portiston (pohr-TEES-tohn)   a porter
la usonan konsulon (lah oo-SOH-nahn kohn-SOO-lohn)
the American consul
Mi deziras kuraciston. (MEE deh-ZEE-rahs koo-rah-
TSEES-tohn)   I want a doctor.
Alvoku policanon. (ahl-VOH-koo poh-lee-TSAH-nohn)
Send for a policeman.

Weather discussions make for pleasant conversation:

Pluvas. (PLOO-vahs)   It's raining.
Neĝas. (NEH-jahs)   It's snowing.
Estas bona (malbona) vetero. (EHS-tahs BOH-nah, mahl-
BOH-nah, veh-TEH-roh)   It's fine (bad) weather.
Estas varme (malvarme). (EHS-tahs VAHR-meh, mahl-
VAHR-meh)   It's warm (cold).
Estas al mi varme (malvarme). (EHS-tahs ahl MEE VAHR-
meh, mahl-VAHR-meh)   I'm warm (cold).

Adjectives, as said before, end in *-a*, regardless of gender,
add *-j* if used in the plural, and *-n* if part of a verb-object. The
prefix *mal-* generally indicates the opposite of a positive
quality (*bela*, "beautiful"; *malbela*, "ugly"). For "more" use
pli, for "most" use *la plej*:

granda (GRAHN-dah)   large, big
malgranda, eta (mahl-GRAHN-dah, EH-tah)   small, little
varma, malvarma (VAHR-mah, mahl-VAHR-mah)   hot,
cold
bona, malbona (BOH-nah, mahl-BOH-nah)   good, bad
unua (oo-NOO-ah)   first
lasta (LAHS-tah)   last
vera (VEH-rah)   true
libera, neokupita (lee-BEH-rah, neh-oh-koo-PEE-tah)
free
mallibera, okupita (mahl-lee-BEH-rah, oh-koo-PEE-tah)
not free

Esperanto verbs can be used in their practical entirety, by
practicing the few simple rules given above. Change *-i* to *-as*
for the present, to *-is* for the past, to *-os* for the future, to *-u*
for the imperative, and use subject pronouns as in English.

aĉeti   (ah-CHEH-tee)   to buy
vendi   (VEHN-dee)   to sell
vidi   (VEE-dee)   to see
viziti   (vee-ZEE-tee)   to visit
paroli   (pah-ROH-lee)   to speak
danki   (DAHN-kee)   to thank
demandi   (deh-MAHN-dee)   to ask
peti   (PEH-tee)   to ask for
pagi   (PAH-ghee)   to pay
manĝi   (MAHN-jee)   to eat
trinki   (TREEN-kee)   to drink
bani   (BAH-nee)   to bathe
lavi   (LAH-vee)   to wash
razi   (RAH-zee)   to shave
foriri   (foh-REE-ree)   to go away, depart
iri   (EE-ree)   to go
veni   (VEH-nee)   to come
marŝi   (MAHR-shee)   to walk
eniri   (eh-NEE-ree)   to go in
eliri   (eh-LEE-ree)   to go out
ripozi   (ree-POH-zee)   to rest
enlitiĝi   (ehn-lee-TEE-jee)   to go to bed
scii   (STSEE-ee)   to know (a fact)
koni   (KOH-nee)   to know (a person), be acquainted with
renkonti   (rehn-KOHN-tee)   to meet
trovi   (TROH-vee)   to find
halti   (HAHL-tee)   to stop
fumi   (FOO-mee)   to smoke
fari   (FAH-ree)   to do, make; for "to have something
    done," use suffix *-igi* on the root of any verb: *farigi* (fah-
    REE-ghee), to have done; *mi skribis leteron*, I wrote a
    letter; *mi skribigis leteron*, I had a letter written.
esti   (EHS-tee)   to be
havi   (HAH-vee)   to have

Esperantists claim that Dr. Zamenhof's language is the
simplest of any to learn. For people who know a Western
tongue, this is probably true. Gauge yourself by your understanding of the following paragraph, remembering the few
easy rules that have been interspersed with our speaking
material:

*La inteligenta persono lernas la Interlingvon Esperanto rapide
kaj* (this word, by the way, means "and," and is taken from

the Greek) *facile*. *Esperanto estas la moderna, kultura, neŭtrala lingvo por ĝenerala interkomunikado. La Interlingvo estas simpla, fleksebla, praktika solvo de la problemo de internacia interkompreno.*

Esperantists also claim that their tongue is a steppingstone to the study of foreign languages, and that school children who have had a year of Esperanto later make giant strides in French, Spanish, and German.

But aside from all this, Esperanto is a practical tourist language, which will help you out in the most unexpected places. So,

Lernu paroli Esperante!

chapter ten

who said latin is dead?

Why do we still study Latin? Because it is a language of culture, literature, and philosophy, a sample of the ancient Indo-European from which our modern Western languages sprang. Because Latin, more than any other language (with the possible exception of Greek) is the vehicle of Western thought, the carrier of the common concepts upon which our civilization rests. Because Latin, more than any other language, enters into the great word stock of the English tongue.

This you can easily prove by running your eye over a few pages of your dictionary. Despite the fact that English is originally and basically Germanic (our most frequently used words, such as "and," "but," "of," "to," "for," "I," "you," "go," "come," "house," "rain," "good," "bad," are Anglo-Saxon), you will find that about 75 per cent of the words listed either came to us directly from Latin, or passed from Latin into French or Italian and then into English, or came to us from Greek through Latin.

A few examples? "Item," "data," "exit," extra," "bonus," "alibi," "propaganda" are pure, unchanged Latin, at least in written form. "Quiet," "ulcer," "history," "popular," "necessary" merely drop or change a Latin ending. "Very" is French *verai, vrai* ("true," "truly"), but that comes from Low Latin *veracus*. "Pay" is French *payer*, but Latin *pacare* is the original (*pacare* meant "to appease, pacify"; what better way of appeasing than with money?). "Money" itself is French *monnaie*, "coin," but that comes from Latin *moneta* (originally from the verb *monere*, "to warn"; the sacred geese of the temple of Juno in early Rome gave warning with their cackling that the Gauls were trying to scale the walls, so the attribute *Moneta*, "the Warner," was applied to this particular Juno; later the temple was turned into a mint, and the word *moneta* was passed on to the product of the mint). "Influenza" is Italian (the disease was at one time thought to be due to the "influence" of the stars); but Italian got it from Latin *influere*, "to flow in." "Buffalo" is Italian, but comes from Latin *bubalus* or *bufalus*, "wild ox." "Dish" comes from Greek *diskos*, but through Latin *discus*. "Economy" (literally "house management") travels from Greek to Latin to French to English. "Priest" comes from Greek *presbyteros*, "elder," but through Latin *presbyter*. Anyone who has studied Latin knows the meaning of thousands of English words.

But has Latin any value as a tourist language? Yes. Surprisingly, the tongue of Caesar, Cicero, and Virgil is much used for international exchanges, and is frequently employed as a stopgap in lands whose spoken tongues stem from it.

Every truly educated person in France, Spain, Italy, Portugal, and Latin America has some knowledge of Latin—usually far beyond that acquired in our all too brief high school courses. In non-Romance countries such as Germany, Holland, Sweden, Norway, the physician, lawyer, judge, even the scientist or engineer, is almost certain to know Latin. The Catholic priest, often the Protestant minister and Jewish rabbi as well, can speak Latin fluently.

This widespread use of Latin goes back to the Middle Ages, when it was the international language of Western scholarship, and a student or professor could go from Oxford in England to the Sorbonne in Paris, Bologna in Italy, Heidelberg in Germany, Salamanca in Spain, even Prague in Bohemia and Cracow in Poland, using the same Latin everywhere, not only in classroom lectures and discussions, but in his everyday relations with his fellow scholars.

Latin had been the universal spoken tongue in the Roman Empire of the West before its fall. It had been the universal language of Western Christianity in the early days of conversion. When the Roman Empire of the West fell, in the fifth century A.D., non-Latin-speaking peoples poured into western Europe, and the use of Latin dwindled. The masses spoke a vulgar form which ultimately gave rise to the Romance tongues; but the use of Latin continued among the educated, with little change in grammar and many modifications of vocabulary. This learned Latin was used not only in the churches and monasteries, but in the royal courts and in legal documents of every country in western Europe until the dawn of modern times.

In England, Latin was spoken along with the French of the Norman conquerors until both languages were superseded by the popular English of the lower classes. As late as 1325 all conversation at Oxford had to be in Latin or French, and the use of English in court and university circles did not become general until the end of the fourteenth century. But England was a radical innovator in the medieval world. In France, Latin remained the legal and court language until the days of Francis I, in the early sixteenth century. As late as 1852, Latin continued to be the language of instruction at most Italian universities.

The Western Church, undivided until the days of Luther and Henry VIII, resolutely stuck to Latin, and Roman Catholic priests, even today, must know it well enough to conduct their services and read their breviaries. But most of them know it far better than that, and are able to converse in it with one another.

The Latin tradition was strong in the United States down to the days of Longfellow and Grandgent, and no high school student escaped it. Even today, in a world where academic learning has given way to science and pseudo-science, Latin continues to be one of the favorite tongues of American high schools. In western European countries it is more often a must, for the link between scientific terminology and the languages that supply most of that terminology, Greek and Latin, strikes the European more forcibly than it does us. How can a physician escape Latin when he has to deal with the Latin names for most parts of the body? How can the lawyer or politician get away from Latin when he must deal in alibis and aliases, nolle prosequis and *in rems*, deficits and agenda, and quorums and vetoes? How can the scientist flee from words like quantum, inertia, and radioactivity?

Therefore the tourist who has no other choice may find that he can occasionally fall back on Latin, particularly in his dealings with the more cultured people in the lands of his travels. He may, as happened to a friend traveling in Hungary, get directions in Latin from a priest, or, as happened to another traveler in Rumania, use Latin in addressing a peasant, be understood, and manage to understand the essential parts of the reply in Rumanian.

What kind of language is Latin? Does it consist exclusively of the military terminology used by Julius Caesar in his front-line dispatches from the Gallic War, or of the involved sentences, often half a page long, used by Cicero in his flowery invective against Catiline the conspirator, or of the resounding, picture-evoking descriptions with which Virgil intersperses his account of the wanderings of Aeneas after the fall of Troy?

What most Latin students (and teachers) forget is that these works now used for school purposes bear the same relation to the spoken tongue of the Roman Republic and Empire that Eisenhower's communiqués from North Africa, Clay's speeches in the Senate, and the verses of Robert Browning and Dylan Thomas bear to everyday spoken English. There was a military, an oratorical, and a literary Latin; there was also a spoken Latin, uttered in short, choppy sentences, with a minimum of subordinate clauses, and larded with slang and vulgarisms. Plautus, who wrote plays dealing with the life of the lower classes in the third century B.C., has left us some interesting samples of the earlier stages of this popular language, and Petronius and Apuleius give us equally fascinating insights into the later stages. But the writers of the early Christian Church, whose main concern was to convert pagans into Christians and hold converted Christians in line so they wouldn't backslide into paganism, are even more typical. Many of their works are frankly propagandistic in nature. It is an axiom of propaganda that it can't be over the heads of the listeners, under penalty of losing its propaganda value.

The Catholic Church has preserved this popular Latin as it was spoken, say, in the fifth century A.D., the period of the Empire's downfall. Pronunciation may vary slightly from country to country, but no more so than do the dialects of the modern spoken tongues. This Latin is substantially what passed on into the medieval world and turned into the language of international scholarship. It was somewhat refined by puristic influences during the Renaissance, but remained generally the same. You can use it today with millions of people. By international convention, it may be used in telegrams. Around the turn of the century, an illustrious Berlin professor who had suffered an accident received an inquiry as to his health from the Italian Minister of Education. His reply: *"Caput ossis femoris fractum. Spero consolidationem. Gratias multas."* ("Hipbone broken. Hope it will heal. Many thanks.")

A truly "dead" language does not grow. International Latin does. Throughout the ages, words and expressions have been constructed and added to the language to keep it current as a medium of communication. How would you express "railroad," "armored cruiser," "postal money-order," concepts which the ancient Romans did not have? By coinages such as *via ferrea* ("iron road"), *loricata navis* ("breast-plated ship"), *diribitoria chartula* ("small paying card"). How would you say "A-bomb," "radiogram," "radio newscast"? By the use of *globus atomica vi displodens* ("ball exploding by atomic power"), *nuntium per aetherias undas missum* ("message sent over the air waves"), *radiophonica diurnorum actorum communicatio* ("radiophonic communication of daily happenings"); note that *acta diurna,* "daily events," was the name of the daily gossip sheet that was posted up in the Forum in ancient Roman times.

"Bombing plane" is *velivolum ignivomis globis verberans* ("sail-bearing flying machine striking with fire-vomiting balls"). "Black market" is *annona excandefacta* ("white-hot market"). "Communist" mildly comes out as *aequandorum bonorum fautor* ("partisan of wealth equalizing"). "Matches" are *ramenti sulphurati* ("brimstoned chips"), and the very modern American "O.K." is translated by the very ancient *amen.*

Even American place names are translated into "modern" Latin, with "Green Bay," Wisconsin, coming out as *Sinus Viridis,* "Springfield" as *Campifons,* and "Little Rock" as *Petricula.* The Vatican takes care of keeping the language abreast of the times, issuing a periodic word list of current coinages, prepared by Monsignor Antonio Bacci, Pontifical Secretary of Briefs to Princes, and one of the greatest living authorities on Latin.

Latin grammar is the learner's bugaboo. This is because Latin, like all Indo-European languages at their outset (and this includes Anglo-Saxon, the direct ancestor of English), has full-fledged declensions and conjugations, with nouns and adjectives taking on different endings according to their number, gender, and use in the sentence. Verbs change their endings to denote differences of person, number, tense, mood, and voice. How could a people, many of whom were illiterate, speak such a "complicated" tongue? Of course they did not have to learn it out of a grammar, as does our high school student today. They grew up using the various forms of words automatically, in given contexts, even if they couldn't tell you why they used them in those contexts, other than, "That's how I've always heard it."

For our purpose, which is neither literary nor scientific, we, too, can skip most of the grammatical explanation and learn the words in given contexts.

Latin pronunciation is made easier by the fact that there is no modern standard. The ancient tongue distinguished between long and short vowel sounds (*venit,* "he comes," for instance, had a short *e* and was pronounced WEN-it, while *vēnit,* "he came," sounded as WAY-nit). Speakers of "modern" Latin, particularly in the Romance countries, seldom bother to make the distinction, which disappeared from spoken Latin as the language turned into Romance, between 400 and 800 A.D.

For the vowels, this was the classical scheme:

Ā, like *a* in "father"	A, the same sound, but shorter
Ē, like *a* in "fate"	E, like *e* in "met"
Ī, like *i* in "machine"	I, like *i* in "it"
Ō, like *o* in "no"	O, like *aw* in "awful" cut very short
Ū, like *oo* in "food"	U, like *oo* in "good"

Latin also had four diphthongs:

AE like English "eye," or *i* in "life."
OE like *oy* in "boy" (but in present-day church pronunciation, both AE and OE sound as *ay* or *eh*).
AU like *ow* in "how."
EU like the *e* of "met" quickly followed by the *oo* of "good."

The Romans did not indicate long or short values over their written vowels, and we shall follow their practice. Also, they used the sign I for the sound of *y*, as well as for the long or short vowel *i*. What is spelled in most modern Latin books *juvenis* (YOO-weh-nis), "young," was originally written IUVENIS. In addition, the sign V, which stood for the sound of *w* in written Latin, was also used for the long or short vowel *u*. The Romans inscribed as PVBLICVS what would today be printed *publicus*. By the time the U-symbol was created and used for the vowel sound, the Latin *w* sound, which continued to use the symbol V, had come to be pronounced like present-day English *v*, and that is the way you will generally hear it from a Romance speaker of Latin.

Classically, the written letter C was always pronounced like *k*, and G was always hard, as in "get"; but modern speakers tend to pronounce C and G before E and I in the fashion of their own modern languages, so don't be surprised if *Cicero*, which you learned as KEE-keh-ro, comes out as TSEE-tseh-ro in the mouth of a German, CHEE-cheh-ro in that of an Italian, SEE-seh-ro in that of a Frenchman, and THEE-theh-ro in that of a Spaniard. The group SC before E and I was *sk* in classical times, but most modern speakers will pronounce it Italian fashion, *sh* (SHEE-o instead of SKEE-o for *scio*, "I know"). TI before a vowel was *tee* classically, but is often pronounced *tsee* today (*Iustitia*, classically yoos-TEE-tee-ah, today yoos-TEE-tsee-ah).

We have reason to believe that Roman R was trilled, as in modern Italian or Spanish, and that Roman S was always hard, as in "case," never sounded like a *z* as in "houses." For B, D, F, H, L, M, N, P, QU, T, an English pronunciation will do, though T and D were probably pronounced with the tip of the tongue against the back of the upper teeth instead of against the upper gum ridges as in English.

We may now pass on to some expressions of Roman politeness:

Ave. (AH-way; literally "Hail") or *Salve* (SAHL-way, "Be safe and sound"); this served the Romans for "Good morning," "Good afternoon," "Good evening," "Hello," "How are you?"

Si tu vales, ego valeo. (SEE TOO WAH-lays, EH-go WAH-leh-o) If you are well, I am well. (This was a favorite formula for starting an ancient letter, but usable in conversation too.)

Quis loquitur? (QUIS LO-quit-oor) Who is speaking? (This may be used as a telephone "Hello," though the

Romans, as is well known, had no phones.)

Impetro (EEM-pet-ro), or *te rogo* (TAY RO-go). I beg you, please.

Gratias tibi ago. (GRAH-tee-ahs TIB-ee AH-go)   Thank you.

Ignosce. (eeg-NO-skay or eeg-NO-shay)   Pardon me.

Poenitet me. (POY-nit-et MAY), or *dolet me* (DO-let MAY)   I'm sorry.

Nihil est. (NEE-hil EST)   It's nothing, don't mention it.

Libenter. (lee-BEN-tehr)   Gladly.

The polite forms of address found in most modern languages were nonexistent in ancient times. The Romans, more democratic in this respect than their descendants, addressed any single person, whether he was emperor or slave, as *tu* (TOO). *Vos* (WOS) was used for a plural audience. But since Latin verb forms indicate clearly by their endings who the subject is, *tu* and *vos*, along with *ego* (EH-go), "I," *nos* (NOS), "we," and various words used for "he," "she," "it," "they," are normally omitted, unless they are meant to be stressed, as in the above *Si tu vales, ego valeo.* Ordinarily, "you are well" is simply *vales* if the "you" is singular, *valetis* (wah-LAY-tis) if "you" is plural.

Here are some common and useful expressions:

Da mihi. (DAH MEE-hee)   Give me.

Dic mihi. (DEEK MEE-hee)   Tell me.

Affer mihi. (AHF-fehr MEE-hee)   Bring me.

Ostende mihi. (aw-STEN-day MEE-hee)   Show me.

Ubi est? (OO-bee EST)   Where is?

Ubi sunt? (OO-bee SUNT)   Where are?

Ecce. (EHK-kay or EH-chay)   Behold, Here is, Here are.

Quo vadis? (QUO WAH-dis)   Where are you going? (Note that *ubi* is "where" without motion, *quo* is "whither.")

Qua via? (QUAH WEE-ah)   Which way?

Dextera manu. (DEK-steh-rah MAH-noo)   On (or to) the right.

Sinistra manu. (see-NEES-trah MAH-noo)   On (or to) the left.

Vade mecum. (WAH-day MAY-koom)   Go with me.

Intro veni. (EEN-troh WEH-nee)   Come in.

Quid agis? (QUID AH-gis)   What are you doing?

Quid agitur? (QUID AH-git-oor)   What's going on?

Volo. (WOH-loh) I want.

Loquerisne latine, anglice, gallice, italice, hispanice, teutonice? (loh-quay-RIS-nay lah-TEE-nay, AHN-glee-kay, GAHL-lee-kay, ee-TAH-lee-kay, his-PAH-nee-kay, teh-oo-TOH-nee-kay) Do you speak Latin, English, French, Italian, Spanish, German?

Paulum. (POW-loom) A little.

Quantum? (QUAN-toom) How much?

Quid magis? (QUID MAH-ghis) What else?

Nihil magis. (NEE-hil MAH-ghis) Nothing else.

Loquere lentius. (LOH-quay-ray LEN-tee-oos) Speak more slowly.

Aspice! (AHS-pee-kay) Look!

Intellegisne? (in-tel-lay-GIS-nay) Do you understand?

Non intellego. (NOHN in-TEL-lay-go) I don't understand.

Scisne? (SKIS-nay or SHIS-nay) Do you know?

Nescio. (NAY-skee-o or NAY-shee-o) I don't know.

Potesne? (paw-TES-nay) Can you?

Non possum. (NOHN PAWS-soom) I cannot.

It will be noticed from some of the above examples that in asking a question that does not have a specific interrogative word, such as "Where?" "When?" "What?" the interrogative particle *-ne* is appended to the verb. If you want to make the question negative, use *nonne* before the verb: *Nonne intellegis?* (NOHN-nay in-TEL-lay-gis) Don't you understand?

Let's try some conversation:

Ignosce, amice, ubi est Via Flaminia? (eeg-NOS-kay, ah-MEE-kay, OO-bee EST WEE-ah flah-MEE-nee-ah) Pardon me, friend, where is the Flaminian Road?

Perge recta, viator, usque ad viam tertiam; ibi est Via Flaminia. (PEHR-gay REHK-tah, wee-AH-tohr, OOS-quay ahd WEE-ahm TEHR-tee-ahm; EE-bee EST WEE-ah flah-MEE-nee-ah) Go straight, stranger, as far as the third street; there is the Flaminian Road.

Ecce ecclesia Sancti Pauli Extra Muros. (EHK-kay ehk-KLAY-see-ah SAHNK-tee POW-lee EHKS-trah MOO-rohs) Here is the Church of St. Paul Outside the Walls.

Quo vadimus nunc? (QUO WAH-dee-moos NOONK) Where are we going now?

Ad quaerendum prandium. Esaurio atque sitio. Latrat

stomachus. (AHD quay-REN-doom PRAHN-dee-oom. eh-SOW-ree-o AHT-quay SIT-ee-o. LAH-traht STO-mah-koos) To get something to eat. I'm hungry and thirsty. My stomach is barking. (Idiomatic for "I'm starving.")

En taberna Aurei Cervi. Bonum vinum praebent. (AYN tah-BEHR-nah OW-reh-ee KEHR-wee. BAW-noom WEE-noom PRAY-bent) There's the Golden Stag Inn. They've got good wine.

Quid emere vis? (QUID EH-may-ray WIS) What do you want to buy?

Saponem atque luciferos emere volo. Habesne? (sah-PO-nem AHT-quay loo-KEE-feh-rohs EH-may-ray WOH-loh. hah-BAYS-nay) I want to buy soap and matches. Have you any?

Habeo. (HAH-bay-o) I have.

Quantum tibi dare debeo? or *Quanti indicas?* (QUAHN-toom TIB-ee DAH-ray DAY-beh-o, QUAHN-tee in-DEE-kahs) How much do I owe you?

Libras quingentas et quadraginta. (LEE-brahs quin-GHEN-tahs et quah-drah-GHIN-tah) Five hundred and forty lire.

Quid mane ages? (QUID MAH-nay AH-gays) What are you doing tomorrow?

Ad basilicam Sancti Petri ibo; eam videre cupio. (ahd bah-SEE-lee-kahm SAHNK-tee PET-ree EE-bo; EH-ahm wee-DAY-ray KOO-pee-o) I'm going to St. Peter's; I want to see it.

Heri eam vidi. (HEH-ree EH-ahm WEE-dee) I saw it yesterday.

Qui es? (QUEE EHS) Who are you?

Civis americanus sum. (KEE-wis ah-may-ree-KAH-noos SOOM) I'm an American citizen.

Serve, affer mihi ampullam cerevisiae. Festina! (SEHR-way, AHF-fehr MEE-hee ahm-POOL-lahm kay-ray-WEE-see-ay. fehs-TEE-nah) Waiter, bring me a bottle of beer. Speed it up!

Mox venit! (MAWKS WEN-it) Coming right up!

Many of the most common objects and practices of our civilization would have mystified the ancient Romans. There is, for example, a perfectly good Latin verb that means "to smoke" (*fumare*, foo-MAH-ray), but it is not used for a person who smokes. Cigars, cigarettes, tea, coffee, chocolate, tomatoes, Indian corn, all came to the Western world long after the fall of the Roman Empire. Fortunately, words for them are largely international, and will be generally understood, even if one does not wish to use the "modern" Latin coinage. *Ascensor* (ahs-KEN-sohr, elevator), *cinematographum* (kin-ay-mah-TOH-grah-foom, movies), *televisio* (tel-ay-WEE-see-o, TV), even *statio* (STAH-tee-o, station), in the modern railway sense, would have puzzled the ancients. But then, wouldn't Shakespeare and even Dickens have thought "penicillin" and "Univac" to be some kind of double talk?

Try some phrases which a Roman centurion might have used:

Calet aer. (KAH-let AH-ehr) It's warm.
Frigus est. (FREE-goos EST) It's cold.
Ningit hodie. (NIN-git HOH-dee-ay) It's snowing today.
Pluit. (PLOO-it) It's raining.
Serena est tempestas. (say-RAY-nah EST tem-PES-tahs)
    It's fine weather.
Immitis est tempestas. (im-MEE-tis EST tem-PES-tahs)
    It's bad weather.
Da mihi segmentum panis. (DAH MEE-hee seg-MEN-toom PAH-nis) Give me a slice of bread.
Poculum aquae cupisne? (PAW-koo-loom AH-quay koo-PIS-nay) Do you want a glass of water?
Cauponam quaero. (kow-PO-nahm QUAY-ro) I'm looking for a hotel.
Ubi est balneum, triclinium? (OO-bee EST BAHL-nay-oom, tree-KLEE-nee-oom) Where is the bathroom (dining room)?
Mihi necesse est (MEE-hee nay-KEHS-say EST) I need
vigil (WEE-gil) a policeman
medicus (MAY-dee-koos) a doctor
bajulus (BAH-yoo-loos) a porter
interpres (in-TEHR-prays) an interpreter

In combination:

Vigilem (medicum, bajulum, interpretem) arcessere volo.
    (WEE-gil-em, (MAY-dee-koom, BAH-yoo-loom, in-TEHR-pray-tem) ahr-KES-say-ray WOH-lo) I want to send for a policeman, doctor, porter, interpreter.

As in many modern languages (German, Russian, etc.), Latin nouns have cases and change their endings according to how they are used in the sentence. An -*m* ending (-*um*, -*am*, -*em*) is most frequent when the noun is the direct object, while -*us* or -*a* often appears when it is the subject. There is also a genitive, used where English would use "of"; here the ending is -*ae*, -*i*, or -*is* (*Da mihi poculum aquae, ampullam vini, segmentum panis.* "Give me a glass of water, a bottle of wine, a slice of bread"). The complete list of cases and declensional endings is lengthy and complicated when you are learning it as an adult out of a grammar, but it can also be assimilated by constant use and infinite repetition, as when a child learns his own native tongue.

Adjectives also have endings, so that *bonus pater*, "the good father," when father is the subject, becomes *bonum patrem* if used as the object of a verb, while "of the good father" becomes *boni patris*.

Verbs, too, have endings. The infinitive generally ends in -*re*, the first person singular of the present in -*o*, the second singular in -*s*, the third singular in -*t*; the first person plural ends in -*mus*, the second plural in -*tis*, the third plural in -*nt*. These endings usually suffice to indicate "I," "you," "he," "we," "they." Imperative forms usually end in -*a*, -*e*, or -*i* if you are commanding a single person, in -*te* if you are commanding more than one.

There are three verbs it is important to know in full, at least in the present tense: *habere* (hah-BAY-ray), "to have"; *esse* (EHS-say), "to be"; and *velle* (WELL-ay), "to want." The last two are quite irregular.

habeo (HAH-bay-o)   I have
habes (HAH-bays)   you (singular) have
habet (HAH-bet)   he, she, it has
habemus (hah-BAY-moos)   we have
habetis (hah-BAY-tis)   you (plural) have
habent (HAH-bent)   they have

sum (SOOM)   I am
es (ES)   you (singular) are
est (EST)   he, she, it is
sumus (SOO-moos)   we are
estis (EST-is)   you (plural) are
sunt (SOONT)   they are

volo (WOH-lo) I want
vis (WIS) you (singular) want
vult (WOOLT) he, she, it wants
volumus (WO-loo-moos) we want
vultis (WOOL-tis) you (plural) want
volunt (WO-loont) they want

Volo followed by an infinitive can express "want to." *Sum* followed by a future participle gives you a so-called round-about future, which can replace the regular future (*bibiturus sum*, "I am about to drink," can mean, to all intents, "I shall drink). *Habeo* with a past participle is somewhat slangy, but appears even in classical authors as a replacement for the regular past tense of verbs that take a direct object.

As an example, let's take the verb "to buy," *emere* (EH-may-ray) and, by using *volo*, *sum* and *habeo*, make a start on some Latin sentences:

Emere volo. (EH-may-ray WOH-lo) I want to buy.
Empturus sum. (ehmp-TOO-roos SOOM) I am about to buy, I shall buy (change -*us* to -*a* if subject is feminine, to -*i* if subject is plural).
Emptum habeo. (EHMP-toom HAH-beh-o) I have bought.

Here are some useful verbs in the infinitive, future participle and past participle:

vendere (WAYN-day-ray) to sell; *venditurus* (wayn-dee-TOO-roos); *venditum* (WAYN-dee-toom).
videre (wee-DAY-ray) to see; *visurus* (wee-SOO-roos); *visum* (WEE-soom).
dicere (DEE-kay-ray) to say; *dicturus* (deek-TOO-roos); *dictum* (DEEK-toom).
loqui (LAW-quee) to speak; *locuturus* (law-koo-TOO-roos); use *locutus sum* (law-KOO-toos SOOM) for "I spoke."
gratias agere (GRAH-tee-ahs AH-gay-ray) to thank; *gratias acturus* (ahk-TOO-roos); *gratias actas* (AHK-tahs).
scribere (SKREE-bay-ray) to write; *scripturus* (skreep-TOO-roos); *scriptum* (SKREEP-toom).
rogare (ro-GAH-ray) to ask, ask for; *rogaturus* (ro-gah-TOO-roos); *rogatum* (ro-GAH-toom).
solvere (SAWL-way-ray) to pay, pay for; *soluturus* (saw-loo-TOO-roos); *solutum* (saw-LOO-toom).

edere (EH-day-ray) to eat; *esurus* (ay-SOO-roos); *esum* (AY-soom).

bibere (BEE-bay-ray) to drink; *bibiturus* (bee-bee-TOO-roos); *bibitum* (BEE-bee-toom).

lavare (lah-WAH-ray) to wash; *lauturus* (low-TOO-roos), *lautum* (LOW-toom).

barbam radere (BAR-bahm RAH-day-ray) to shave; *barbam rasurus* (rah-SOO-roos); *barbam rasam* (RAH-sahm).

ire (EE-ray) to go; *iturus* (ee-TOO-roos); use *ivi* (EE-wee), *ivisti* (ee-WIS-tee), *ivit* (EE-wit), *ivimus* (EE-wim-oos), *ivistis* (ee-WIS-tis), *iverunt* (ee-WAY-roont) for "I went," etc.

venire (way-NEE-ray), to come; *venturus* (wen-TOO-roos); use *veni* (WAY-nee), *venisti* (way-NIS-tee), *venit* (WAY-nit); *venimus* (WAY-nee-moos), *venistis* (way-NIS-tis), *venerunt* (way-NAY-roont) for "I came," etc.

invenire (in-way-NEE-ray) to find; *inventurus* (in-wen-TOO-roos); *inventum* (in-WEN-toom).

facere (FAH-kay-ray) to do, make; *facturus* (fahk-TOO-roos); *factum* (FAHK-toom).

fieri jubere (FEE-ay-ree yoo-BAY-ray) to have (something) done; *fieri jussurus* (yoos-SOO-roos); *fieri jussum* (YOOS-soom).

There is another use for Latin, which goes far beyond tourist needs and drops the language squarely into everyone's lap. It is not merely a matter of word derivations and word power, but the actual use of Latin expressions in normal American life. In countries whose languages stem directly from Latin, a far greater number of such expressions are in popular use. In Italy, for example, practically everybody would recognize *punica fides*, "Punic faith," or "absolute untrustworthiness," a byword arising among the Romans at the time of their wars with Carthage, by reason of the fact that the Carthaginians, according to Roman historians, never kept their pledges; but remember, we don't have the accounts of the Carthaginian historians; or *hodie mihi cras tibi*, "Today to me, tomorrow to you," "What happens to me today may happen to you tomorrow."

But even in modern American life, there is a very frequent use of Latin words and expressions. Here is a little quiz on the Latin expressions in English. Try giving the full form if the expression is abbreviated, the literal meaning, the historical or legendary connection if any. Score yourself 2 for every correct answer (there are 50 questions). If your score is over 80, you are a language scholar; between 50 and 80 is fair; below 50 means you should brush up on both your Latin and your English.

I—ABBREVIATIONS

1. A.D.
2. A.M.
3. e.g.
4. lb.
5. etc.

6. n. b.
7. q. e. d.
8. r. i. p.
9. ad lib.
10. op. cit.

II—COMMON EXPRESSIONS

11. Alma Mater
12. bona fide
13. fiat
14. Magna Charta
15. per annum

16. per capita
17. per se
18. verbatim
19. via
20. vice versa

III—LEGAL, POLITICAL AND DIPLOMATIC TERMS

21. pro tempore
22. sine die
23. cui bono?
24. ad valorem
25. non compos mentis

26. status quo
27. casus belli
28. modus vivendi (operandi)
29. persona non grata
30. quid pro quo

IV—LITERARY EXPRESSIONS

31. lapsus linguae
32. inter nos (alia)
33. summum bonum
34. obiter dictum
35. pro bono publico

36. profanum vulgus
37. sub rosa
38. cave canem
39. hic jacet
40. ex libris

V—RELIGIOUS EXPRESSIONS

41. ex cathedra
42. urbi et orbi

43. ora pro nolis
44. nihil obstat

45. imprimatur

VI—FAMOUS SLOGANS FROM ROMAN HISTORY

46. Salus populi suprema lex esto.

47. Vae Victis!
48. Delenda est Carthago!
49. Timeo Danaos et dona ferentes.
50. Morituri te salutamus!

For no extra credit, try a few coined in post-Roman times:
1. E pluribus unum.
2. Sic semper tyrannis!
3. Semper fidelis.
4. Similia similibus curantur.
5. De mortuis nihil nisi bonum.

If we have passed this test, we may safely adopt as our motto: ROMAM EAMUS, ET LATINE LOQUAMUR (RO-mahm eh-AH-moos et lah-TEE-nay lo-QUA-moor), "Let's go to Rome and speak Latin!"

Answers to quiz questions:

1. *Anno Domini,* "in the year of the Lord."
2. *ante meridiem,* "before noon."
3. *exempli gratia,* "for the sake of an example."
4. *libra,* "pound."
5. *et caetera,* "and other things."
6. *nota bene,* "note well."
7. *quod erat demonstrandum,* "which was to be proved."
8. *requiescat in pace,* "may he rest in peace."
9. *ad libitum,* "at one's pleasure."
10. *opere citato,* "in the aforementioned work."
11. "fostering mother"; said of the college where one was educated.
12. "in good faith."
13. "let it be done"; said of an arbitrary measure.
14. "Great Charter"; the document which the English barons forced King John to sign, and which contains the germs of modern freedoms.
15. "by the year."
16. "by the head."
17. "by itself" or "in itself."
18. "word for word."
19. "by way of."
20. "with the order inverted."
21. "for the time being."
22. "without a day"; said of an adjournment when no date is fixed for the assembly to reconvene.

23. "to whose advantage?"; said of a mysterious happening, usually a crime; if we can discover who will benefit from it, we have a possible culprit.
24. "to the value"; said of a tariff on imported goods, levied at a given rate of their invoiced valuation.
25. "not of sound mind"; applied especially to one who has made a will.
26. "the situation in which"; the existing state of affairs.
27. "the occasion of war"; the incident which gives rise to hostilities.
28. "way of living," "way of operating"; the first is applied especially to diplomatic arrangements by which peaceful coexistence is achieved.
29. "a not pleasing person"; said usually of a diplomatic representative who has offended the nation to which he is accredited.
30. "what for what"; that which is given in return for something received.
31. "slip of the tongue"; *lapsus calami* is "slip of the pen."
32. "between us"; *inter alia* is "among other things."
33. "the greatest good"; that which we should most strive for.
34. "incidental remark."
35. "for the public good."
36. "the fickle crowd."
37. "under the rose"; something done surreptitiously.
38. "beware of the dog"; sign found on a Pompeian gateway.
39. "here lies."
40. "from the books"; the owner's name follows.
41. "from the chair"; by virtue of one's office; the Catholic Church claims that the Pope is infallible only when he speaks *ex cathedra*.
42. "to the city and to the world"; the Pope's addresses are sometimes so described, when he speaks not only to the city of Rome, but to the entire world.
43. "pray for us"; a common invocation to the Virgin Mary and the saints.
44. "nothing hinders"; often appears on books to which no objection has been found by the church authorities.
45. "may be printed"; as above.
46. "The welfare of the people shall be the supreme law." Taken from the most ancient body of Roman law, this is probably the first "general welfare" clause in existence.

47. "Woe to the conquered!" Said to have been uttered by Brennus, chief of the Gaulish tribes that besieged and almost took Rome in the early days of the Republic. Appeasers among the Romans had tried to buy off the Gauls with gold, but it was noticed that the Gauls tried to use weighted scales. When the Romans protested, Brennus threw his sword on the scales and uttered the famous phrase. A Roman leader, fed up with appeasement, threw his own sword on the scales and shouted: "Rome will be ransomed with iron, not with gold!" The fighting broke out again, and the infuriated Romans finally put the Gauls to flight.

48. "Carthage must be destroyed!" After the second Punic War, which the Romans had won by the skin of their teeth, and in the course of which Hannibal had almost taken Rome, Cato the Elder, Grand Old Man of the Roman Republic, ended all his Senate speeches with this phrase. He finally had his way, and the third Punic War saw the end of Carthage.

49. "I fear the Greeks even when they bear gifts." In Virgil's *Aeneid* this famous line is spoken by Laocoön, the Trojan high priest, when he first glimpses the Greek wooden horse.

50. "We who are about to die salute you!" Said to have been spoken by the gladiators in the arena as they saluted the Emperor before the games began.

1. "Many out of one"; symbol of American Federal Union.

2. "Thus always with tyrants"; State motto of Virginia.

3. "Ever faithful"; motto of the United States Marine Corps.

4. "Like is cured with like"; motto of the homeopathic school of medicine.

5. "Concerning the dead, nothing but good"; only good should be spoken about those who have passed on.

chapter eleven

african tongues

Of the world's 2,796 known languages, 570 are spoken on African soil. Some, like Arabic, are widespread and highly cultural. Others, like Rundi and Kanuri, are small and obscure. All are important to us Americans, particularly at the present moment, when colonialism seems to be on its last legs, and independent but turbulent nations, unsure of themselves or their future, are rising to replace it.

It is interesting that of the 570 African languages, over 500 are spoken by Negro groups. It is equally interesting that by far the major tongue of Africa, Arabic, is non-African in origin.

The native African tongues can be rather neatly classified into two great divisions, with the southern edge of the Sahara as their oversimplified border line. South of that line, the people are predominantly black, and their languages, however infiltrated, are decidedly native African. North of the line, which in the eastern part of Africa slopes to the southeast, so as to include Ethiopia and Somalia in the northern division, the people are predominantly of the white race, however much of their blood may have become intermingled with Negro blood, and their languages are predominantly of the Hamitic and Kushitic stocks, which means that they bear a distant relationship to the Semitic language spoken by the Arabs of the Mediterranean coast. (It may be well to remember that "Semitic" and "Hamitic" come from the names of two of Noah's sons, Shem and Ham, who parted company, speaking different but still related tongues, after the Tower of

Babel episode. "Kushitic" comes from the name of the ancient land of Kush, or Cush, adjoining Egypt. The experts consider Semitic, Hamitic, and Kushitic languages as all forming part of one big language family.) Of the 570 languages of Africa, only 46 are of the Semitic-Hamitic-Kushitic variety. The remainder (and it is a large remainder) are conveniently described as African Negro tongues.

We must not forget the European languages of colonization. At least five million inhabitants of Africa (and this includes both European colonists and natives who have learned the language) speak good French. Almost as many speak passable English. Then, in the Union of South Africa, there are perhaps three million people, white and black, who can speak Afrikaans, that curious form of Netherlands Dutch which was imported from Holland by the Boer settlers who founded Cape Colony in the seventeenth century, then moved north, changing their speech as they went, until today it presents striking differences from the mother tongue, greater, perhaps, than the divergences between British and American English, which arose about the same period. In the lands held by Portugal there are estimated to be nearly two million Portuguese speakers; one million speakers of Spanish in Spain's former and present possessions; half a million speakers of Italian in Libya, Eritrea, Ethiopia, and Somalia. There are even fifty to a hundred thousand people who remember German in what used to be German East Africa, German Southwest Africa, Togoland, and Kamerun before the First World War.

Then, in the Union of South Africa, there are well over half a million speakers of the languages of India, who have emigrated in large numbers to Africa. The Hindustani and Gujarati of northern India, the Tamil and Telugu of the south of the Indian Peninsula, may be heard in the market places of Johannesburg and other South African towns.

But the languages of Europe and India may be described as a superimposed veneer on the dark skin of Africa—something which may be destined to be erased with the passing of time and the resurgence of African nationalism, or perhaps to blend and mingle with the native tongues into a tongue of the future, as yet unborn.

This is emphatically not true of the two big Semitic tongues of Asiatic origin—the Arabic of the Mediterranean coast and the Amharic of Ethiopia. Both have acquired such prestige and such numerical concentration in their respective areas that their disappearance or absorption is inconceivable.

If we begin our linguistic tour of Africa from the north, what we find, in an unbroken line that runs from Nasser's Egypt on the east to Moroccan Casablanca on the west, is Arabic, the great language of the Koran and the Moslem world. Arabic is not native to North Africa. It overran the region back in the seventh century A.D., when Mohammed's followers, issuing in fanatical hordes from the heart of Arabia, planted their own crescent in the place of the cross over all North African lands, giving the local populations their choice between the Koran and the sword, and going on to sweep across the Strait of Gibraltar into Spain, most of which they held for many centuries, and even into France, from which they were driven back by the Frankish hosts of Charles the Hammer at the great Battle of Tours, in 732. It is interesting to speculate what might have happened if the Franks had lost that battle and the Moslems had won it. The chances are that we of the Western world would today be worshipping Allah instead of Christ and speaking some form of Arabic instead of English, French, German, Spanish, Italian, and the other languages of western Europe.

But the Franks won and the Moslems didn't, and the Moors and their Arabic tongue were eventually thrown back across the Straits into North Africa, which they continued to hold. Arabic today is the spoken tongue of over forty million people in Egypt, Libya, Tunisia, Algeria, and Morocco, as well as of millions more in what we choose to call the Middle East—Syria, Lebanon, Jordan, Iraq, and Arabia. It is also the religious tongue of hundreds of additional millions in Iran, Pakistan, India, Indonesia, and many other regions that adopted Islam but did not go over to Arabic as a popular tongue.

There are two observations to be made about Arabic in North Africa. The first is that while the written language is one (the classical Arabic in which the Koran was written), the vernacular dialects are many, and quite different. Each North African country has its own, and there are further variants in the Middle Eastern countries we have mentioned. The second is that all the way along the line, from Morocco to Egypt, Arabic is interspersed with what might be called pockets of resistance consisting of an older, native tongue,

Berber. Berber is of the Hamitic stock, which makes it a closer relative to the ancient Egyptian of the hieroglyphic inscriptions than to present-day Arabic. Back around 1000 B.C., long before the Arabs, or even the Romans, started out on a career of conquest, all of North Africa spoke Hamitic languages, of which ancient Egyptian was the most notable. The others were called Libyco-Berber or Numidian (the latter name was preferred by the Romans). The first Semitic speakers to get into Africa were the Carthaginians, who were colonists from the Phoenician cities of Tyre and Sidon. They held themselves separate from the native Numidians, though they used them as mercenaries in their armies; but in the hour of Carthage's extremity, the Numidians turned against their Carthaginian overlords and joined the Romans, and that marked the end of Carthage and of the first Semitic experiment in North Africa. Under the Roman Empire, Latin and Greek became widespread in the entire region, but the backwoods continued to speak Numidian, or Berber. When the Arabs came, most of the Berber tribes were converted to Islam, but many of them went right on speaking their ancient tongue, and they still do today, to the tune of about six million speakers.

Best known and most picturesque of these Berber tongues is the Tamashek of the Touaregs, the fierce veiled men of the central Sahara, who still use a system of writing inherited from their ancestors, the ancient Numidians. Other isolated groups are the Shluh or Shilh speakers of Morocco and the Kabyles of Algeria and Tunisia. There is even a small group of Berber speakers in northern Egypt. In the Canary Islands there was, until recently, a Berber tongue called Guanche, but it became extinct in modern times.

The other great Semitic wave came to Africa from southern Arabia, and it became the ruling class of Ethiopia. Over six million inhabitants of central Ethiopia speak Amharic, a language of South Arabian origin. The rest of Ethiopia and surrounding regions use Kushitic languages, distantly related to both Semitic and Hamitic. The best known of these are Dankali, Galla, Sidama and the Somali of the three Somalilands. Ancient Egyptian survives in Coptic, used as a liturgic language in the Ethiopian Christian Church.

If, starting from the west coast of Africa, you draw a line eastward from the mouth of the Senegal River, then extend it northeast to Asswan, where Nasser is building his dam, then bend it again in a south by east direction to Mombasa, on the east coast, you will have approximately the border between the Semitic-Hamitic-Kushitic languages of the north and the African Negro languages of the south. But you must remember that "African Negro languages" is a geographical and ethnological rather than a strictly linguistic concept. Within Negro Africa there are three well-defined language areas, just as there are three in the north of the Continent.

If you draw another line across Africa, this time from Cross River on the west coast, eastward to Lake Albert, then south to Lake Victoria, then east again to Mombasa, where it will join your first line, you will have enclosed between your two lines a vast area in which are spoken no fewer than 435 of the African languages—a clear and overwhelming majority. These central African tongues show great diversity, and some experts deny that they really belong to a single family. But most of the people who have studied them agree in considering them of one basic stock. To these languages the geographical name Sudanese-Guinean has been applied, since they extend from the Gulf of Guinea to the Sudan. Some people feel that they are the "purest" African languages, because the most typical specimens of the black race come from the region around the Gulf of Guinea. These are the languages spoken by the African slaves who were brought to America, both North and South, and it is words from these languages that have gotten into both American English (*jazz, juke, tote, hoodoo, voodoo,* possibly *banjo* are samples) and Brazilian Portuguese (*samba, conga* and *carioca* are three such words that have eventually reached us).

Antiquity knew next to nothing about these Sudanese-Guinean languages, or the others farther south. Herodotus tells the story of a Phoenician expedition that circumnavigated Africa about 600 B.C.; it took them three years to do it, and if they brought anything back with them it was lost. A Carthaginian explorer, Hanno, sailing out of the Mediterranean into the Atlantic, got as far as Sierra Leone around 520 B.C. He brought back with him one word that has reached us, *gorilla.* Nero sent an expedition to discover the sources of the Nile, but if you have followed our geography you will see that the Roman explorers moved largely in Hamitic-speaking territory, and at any rate they did not reach their destination. West African empires like ancient Ghana flourished around the seventh century A.D., but medieval Europe knew nothing about them and cared less. Down to the fifteenth century only a score or so of African Negro words were known to the Europeans. Then the Arabs began to get down into the black lands in earnest, and information became more plentiful. By the sixteenth and seventeenth centuries, Italian missionaries and explorers like Pigafetta and Brusciotto began to describe some African Negro languages. Today we know a good deal about them. Many have been reduced to written form, and literacy is becoming more widespread, though it still seldom gets beyond 5 to 10 per cent of the native populations.

In the Sudanese-Guinean group there are many languages of which people have heard, Ibo, Fanti, and Ewe among them. But there is one that tends to outstrip all others, the Hausa of northern Nigeria, spoken by over ten million inhabitants of the region and spreading over vaster territories as time goes on. Hausa has not one, but two written forms, for Arab missionaries adapted the Arabic alphabet for the use of Hausa speakers who wished to read the Koran, then Christian missionaries repeated the job for those who wanted to read the Bible. But Hausa, while it is a flourishing trade language in Nigeria and the Sudan, cannot be properly described as yet as a cultural or literary tongue. For that we shall have to go to another great African Negro language, of which we shall speak presently.

South of the line from Cross River to Mombasa lies the family that is perhaps most characteristic of African Negro culture and civilization, the great Bantu group. It occupies the rest of Africa, save for the extreme south and southwest, where we have European languages (English and Afrikaans) and the third, rather small division of native Negro tongues, the Hottentot-Bushman.

Sudanese-Guinean numbers 435 languages. The Bantu family has 83, though the total number of Bantu speakers is at least as great as that of Sudanese-Guinean. In the Hottentot-Bushman division are only six tongues, but they are extraordinary tongues, possessing sounds that no other language in the world utilizes. These are the clicks (dental, lateral, palatal, and guttural), which resemble the smacking of one's lips, or the clucking sound with which one summons chickens or encourages horses. Not that these sounds are difficult to produce. Anybody can click and cluck. The trick is to fit the clicks and clucks into the pattern of ordinary speech. Try, for example, to get your click right at the beginning of a word, so as to produce (click)*osa*. (This is actually the name of a language that uses clicks, and it is conventionally spelled *Xhosa*, with *xh* used to represent the clicking sound.)

An even better trick is to get the click into the body of a word, between two vowels (try *easy*, replacing the *s* with a click). In the Hottentot branch of the family there are only four clicks; in the Bushman, there are seven. Early European explorers in Hottentot-Bushman territory were so startled by these language sounds that the Portuguese regarded them as a form of stammering, while the Dutch compared them to the gobbling of a turkey. "Hottentot" is actually a constructed word, devised by the explorers to imitate the stammering sounds they thought they heard. The Hottentots' name for themselves is Khoi-Khoin, "men of men."

The story of the Hottentot-Bushman race would be an interesting one, if we only knew more about it. At one time, it seems, they covered far more territory than they do today. Herodotus even describes the sounds of the language spoken by cave dwellers in what today is Ethiopia, and his description sounds as though they may have had the clicks. About three thousand years ago, however, the Bantu tribes that had been concentrated in the region of the great African lakes began a vast career of expansion to the south and west, and before them the Hottentot-Bushman groups retreated, until they were forced back into the thirsty wastes of the Kalahari Desert and southwest Africa. Their numbers dwindled, and their standards of living sank to an unbelievable low. Yet at one time they must have enjoyed a higher culture. The rock paintings of the Bushmen still amaze modern artists by their beauty of color and precision of form.

There was always war between the Bantu and the Hottentot-Bushmen. Yet it is a curious fact that such peaceful contact as there was between the two groups led to the assimilation of the clicking sounds by the Bantu tribes that were closest to the Hottentots, so that today the clicks are better studied in the mouths of southern Bantu groups like the Kaffirs and Xhosas than in those of the timid Bushmen, who sometimes conceal their own language in the presence of strangers, and speak only in the tongue of their Bantu neighbors and enemies. That racial intolerance is not confined to the white race is shown by the treatment inflicted upon the peaceful Hottentot-Bushman groups of southwest Africa by the warlike Bantu tribes of the Hereros, sometimes called the "Black Herrenvolk" of Africa.

What of the Bantu group, that constitutes the predominant element of Africa south of the Gulf of Guinea, with a numerical contingent that is probably the equal of the other two Negro groups combined? Racially, the Bantu tribes are sometimes called "Negroid," as opposed to the Sudanese-Guinean, which are pure Negro. In varying degrees, the Bantu show an admixture of non-Negro blood, and it is supposed that somewhere in prehistory they may have become mixed with peoples of Hamitic stock, possibly groups of colonists from ancient Egypt, though the Egyptians have left us no record of any such migration. The name Bantu means "men," and it was devised in 1856 by Dr. W. H. Bleek, librarian of the government of Cape Colony and an intense student of the African languages.

Speakers of Bantu languages show great diversity of racial type, ranging all the way from the brownish Pygmies of the Central African forests to the tall, handsome Zulus and Kaffirs of South Africa, where the Hamitic strain, if one there was, must have been quite strong. From their original homeland in the lake region, the Bantu peoples expanded southward and westward, even crossing the Mozambique Channel to the island of Madagascar, where they found people of an altogether different, non-African race, the Hovas, who had apparently migrated by an overseas route from Malaya or Indonesia, and whose language, Malagasy, is of the same stock as Indonesian, Hawaiian, Samoan, Tahitian, and the Maori of New Zealand.

The least common denominator among the so-called Bantu races is the Bantu form of speech. The 83 known Bantu languages show far greater similarity than do the more numerous Sudanese-Guinean idioms. It is easy to trace words and forms from one Bantu language to another, and it is not at all difficult to take one of them and use it as a sample of the group.

Two tongues stand out from the Bantu group as having been heard of by practically everybody who reads historical fiction. One of them is Zulu, the tongue so often described in the entrancing novels of H. Rider Haggard. What male reader of the adult generation does not recall the story of

King Chaka and his Zulu *impi* ("army"), armed with *assegais* and *knobkerries?* (The first word, meaning "javelin," is, like so many Bantu words, of Arabic-Berber origin; the second is a mixture of South African Dutch and Hottentot, and means "war club".) Who does not recall King Cetewayo and the disastrous defeat he inflicted on the British at Isandhlwana in 1879, or picturesque words like the Afrikaans *voortrekker* ("early settler," "pioneer"), the Zulu *inkosikazi* ("chieftainess"), or the names of peoples like the Amazulu, the Matabele, or the Kaffirs, whose name is Arabic for "infidels"?

chapter twelve
swahili

Zulu, for all its three million speakers and its words of literary interest, is still not the major Bantu language. Swahili, with nearly ten million speakers, a sphere of influence that covers the entire central East African coast and extends across the Congolese Republic, a high rate of literacy, at least for Negro Africa, and a flourishing literature that has such feathers in its cap as books of native poetry, a dozen newspapers, and a full translation from the French of some of Molière's comedies, presented on the Zanzibar stage, is not only the chief Bantu language, but also the worthiest and most dignified representative of all African Negro tongues.

Swahili itself is an Arabic word. *Sāhil* is Arabic for "coast" and the Wa-Swahili were named "coast people" by the Arab traders who were already on the scene when Vasco da Gama arrived in Zanzibar in 1498. The spreading of Swahili seems to have been largely the work of those same Arab traders. It was they who gave Swahili its first written form, in Arabic characters, then carried it on, during the eighteenth and nineteenth centuries, to cover the entire region between the white Nile and the Zambesi.

Today Swahili is a current language in Tanganyika, Kenya, southeastern Somalia, Uganda, Ruanda, Nyasaland, parts of Mozambique and Rhodesia, the Congo, Zanzibar, northwestern Madagascar, and the island of Réunion. There are three chief dialects, that of Zanzibar, that of Mombasa, and the Kingwana of the interior, but they are all mutually intelligible. There is a standardized literary and poetic form of the language, called *ki-ngozi*. There is even a "Union Swahili," put together by the missionaries to facilitate their work of spreading the Gospel; but despite their efforts, most Swahili speakers remain Moslems.

The language may be described as a somewhat archaic form of Bantu, with copious admixtures of words from Arabic, Persian, the languages of India, Portuguese, German, and English. Its fulcrum is Zanzibar, or Zanquebar, the "land of Zenj," a sultanate which is also a British Protectorate. The "protection" was first extended in 1890, and it is indicative of the colonial mentality of the period that it involved compensation to Germany in the form of the cession of the island of Helgoland in the North Sea, and to France in the form of renunciation of British claims to Madagascar. Colonial interest had been aroused previously, in 1873, in connection with the suppression of the region's prosperous slave trade.

Bantu languages had been first described by Pigafetta in the late sixteenth century, and by Brusciotto in the seventeenth. Comparing these descriptions with a present-day Bantu language like Swahili, we come to the conclusion that there has not been too much change.

Swahili is a fair representative of the Bantu tongues. It is also a complete refutation of the idea held by so many that languages of "primitive" groups are necessarily primitive, consisting largely of grunts, groans, and mixed-up ideas. Swahili has a euphony that makes it comparable to Italian, with clear, distinct sounds, vocalic endings, and a most pleasing syllabic arrangement consisting for the most part of consonant-plus-vowel. It is capable of such absolute precision that the Swahili version of the Pentateuch contains fewer words than the Hebrew original, without the slightest loss or distortion of meaning. Its grammatical and syntactical structure is logical, one might almost say to the point of being philosophical. The rules may seem a trifle complicated (though certainly not to the same extent as those of Latin, Greek, Sanskrit, or Russian); but once you know them, they work with a minimum of exceptions. The vocabulary is extensive (the missionaries who translated the Bible into Swahili were forced to use very few foreign words): but more than that, it is extensible to the point of infinity, and shows remarkable adaptability to new ideas. Using Swahili roots, prefixes, and suffixes, it would be no more difficult to construct in the language the vocabulary of nuclear fission (or of any other scien-

tific, philosophical, or literary topic) than it is in languages
like the modernized Irish of Éire or the modernized Hebrew
of Israel. Even as it stands today, the tongue is rich in words,
ideas, and concepts, and capable of conveying subtle differences and shades of meaning that escape even the most refined
Western languages. Certainly it is adequate, and more than
adequate, to serve the present needs of its speaking community, and its capability for infinite growth is such as to
guarantee that if some day there arises, south of the Sahara, a
modern, civilized, unified African Negro nation, Swahili will
stand ready to serve it as a common tongue for the black race.

Consider these few examples of specialized words for specialized meanings: *chunga* is the general term for "ants"; but
small ants are *sisimisi*, "red biting ants" are *siafu*, and "white
ants," or "termites," are *mchwa*. *Ulayiti* is English unbleached
"calico," but *kaniki* is "blue calico," and *shiti* is "printed
calico." *Dafu* is a "coconut" that is ready for drinking, but
nazi is a "ripe coconut," ready for eating. *Mave* is "stones" in
general, but *mafya* is "stones suitable to set a pot over a fire."
Mchele is "rice," but *wali* is "cooked rice."

The precision of the Swahili vocabulary is shown by other
forms; *kanda* is not merely a "bag"; it is "a long, narrow bag
made of matting." *Sufuria* is not just a "pot"; it is "a large
metal pot." *Dau* is translated as a "small vessel, made sharp
at the two ends." *Ng'ambo* is not just the "bank" of a stream,
it is the "opposite bank from where you stand." (Other Bantu
languages share the same feature; in Sotho the simple word
ola means "to remove big pieces by hand before sifting.")
There is in Swahili a word that specifically means "to become
bright by rubbing"; but if you mean "to become bright" in
the sense of "shining," you use a different word. A single word
in Swahili means "to become foolish" (*kupumbazika*, just in
case you doubt it). There are, in like manner, single words
that mean, "to become obligatory upon," "to become opposite," "to become spherical." In comparison with the precision
and concision of Swahili, English sometimes assumes the aspect of Basic English, which must use the circumlocution
"without thought of others" to render the concept of "selfish."
Only occasionally does Swahili show the confusion of homo-
phones and homonyms that so often appears in English; one
example is *kucha*, which means both "to fear" and "for the
sun to rise," and its passive *kuchwa*, which covers "to be
feared" and "for the sun to set."

Is Swahili capable of expressing abstract ideas as against concrete objects and actions? There is a prefix *u-*, which forms any abstract noun you may want; *zuri* is "beautiful," *uzuri* is "beauty"; *pana* is "wide," *upana* is "width." In Swahili you have specific words for acceptance, bitterness, old age, deliverance, poverty, resurrection, to mention a few. You even have *usultani*, "sultanship," *uwaziri*, "viziership," *utafiri*, "wealthiness," the quality of being wealthy, as opposed to *mali*, which is the more tangible "wealth." *Kupatanisha* is "to conciliate"; *upatanisho* is "conciliation," and *mpatanashi* is "conciliator." Even a scientifically constructed language like Esperanto could not do much better.

Is Swahili a language suitable for philosophical discussion? Consider these two proverbs, which have no counterpart in the Western tongues: *Fayide yapita kiburi*, "Profit surpasses pride"; and *Akili yapita mali*, "Understanding surpasses property." Other Swahili proverbs are:

Kusema ni kuzuri, na kutokusema ni kuzuri, "To speak is good, and not to speak is good."

Kufa tutakufa wote, "As for dying, we shall all die."

Ulevi huondoa akili, "Drunkenness takes away sense."

Alioko juu, mngoje chini, "He who is there above, await him below." (Pride comes before a fall.)

Asiopo, na lake halipo, "He who is not here, and his business is not here" (like the Italian *Gli assenti hanno sempre torto*, "The absent are always wrong").

Kwamba una kidogo au kwamba una wingi, uwe radhi, "Whether you have little or much, be content."

Jogoo likiwika lisiwike, kutakucha, "Whether the cock crows or not, it will dawn."

Occasionally the Swahili vocabulary shows startling similarities to the Western languages in words that could not possibly have been borrowed. *Mama*, for example, means just that, "mother"; but don't get overconfident and go on to use *papa* for "father," for *papa* means "shark." The word for father is *baba* (a little like the Italian *babbo*), while grandmother is *bibi*, and "aunt" is *babu ndogo*. This vowel alternation in words that have a semantic connection appears elsewhere; *bivu* is "ripe," *bovu* is "rotten." The word for "kiss" is *busu* (could that have come from the archaic English *buss*, or the Spanish *beso*, or the Portuguese *beijo*?): *lulu* is a "pearl," and some pearls are undoubtedly lulus. For sheer beauty of sound coupled with what seems to be a reflection of the meaning, I would recommend the Swahili word for "to caress," *kubembeleza*.

Let us not, of course, forget those words rendered famous by African literature, *bwana*, "master," "sir," "gentleman"; its feminine *mbana*, "lady," "madame" (heard more and more now that women organize safaris of their own); and *mwana*, "girl," "miss"; also *asikari* (or *askari*), "soldier"; and, of course, *safari*, "journey," a word that Swahili has taken from Arabic. A couple of misleading words to go with *papa* are *boi*, which sounds like "boy" but means "water," and *vino* or *wino*, which means "ink."

"Primitive" languages are supposed to make great use of the doubling process (repeating the word to indicate the plural), and a few of them actually do. Swahili, as we shall see, scorns this elementary procedure; but the doubling appears occasionally, to the same extent, perhaps, as in Italian, where *piano piano* means "very slowly" and *forte forte* means "very strong." In Swahili, *mbali mbali* means "different," "divided," "opposite"; *dogo dogo* means "least" (a single *dogo* means "little," and its compound, *kidogo*, uttered twice, means "very little"); *pole pole* means "slowly"; *sava sava* means "equal" (a single *sava* means "same"); *bui bui* is a "spider," and *pilipili* means "pepper," but here the word is borrowed, and it's our own fault if the *p* appears twice.

Animal names, particularly those of big game, often crop up in safari accounts. *Simba* is "lion," but this word is Arabic, and has been carried, in one form or another, to very far places (Singapore is "lion-city," and the native name of Ceylon, Sindhalawipa, means "lion-island"). Native Swahili words are *kiboko*, "hippopotamus"; *kifaru*, "rhinoceros"; *ng'ombe*, "ox," "cattle"; *mamba*, "crocodile"; *tembo*, "elephant"; *chui*, "leopard"; *kima*, "monkey." "River" is *mto*; "interpreter," whom you may need, is *mkalimana*; and "God" is *Mungu*.

Swahili has borrowed extensively from other languages, but we cannot hold this against it, for we have borrowed even more. Arabic, of course, is Swahili's main contributor. There are words like *kitabu*, "book"; *yamkini*, "perhaps"; *hewa*, "air"; *saa*, "hour," "watch," or "clock"; *masikini*, "poor." (This Arabic word, going north into Europe, gave rise to the French *mesquin* and the Italian *meschino*.) *Kamili* means "complete" or "perfect" (the same word as Nasser's first name, Gamal); *amini*, "faithful"; *jini*, "spirit" (our "djinn"); *kathi*, "judge" (our "kadi"); *mskiti*, "church" (our "mosque"); *sheitani*, "devil" (our "Satan"); *kabili*, "tribe"; and, of course, the universal *bakshishi*, "tip," which the Arabs got from the Persians, and which is probably the word heard most frequently by foreigners in the Middle East.

From the Portuguese, Swahili got such words as *bandera*, "flag"; *parafujo*, "screen"; *sabuni*, "soap"; *meza*, "table"; *kasha*, "box" or "chest"; *bastola*, "revolver" or "pistol"; *padri*, "priest." *Kalamu* for "pen" was originally Greek, and *garofuu* for "cloves" seems to be Italian, but *pensil* for "pencil" is pretty definitely English, and so is *daktari*, which Swahili uses interchangeably with the native *mtabibu* or *mganga* for "doctor." In return, we seem to have gotten *papayi*, "pawpaw" (though that was brought to us by the Spaniards). There is a Swahili word, *jambo*, with a plural *mambo*, meaning "affair," that smacks suspiciously of *mumbo jumbo*, while *goober* comes to us not from Swahili, but from a kindred Bantu language.

When it comes to grammar, Bantu in general and Swahili in particular force us to do some revision in our thinking. Our Western languages indicate changes by the endings of a word; the more complicated they get, like Latin or Russian, the more endings they pile up. Therefore, we are in the habit of looking at the end of a word to get our clues as to its function. In the Bantu tongues of Africa, these clues come usually at the beginning of the word, while the end of the word generally remains unchanged. In what might be described as proto-Bantu, the word *Bantu* itself means "men"; the singular, "man," is *muntu;* "thing" is *kintu*, but "things" is *bintu;* "little thing" is *kantu*, "little things" is *tuntu*. As you see, the element *-ntu* ("something that exists") remains unchanged; it is the prefix, *mu-, ba-, ki-, bi-, ka-, tu-*, that gives the word the particular meaning you want it to have. Strange? Yes, but we have something very similar in a Western language that a great many of us know, French. In *written* French, you get *le livre, les livres, la femme, les femmes*, and we confidently assert that French nouns usually form the plural by adding *-s;* but in *spoken* French, what is the only clue you get as to whether the noun is singular or plural? It's *le* or *la* as against *les;* the noun itself sounds exactly the same, whether it has or has not a written -*s* at the end. So consider a language like Swahili as a vast extension of certain features of spoken French.

Swahili does not have masculine, feminine, and neuter nouns, but it does divide its nouns into a large number of classes, each of which calls for a specific handle in the singular, and another specific handle in the plural. The words *muntu*, *bantu*, *kintu* and *bintu* in "general" Bantu appear in Swahili as *mtu*, "man"; *watu*, "men" or "people"; *kitu*, "thing"; *vitu*, "things." *Wa-Swahili* is the "Swahili people," plural and alive; *Ki-Swahili* is the "Swahili language," singular and inanimate.

If you use an adjective with your noun, it must take the same handle as the noun. Therefore, "tall man" is *mtu mrefu* ("man tall"; the adjective follows the noun, but languages like French and Spanish have made us used to this); if you want "tall men," shift from *m-* to *w-: watu warefu.* "Long knife" is *kisu kirefu;* "long knives" is *visu virefu.* Try out the system with a couple of different adjectives, like *zuri*, "handsome," or *kubwa*, "large," "great." That's right: "handsome men" is *watu wazuri*, and "big things" is *vitu vikubwa. Kufa kuzuri* is a "noble death." This system of putting the modifier after the modified word, and of using the same prefix on both, is followed even in interrogative words like "how many?" which is *ngapi.* "How many people?" would be *watu wangapi?* "How many chairs?" would be *viti vingapi?* "How many trees?" (trees are in a different class from chairs) would be *miti mingapi?*

The business of classes and classifying prefixes can get to be a little confusing. "Dates," for example, are *tende;* but the "date tree" goes into another class, and becomes *mtende.* This, however, is no worse than our having to say "pear tree" and "pear," or Italian having to shift from *pero* to *pera.* Swahili has a knack, too, for deriving nouns from verbs by making a change in the beginning and the ending. "To send" is *kutuma* (*ku-* is an infinitive prefix that works just like our "to"); a messenger, "one who is sent," becomes *mtume;* the use of *m-* instead of *ku-* turns the verb into a noun of a specific living class. Note also that while *safari* is a "journey," *msafari* is a "traveler."

The Bantu tongues don't worry about masculine, feminine, and neuter, but they have a way of indicating the feminine if they really want to. Remember the Zulu *inkosikazi* for "chieftainess"? It is formed from the masculine *inkosi*, "chief" (you often hear it as *inkoos'* in South Africa, where it does duty for "thank you"), by the addition of the feminine suffix *-kazi*, which works like our *-ess* in *stewardess*, *abbess*, *actress*. Similarly, Swahili has *kijakazi* for "slave girl," though such things are no longer supposed to exist.

Swahili has a full set of numerals. From 1 to 10 they run: *moja* (1), *wili* (2), *tatu* (3), *nne* (4), *tano* (5), *sita* (6), *saba* (7), *nane* (8), *tissa* (or *kenda*) (9), *kumi* (10). The words for the numbers from 1 to 5, as well as 8, the alternative for 9, and 10, are Bantu, but 6, 7, and the regular 9 are Arabic in origin. From 11 through 19 use *kumi na* followed by the unit figure you want. But 20, 30, 40, etc., up to and including 100 and even 1,000 are pure Arabic. Evidently the Arabs were traders and could really count; the Bantu people didn't care for such material things.

Numerals, by the way, are also expected to take the prefix of the noun they are used with, and, as you probably suspect by this time, they follow the noun and any adjective modifying it. So, for "two bad men," say *watu wabaya wawili*, "men bad two"; for "three fine trees," it's *miti mizuri mitatu*, "trees fine three." One final example of the reversal of Western word order that we find in Bantu and Swahili is "day after tomorrow," which is *kesho kutwa*, with *kesho*, "tomorrow," coming first.

As in most languages, the verb in Swahili plays a predominant role in the sentence. Here, too, it is usually the beginning of the word, not the end, that affords the significant clues.

"To be" and "to have" are expressed in simple ways that remind you of Russian. The verb "to be" is omitted in the present tense (though not in the past), and a very simple statement results: *Simba mui*, "The lion (is) bad"; *mimi mkubwa*, "I (am) great." *Mimi* is the word for "I," but when used with an expressed verb it becomes *ni*. "To have" is transformed into "to (be) with," and "I have it" is translated by *ninalo* which is literally "I (am) with it." One wonders whether the arty slang expression, "Are you with it?" could have been borrowed from Swahili. "You" is *wewe*, but when used with a verb it is shortened to *u*. The *yeye* that means "he" or "she" becomes *a*; "it" is *ki*; "we" is *tu*; plural "you" is *m-*; "they" is *wa* for persons, *vi* for inanimate objects. Suppose now we take a verb like *kupenda*, "to love." *Ku-*

is the infinitive sign, corresponding to our "to," and disappears in all other forms of the verb. The prefix that indicates present action is *na*, and it comes between the subject
pronoun and the verb root. Therefore, "I love" is *ni-na-penda;*
"you love" is *u-na-penda;* "he or she loves" is *a-na-penda;*
"we love" is *tu-na-penda;* "you (plural) love" is *m-na-penda*,
"they love" is *wa-na-penda.* If you want "I have loved" instead of "I love," change the tense prefix from *na* to *me* (*ni-
me-penda*, "I have loved"); if you want "I loved," shift from
na to *li* (*ni-li-penda*, "I loved"); if you want "I shall love,"
use *ta* (*ni-ta-penda*, "I shall love").

This is fairly simple, and looks like a Latin or Spanish verb
in reverse, with prefixes taking the place of endings; in fact,
it looks even more like English ("I-do-love," "I-have-loved,"
"I-did-love," "I-shall-love"). But Swahili gives you a few
more complications. As in many other languages (Arabic, for
instance), the object pronoun becomes part of the verb instead of going before it as a separate word, as it does in French,
or coming after it as a separate word, the way it does in
English. "Me" is *ni*, the same word that is used for "I." "He
loves me" becomes *a-na-ni-penda* ("he-does-me-love"). "I
loved them" is *ni-li-wa-penda* ("I-did-them-love"). "They will
love us" is *wa-ta-tu-penda* ("they-will-us-love").

But this is only a beginning. If your sentence is to be negative, you use an entirely different set of subject pronoun
prefixes: *si* for "I-not," *hu* for "you-not," *ha* for "he-or-she-
not," *hau* or *haki* for "it-not," *hatu* for "we-not," *ham* for
"you-not," *hawa* for "they-not" if "they" stands for people,
hai or *havi* if "they" stands for things. You also change the
final -*a* of the verb to -*i*. "I shall not love" therefore comes out
as *si-ta-pendi* instead of *ni-tᵣ-penda*, which is "I shall love."
"He will not love you" becomes *ha-ta-wa-pendi* ("he-not—
will—you—love-not").

If you want the passive instead of the active ("I am loved"
instead of "I love"), insert *w* before the final vowel of the verb
(*kupenda*, "to love"; *kupendwa*, "to be loved"; *ninapenda*, "I
love"; *ninapendwa*, "I am loved"; *watapenda*, "they will love,"
watapendwa, "they will be loved").

There is, of course, far more. There are other tenses, other
prefixes that show the action taking place in a certain fashion
("to make one love," for instance). There are even participles
used as complete subordinate clauses: *mtu anayesimama*, "the
man who-is-standing"; *watu wanaosimama*, "the men who-

are-standing"; *meno yatakayouma,* "the teeth which-will-ache"; *nyumba nisiyoinunua,* "the house which-I-shall-not-buy." "When he will look" is *a-ta-ka-po-tazama,* which can be analyzed as "he-will-and-when-look." This verb system gives Swahili both elasticity and expressiveness. Consider, for instance, *mtungi u-na-jaa,* "the water-jar is getting-full"; *mtungi u-me-jaa,* "the water-jar is-full"; *mtungi u-lio-jaa,* "the full water-jar"; *mtungi u-sio-jaa,* "the not-full water-jar."

All this grammar, and much more, is for those who want to handle Swahili fluently, or as a literary tongue. Few African travelers, even on an extended safari, will want to do that. They will prefer to rely on the services of their *mkalimana.* But this does not mean that they should not be able to say a few words to the people around them, just to let them know that they appreciate the fact that their language is indeed a language. This is made easy by the fact that Swahili has extremely easy sounds and rules of pronunciation. All you have to do is to give vowels their Italian or Spanish value (*a* = AH; *e* = EH; *i* = EE; *o* = OH; *u* = OO); the consonants their English value; and remember to put the stress always on the next to the last syllable.

Here are a few elementary Swahili phrases:

Salam alekum. "Hello, Good day!" (This is pure Arabic, and means "Peace be with you!" The reply is *Alekum salam.*)
Kwaheri. "Good-by."
Unataka nini? "What do you want?"
Saa ngapi? "What time is it?"
I napata duhuri. "It is noon."
Kesho u subuhi. "Tomorrow morning."
Ngapi gima yake? "How much?"
Gali sana! "Too much!"
Unanenda wapi? "Where are you going?"
Ndio. "Yes."
Siyo, or *hapana.* "No."
Njo hapa! "Come here!"
Upezi. "At once."
Simameni! "Stop!"
Ngoja! "Wait!"
Unasema ki-ingereza? "Do you speak English?"
Kidogo. "A little."
Sana. "Very (much)."

Leo yuko jasho. "It's warm today."
Leo magira mzuri. "It's fine weather today."
Siwesi ninahuma. "I'm ill."
Hali gani or *Hu jambo?* "How are you?"
Hali njema or *Njema.* "I'm well." (This reply is com-
pulsory as an answer to the question "How are you?" or
"How are things?" or "What's the news?" Then you may
add *lakini,* "but," with an explanation that you're really
feeling very bad, that things are in terrible shape, or that
you are the bearer of awful news.)
Asante. "Thank you."
Tafadhali. "Please." (Don't be surprised if you don't hear
this Arabic word too often. The African is very polite,
but he seldom says "please" or "thank you.")
Karibu chakula. "Come and eat." (This is a must if you
happen to be eating and someone approaches. The
African is nothing if not hospitable.)
Pole or *poleni.* "Sorry." (This is not only an apology, but
also an expression of sympathy which must be used if
anyone tells you a tale of woe. In fact, Africans will often
say as they relate their stories: *Tufani pole,* "Give us
your sympathy.")

As a final sample of Swahili, we might offer the Bible
translation of John 3:16: "For God so loved the world, that he
gave his only begotten Son, that whosoever believeth in him
should not perish, but have everlasting life." This is the way it
appears in the American Bible Society's *Book of a Thousand
Tongues,* in the three main dialects, the Kingwana of the
interior, the Mombasa, and the Zanzibar:

*Sababu Mungu alipenda ulimwengu hivi, ye alikupa Mwana
yake muzaliwa pekee, hata mutu gani anaamini ye, asi-
potele, lakini apate uzima ya milele.*

*Kwani Mwenyiezi Mngu jinsi alivyoupenda ulimwengu,
amewapa watu Mwanawe mzaliwa pekee, killa nwenyi
kuamini kwakwe asipotee, awe na uzima wa milele.*

*Kwani kwa hivyo, Mungu alivyoupenda ulimwengu, alimtoa
Mwana wake wa pekee, kila amtegemeaye asiangamie, ila
apate uzima wa kale na kale.*

Armed with all this, the next time you go on safari, you will
be able to say: *Tunasema kidogo ki-swahili,* which means, of
course, "We speak Swahili a little."

chapter thirteen
the languages of asia

Asia is a vast linguistic world in its own right. The tongues of this great continent are as varied and picturesque as their speakers, and run into the number of several hundreds, distributed among most of the world's great language families: Indo-European, Semitic, Ural-Altaic, Sino-Tibetan, Japanese-Korean, Dravidian, Malayo-Polynesian. This is as it should be, for Asia contains about half of the world's total population.

In the great expanses of the Soviet Union in Asia, covering the entire northern half of the Asian continent, are found native tongues of the Uralic and Altaic stock, which are linked on the one hand with Finnish, Estonian, and Hungarian, on the other with Turkish. But everywhere there are infiltrations of Russian, the great Eurasian language that extends for six thousand miles from Leningrad to Vladivostok. It is perhaps an exaggeration to say that all the inhabitants of the Soviet Union in Asia have learned Russian to the point of mastery, but as the "binding tongue" of the USSR and the official language of the Soviets, Russian has made great strides.

Among the native languages of Altaic or Turkic stock, the most important is Uzbek, with perhaps five million speakers. Kazakh, Kirghiz, and Turkoman are in this group, as well as the Azerbaidjani of the Iranian border, and there is a further link with Mongolian, Manchu, and Tungus. On the Uralic side are western Siberia's Vogul, Ostyak, and Samoyed (this last name means "self-eating" or "cannibal," for the first Russian settlers accused the natives of cannibalism).

The languages of the Uralic and Altaic families share many structural features, though the vocabulary resemblances between the two are difficult to determine. They are agglutinative, which means that they keep on piling suffix after suffix on a root, until they achieve words of very respectable length, like the Turkish *sevildirememek*, "to be impossible to be made to be loved." They utterly lack the concept of grammatical gender, though they do have the concept of number. This means that in many of them the same word is used for "he," "she," and "it." (This surprises us until we stop to think that in English no distinction of gender is made in "they," which applies indifferently to men, women and things.) Another characteristic is that of vowel harmony, which means that if the root word has a front vowel, like *e* or *i*, the suffixes attached to it must likewise have front vowels; but if the root has a back vowel, like *a*, *o* or *u*, a back vowel must appear in the suffixes. This means that in Turkish *baba*, "father," has a plural *babalar;* but *dil*, "language," has a plural *diller*.

Other languages spoken on Soviet Asiatic soil, on the border line between Europe and Asia, are Armenian and the Caucasian tongues. Armenian constitutes a separate branch of Indo-European, with an ancient and flourishing culture. Its present-day speakers, however, number less than three million, of whom about two million are in the Armenian Soviet Republic and another million scattered over Turkey.

The Caucasus region in the Middle Ages was nicknamed the "Mountain of Tongues," and this description still holds, for the two or three million inhabitants of this area speak some seventy different languages, of which the best known are Georgian (the native language of Stalin, or Dzhugashvili, to give him his authentic Georgian name), Lesghian, Laz, Avar, and Circassian. These languages are characterized by the extraordinary richness of their system of consonant sounds.

The linguistic picture of the Soviet Union in Asia is rounded out by some mysterious tongues of Kamchatka and the extreme eastern corner of Siberia, described as Hyperborean or Paleo-Asiatic (Yukagir, Chukchi, Kamchadal, etc.), which have only a few thousand speakers and no ascertainable connection with any major language group.

Great variety appears in the linguistic picture of Asia as we advance farther south. In the eastern part of the continent is the great Sino-Tibetan family, which includes Chinese in all its varieties, Burmese, Thai, and Tibetan, with a total speaking population of well over seven hundred million; this vast total, placing Sino-Tibetan as second only to Indo-European in number of speakers, is mostly due to Chinese, with its six hundred and more million speakers. The areas covered by Sino-Tibetan include China, Manchuria, Formosa, Thailand, Burma, and parts of Nepal and Bhutan. These tongues distinguish themselves by their monosyllabic, isolating structure and their use of tones to distinguish among different meanings of what otherwise appears as the same word. A more comprehensive idea of their general nature will appear in our Chinese chapter.

There may be a link between Sino-Tibetan and the Vietnamese, Khmer and other languages of Vietnam, Cambodia, and Laos, but there is no certainty about this. The total number of speakers of these so-called Austro-Asiatic tongues approaches thirty million.

Malaya, Indonesia, and the Philippines are representative of the vast Malayo-Polynesian family of languages, which further extends across the Pacific and Indian Oceans to cover such far-flung insular regions as New Zealand, Hawaii, Samoa, Tahiti, the Solomons, and Madagascar.

These are languages of simple structure and easy sounds, and the links among them are easily discernible. "Five," for example, is *lima* in Indonesia, the Fiji Islands, Samoa, and Hawaii, *rima* in New Zealand and Tahiti, *dimi* in Madagascar. "Nine" ranges from Indonesian *siwa* and Fijian *tsiwa* to Hawaiian and New Zealand *iwa*, Samoan *iva* and Madagascar *sivi*.

Best known in this group are the new *Bahasa Indonesia*, or "Language of Indonesia," which is replacing the older Malay; the other spoken tongues of Indonesia (Javanese, Sundanese, Madurese, Balinese, Dayak, Batak); the Tagalog, Bisaya, and Ilocano of the Philippines; the Polynesian tongues of Hawaii and Tahiti; the Malagasy of Madagascar; the Maori of New Zealand. Indonesian in theory holds sway over a population of some eighty-five million, but although it is taught in the schools, it is a question to what extent it has replaced the local languages or the Malay which was used as a sort of *lingua franca* in what used to be British Malaya and the Dutch East Indies.

Japan and Korea form a separate family, with some linguists denying the existence of a link between them, others stressing their structural similarities. Speakers of Japanese are rapidly approaching the one hundred million mark, those of Korean are at least thirty million.

While the structure of Japanese will be brought out in the Japanese chapter, it may be well to stress at this point that there is no link between Japanese and Chinese, save for the fact that Japanese has borrowed the Chinese system of writing and a considerable number of cultural loan words.

In the northernmost Japanese island of Yezo or Hokkaido are a few thousand speakers of a mysterious tongue called Ainu, which apparently has no connection with any of the neighboring languages. It may possibly be related to the Hyperborean tongues of eastern Siberia.

The vast subcontinent consisting of India, Pakistan, and Ceylon is subdivided linguistically between two great families, the Indo-European, in its Indo-Iranian branch, and the Dravidian. The latter name was coined from the name of a district in southern India, and the south of India, also known as the Dekkan, is Dravidian-speaking, with four main languages of the family predominating: Tamil, Telugu, Kanara, and Malayalam. The first two come close to forty million speakers each, the latter to twenty million. Tamil is also a minority language on the large independent island of Ceylon, sharing the linguistic honors with Indo-Iranian Singhalese.

The Dravidian languages seem to constitute an older linguistic stratum in the Indian subcontinent, representing perhaps the original speech before the coming of Indo-European invaders from the north. If so, they share this distinction with an apparently even older layer of Munda languages, most of which are concentrated in the eastern part of India, near the border of East Pakistan. There are Dravidian islands in central India, and even one, Brahui, in Beluchistan.

The rest of India and Ceylon and practically all of Pakistan, East and West, are of Indo-Iranian speech, with the Hindi of India and the Urdu of West Pakistan together forming Hindustani, the world's third most widely spoken tongue. Hindi and Urdu have replaced English as the official tongues of India and Pakistan, respectively, but attempts to force them upon speakers of other languages have met with pronounced resistance.

Other languages of Indo-Iranian stock are the Bengali of East Pakistan and the Calcutta region of India, with close to eighty-five million speakers and a flourishing literature, of which the poetry of Rabindranath Tagore is representative; the Bihari of eastern India (thirty-five million); the Marathi or Maharashtrian, the Punjabi, Rajasthani, and Gujarati of western India, with speaking populations of about thirty-five million for the first two, twenty million for the last two. Other Indo-Iranian languages of India with speaking populations ranging from three to fifteen million are Oriya, Assamese, Sindhi and Kashmiri. Singhalese, the predominant and official language of Ceylon, is also of Indo-Iranian stock. All of these languages proudly claim descent from Sanskrit, oldest recorded Indo-European tongue, and from the medieval Prakrits of which one, Pali, is the sacred language of Buddhism.

There has been, however, a vast structural change from Sanskrit to the modern Indian tongues, with a great simplification of noun and verb systems.

To the northwest of India and West Pakistan lie the Iranian tongues, closely allied to the languages of northern India. Of these the chief are the Persian of Iran and the Pashto of Afghanistan. Persian in particular has a long and glorious history, which goes back to the cuneiform inscriptions of Darius and Artaxerxes, through the Avestan of Zoroaster, to the modern Persian of Firdausi and Omar Khayyám. These languages, too, have greatly modified their structure. Like Urdu, they are filled with Arabic words brought in at the time when their speakers were converted to Islam.

As we approach the Persian Gulf and the Mediterranean, the language picture begins to embrace the two great Semitic languages of modern times: the Arabic which originated in the Arabian Peninsula but now covers Iraq, Syria, Lebanon, Jordan, then goes on to overspread all of North Africa; and the modernized Hebrew of Israel.

Arabic is a tongue of harsh guttural sounds, glottal stops, pharyngeal consonants, and an emphatic, powerful rhythm. Its prototype is the classical Arabic of the Koran, still widely used both as a religious and a written language; but the modern spoken vernaculars of the various Arabic-speaking countries show strong divergences. Arabic, one of the world's thirteen leading tongues, is official and current in countries whose total population approaches one hundred million (but most of them are in North Africa), and is used as a religious language wherever there are Moslems, which means that its influence is felt in the Balkans, in Central Africa, in both Russian and Chinese Turkestan, in Iran, Afghanistan, Pakistan, northern India, and even Indonesia. Originally Indo-European languages such as Persian and Urdu have been changed almost beyond recognition by the addition of Arabic vocabulary elements.

Hebrew, in its Israeli version, is still basically the ancient tongue of the Scriptures and the Mishnah, with the addition of a coined modern vocabulary. It is now the spoken and official language of a population that is rapidly approaching two million, and is also a key to the vast treasure house of Hebrew tradition and learning throughout the world, wherever Jewish communities exist.

The last important language of the Asian continent is the Turkish that occupies Asia Minor and belongs to the Turkic or Altaic family that is so widespread in the Soviet Union in Asia. But the Turkish language appears also on the European continent, in and around the Istanbul region and throughout the Balkans.

No fewer than six of the world's thirteen leading languages (Chinese, Japanese, Hindustani, Indonesian, Arabic, Bengali) are of Asiatic origin. Today, Arabic is best described as Afro-Asian, while originally European Russian may well be described as Eurasian.

Outside of these, the list of Asian languages with speaking populations of over twenty million is quite imposing: Bihari, Telugu, Tamil, Korean, Marathi, Turkish, Vietnamese, Punjabi, Gujarati, Rajasthani, Kanarese, Malayalam, Burmese, Thai, Persian. If Chinese is split up into its constituent "dialects," we may add Mandarin, Cantonese, Wu, and Min.

chapter fourteen

would you care to say it in chinese?

Some years ago, my Chinese informant, Dr. Charles Wan, invited me to dine with him in a real Chinese restaurant. Among linguists an informant is not a sinister character of the spy class, but simply a cultured native speaker who demonstrates in the classroom the pronunciation of a foreign language. Wan was a native of Chungking, a member of the Chinese Nationalist Ministry of Information, and a most intelligent and amiable gentleman. His Mandarin Chinese was impeccable. That, perhaps, is why we had trouble. He began to explain to the restaurateur, who was from Canton, just what dishes he wanted. The Cantonese shook his head. "Better write it," he said in English. When Wan gave him the order in graceful Chinese longhand, he beamed understandingly. Every succulent item of the dinner was in full accordance with Wan's written specifications, which he could never have made intelligible to the restaurateur in spoken words.

Written Chinese is one and indivisible throughout the entire vast Middle Country; but spoken Chinese is a conglomeration of mutually incomprehensible dialects (some call them languages), as different from one another as are French, Spanish, and Italian, or English, German, and Dutch.

There are on the Chinese mainland well over six hundred million people—more than three times as many as in the United States. Of these, nearly five hundred million Chinese speak Mandarin dialects which belong to the same dialectal group as the Peking Mandarin used at the old imperial court in Peking. Since the advent of the Republic of China, Peking

Mandarin has been called *Gwo-yü*, the "national tongue." But the remaining hundred fifty million speak such widely diverging "dialects" as Cantonese, the Wu of Shanghai, and the Min of Fukien and Taiwan Provinces. Yet they all read and write alike, for written Chinese is made up of symbols that represent not sounds, but ideas. Thus the word for "man" may be pronounced *ren, nyin, nen, len, yen,* in different sections of China; but the written symbol never changes. It is like the limited system of international symbols we have in the West: *1,000* is "thousand" to us, *tysyacha* to the Russian, *mille* to the Frenchman; *$10* is "ten dollars" to the American, *diez pesos* to the Mexican; *NaCl* is "sodium chloride" to the American chemist, *cloruro di sodio* to the Italian. But the written symbol is clear to all.

Legend has it that the Emperor Fu-hsi, about 2800 B.C., thought of combinations of straight and broken lines to replace the knotted cords that were used to transmit simple messages. Then a sage, ordered by a later emperor to improve the original set, was inspired by the marks of birds' claws in the sand to devise hundreds of additional characters.

It seems more likely that the earliest characters were simply pictures—a circle with a dot in the center to represent "sun," a crescent to indicate "moon," and so forth. Then, with the passing of time and the growth of ideas, characters were combined to convey new meanings. Many of these combinations are obvious even today. The symbol for "bright," for instance, is a combination of "sun" and "moon"; the "tree" symbol repeated twice is "forest"; the "sun" over the "horizon" is "dawn"; "eye" plus "water" gives "tears"; "mouth" plus "bird" gives "singing"; "woman" plus "broom" equals "housewife," whereas "woman" under "roof" equals "peace"; but the two-women symbol equals "pretty" or "cunning"; three women, "adultery" or "treacherous." The "woman" symbol enters into the characters for "beautiful," "graceful," "elegant," "jealous," "lady-like," "false" and "uncanny." The "man" symbol is said to enter into six hundred combinations, the "tree" symbol into nine hundred.

Chinese characters are picturesque. The symbol for "words," for instance, is a "tongue" with "vapor" or "steam" above it. Can it be that the Chinese thought of "hot air" before we did?

The maze of characters in written Chinese is at first bewildering. Actually, the situation is not quite so bad as it looks. There are 214 simple characters or radicals, and about 900 phonetics, and it is just a matter of combining them. Comprehensive Chinese dictionaries list some 40,000 compound characters, but only 5,000 or so are in general use, and there is a movement afoot to simplify and reduce even these. Compound characters usually consist of two parts; one, the radical, conveys the general idea, the other, called "phonetic," gives a clue to the pronunciation. The character for "horse," originally a picture of a horse, is pronounced *ma*. The word for "mother" is also *ma*, spoken in a different key. The written symbol for "mother" is a combination of the "horse" symbol and the "woman" symbol, meaning that the word has something to do with a woman and is to be pronounced somewhat like the word for "horse."

Experiments in picture writing of English words with imaginary Chinese characters are tried occasionally by linguists with time on their hands. "Pear," for instance, could be represented by a picture of the fruit; "pair" would be made by combining two strokes with the pear symbol, and "pare" would be a knife and a pear. "Pear" would give the clue to the pronunciation; the two strokes or the knife would serve to set the meaning. "Mail" could be represented by a picture of an envelope; then "male" would be the envelope with the symbol for "man"; and "coat of mail" would be a coat combined with the envelope.

The universal written tongue of China, in its more literary version as against the colloquial style, is called *Wen-li*. On a printed page, Chinese characters are read down vertical columns, and columns progress from right to left.

Spoken Chinese (*Gwo-yü*, the language of the five-hundred-million majority, and widely understood by the one-hundred-and-fifty-million minority) has interesting features, too.

In the first place, all Chinese characters stand for one syllable. Some say this was always true; others claim that the syllables are cut down from longer words—a tendency appearing also in English. where "telephone" becomes "phone" and "airplane" becomes "plane." Second, Chinese lacks a good many sounds appearing in English, though it also has a few sounds that English lacks. Third, words generally end in vowels, in *n* or in *ng*. These restrictions mean that there is a definite limit to the combinations that can make up a word. Actually, 420 one-syllable combinations are in use. How, then, can the enormous total of 40,000 word-ideas of the dictionaries be accounted for, or even the 5,000 in common use?

In Chinese, as in English, two words with entirely different meanings can be pronounced alike and written differently— like our "meat," "meet" and "mete," or our "right," "write," "rite" and "wright." In actual speech, such words, in both English and Chinese, are distinguished by the way they are used in the sentence. If I say, "Please write the letter," it will not occur to my hearers that I am saying "right" or "rite" the letter, while if the word appears in writing, the distinctive spelling of the English and the distinctive symbol of the Chinese will keep one from misunderstanding.

Again, two or more one-syllable Chinese words can form compounds, like "railroad" or "foxhole," which carry a meaning not exactly contained in any one of the parts. Our compound words are often picturesque. The Chinese are no less so: "cream," for example, is "milk-skin"; "lantern" is "lamp-cage"; "strait" is "sea-waist"; "parent" is "father-mother"; "God" is "upper-ruler." The generic compound for "clothing" is *i-shang*, where *i* means "upper clothing," *shang* "lower clothing"; "coat-pants," as it were. Often Chinese uses a compound where we would be satisfied with one of the parts: "way-path" for "way," "look-see" for "see."

Chinese has a third resource that has no exact counterpart in English. These are the tones of the voice, which we use to indicate varieties of emotion, or to distinguish between a statement and a question or command, but which are used in Chinese to convey different meanings of the same sounds. The *ma* that customarily means "mother" and the *ma* that usually means "horse" are pronounced in different tones, while two other tones for *ma* mean "flax" and "scold" or "curse," and a toneless use of the word at the end of a statement turns it into a question.

These tones cause Westerners the most trouble. It is easy enough to remember the correct tone of a single word, but in a six- or ten-word sentence, with all the words to be put in their proper tones, you run into snags. An American missionary's wife, learning Chinese in Peiping, once meant to say to her guest: "You are very polite," but said: "You are very hateful" instead, because she said *kèchi* in the wrong tone. There is a Chinese tongue twister that runs as follows: *Māma chí mǎ*, *mǎ màn, māma mà mǎ* ("Mother rides horse, horse slow, mother curses horse").

The Chinese were not always aware of using tones. When the theory was first advanced by some Chinese scholars about 500 A.D., many high-placed Chinese were skeptical. The Emperor Wu Ti, one of the unbelievers, summoned the sage Chou Yung. "Come, tell me," he said, "what are these four tones?" The sage replied, using four words, each clearly exemplifying a different tone. The four words, *tyēn dž shèng jé*, literally meant, "Your Majesty, who has the wisdom of the sages." This ingenious example was too much for His Majesty, who became a firm believer in the existence of tones.

The modern educated Chinese are quite aware of tones, but they are not at all worried by them. They have learned them just as you learned the inflections of the voice that have become second nature to you when you ask questions or issue commands.

There is, to help you out, another typical Chinese-language device: the addition of a classifying or explanatory word. We can say in English "ash" or "ash tree." The latter cannot be confused with the ash from your cigarette. Chinese has dozens of such classifiers, which make the meaning absolutely clear. One, for instance, is applied to round objects, like rings or coins; others work for small things, like pearls and grains of rice; for human beings; for animals; for articles of clothing. The "head" in "fifty head of cattle" has been called the perfect English counterpart of the Chinese classifier.

The Chinese vocabulary is, of course, totally unrelated to the words of Western languages. Each word has to be separately memorized. There are loan words from the tongues of the West, but they are relatively few.

One way of making a start on Chinese vocabulary is to study Chinese place names in the news. Names like Amoy, Quemoy, Tachen, Penghu, Ningpo, Hangchow, Changsha, are not just meaningless jumbles of sounds, but, to a Chinese ear, descriptive of things that are to them as Long Beach, Sandy Hook, Fire Island, and New Haven are to us.

Names like Formosa and the Pescadores Islands mean "Beautiful" and "Fishermen Islands," but they are Portuguese, not Chinese, having been bestowed by the Portuguese explorers who reached some of the island outposts of China before the Chinese themselves did. The Chinese names of these localities are Taiwan ("Terrace Bay") and Penghu ("Dash-ing-Waters Lake"). The word *tai* ("terrace") appears also in Formosa's four chief cities, Taipeh ("Terrace North"), Tainan ("Terrace South"), Taichung ("Terrace Central") and Tai-tung ("Terrace East"). We may assume that the first Chinese to visit the island compared it to a terrace rising from the sea.

Quemoy (this is Fukien dialect; in Mandarin it should be spelled and pronounced Jinmen) is reminiscent of California, for it means "Golden Gate." Matsu, though seemingly Japa-nese, means "Horse Ancestor," a name applied to the sea goddess worshiped by the local fishermen. Other small islands off the mainland, Pai-chüan, Yin-shan, Yu-shan, are "North Dog," "Silver Mountain," "Jade Mountain."

Hainan, off the southern coast, means "South of the Sea," but it may also be a reversal of the name of the sea in which it is located, Nan Hai ("South Sea").

Kowloon ("Nine Dragons") is the point of land close to Hong Kong; its name seems based on legend. Hong Kong itself means "Fragrant Harbor," while Shanghai is "Up Sea" or "Up from the Sea," and Amoy is "Mansion Gate." The three air bases on the mainland, Ningpo, Hangchow, and Changsha, bear names that mean "Quiet Waves," "Square-Boat Region," and "Long Sand." The nearby cities of Foo-chow and Wenchow are "Happy Region" and "Warm Region."

The Chinese capital was Peking, or "North Capital," before the advent of the Republic, which changed its name to Pei-ping, or "Northern Peace," in 1927. The Chinese Communists have restored the old name, which sets the "North Capital" in opposition to Nanking, the "South Capital." Chungking served as a refugee capital for Chiang Kai-shek during the Sino-Japanese War, and has the meaning of "Repeated Felicitations."

The three mainland provinces closest to Formosa are Fukien ("Happy [or "Fortunate"] Construction"), Chekiang ("Twisting River"), and Kwangtung, or, as simplified by English traders, Canton. Kwangtung means "Broad East," and the adjoining province, Kwanghsi, is "Broad West."

Among names of rivers, we find the Yalu or Yalu Kiang ("Duck-green River") and the Huangho ("Yellow River"); both get their names from the color of their waters, the Huang being a muddy yellow, while the snow-fed Yalu is gray-green.

All this gives us an initial vocabulary base. *Kiang* and *ho* both mean "river." *Hai* is "sea," *hu* is "lake," *shan* is "mountain," *chow* is "district," "region" or "department." To these we might add *hsien*, "county," *tao*, "island," *pan tao*, "peninsula," *sheng*, "province." *Pei*, appearing also as *pai*, *pe* or *peh*, is "north," and *nan* is "south"; *tung* is "east" and *hsi* is "west." *Fu* or *foo* is "happy," "fortunate."

Among Chinese provinces, *Honan* is "river south" (south of the Yellow River). *Shantung* is "Mountain East," and *Shanhsi* is "Mountain West" (the provinces are respectively east and west of the T'ai Hang Mountains).

Learning the written Chinese language is almost a lifetime job, although there are movements going on to simplify it. The spoken tongue, on the other hand, is quite accessible and, for an English speaker, not too difficult.

The North Mandarin dialect, on which the National Language is based, is official throughout Red China, including Manchuria, Mongolia, Tibet, and Chinese Turkestan. It is also the official tongue of the Nationalist Chinese on the Island of Formosa. As a popular spoken tongue, it predominates in the northeastern part of China, serving a population of between two and three hundred million. Other dialects and languages spoken on Chinese soil are Southern and Southwest Mandarin, the Wu of the Shanghai region, the Min of Fukien, and the Cantonese of the south, all of which are definitely of the Chinese family. Southern China also has Hakka and Miao, both of the Chinese group, as well as Lolo and Thai, spoken along the borders of Burma and Thailand. Mongolian appears in Mongolia, Tibetan in Tibet, Turki in Chinese Turkestan, and there are remnants of Manchu in Manchuria.

For the spoken north Mandarin, various systems of transcription are used, of which the most popular among English speakers, though by no means the most accurate, is the one devised at Yale University.

Here the four tones of Mandarin are indicated as follows:

1. High and level: ā
2. High and rising: á
3. Low and rising: ǎ
4. Falling from high to low: à

The four tones may be indicated by various English uses of the word *go*. In "I'm going to gō to New York," you have the high level tone that corresponds to 1. In "Gó to New York?" with a mildly interrogative inflection, you have Tone 2. But if you say "Gŏ to New York?" as though you thought the statement preposterous, you approach Tone 3. Finally, in the command "Gò!" you have Tone 4.

Since in Chinese the tones are used to distinguish meanings, not to give expression to emotional states, one must take care not to give a question a rising inflection merely because it is a question, or a command a falling inflection because it is an order. To form a question, Chinese generally uses the toneless word *ma* at the end of the sentence, or repeats the verb putting *bù* or *bú* ("not") before the second use of the verb. Thus, *nǐ lèi* means "You are tired." "Are you tired?" would be either *Nǐ lèi ma* ("You tired?") or *Nǐ lèi bú lèi* ("You tired, not tired"). *Bù* changes to *bú* before another fourth tone. Questions may also be formed with interrogative words like *shémma*, "what?" *dwōshau*, "how many?" "how much?" *sheí*, "who?" In these cases, omit both *ma* and *bú*.

In accordance with the transcriptions used in the Yale System:

a is pronounced for the most part as in "father."

e is pronounced like *e* in "the man" (but in *ye*, pronounce as in "yet").

i as in "machine"; but if followed by *n, m, ng*, as in "it."

o as in "worn."

u as in "super" or "book."

ai as in "aisle."

au as in "how."

ei as in "eight."

ou as in "low."

yu like French *u* or German *ü;* pronounce *i* of "machine" with rounded lips.

er as in "her."

Try this out in a few simple words:

mǎ, "horse"	*shū*, "book"
tā, "he," "she"	*mài*, "sell"
màn, "slow," "be slow"	*mǎi*, "buy"
máng, "busy," "be busy"	*māu*, "cat"
dé, "get"	*lèi*, "tired," "be tired"

lěng, "cold"
yě, "also"
bǐ, "pen," "pencil"
nín, "you"
wǒ, "I"

yǒu, "have"
nyǔ, "female"
nán, "male"
èr, "two"

Among the consonants, *p, t, k, ch, ts* are pronounced with a strong puff of breath; *b, d, g* sound like English *p, t, k* after *s* ("spun," "sting," "sky"), without any puff of breath; this also applies to *j* and *dz,* which are weakly uttered *ch* and *ts. R, ch* and *sh* are pronounced with the tip of the tongue curled upward. *Sy* (which in another system of transcription appears as *hs*) is pronounced with the tip of the tongue against the back of the lower teeth. *H* is more strongly pronounced than in English. *M, n, l, f, y, w* are generally as in English. A few samples:

péng-you, "friend" (give the initial *p* an even stronger puff of breath than you would give English *pen*).

bàu, "newspaper" (pronounce *b* not as in "bat," but rather like the *p* of "spat," with no puff of breath).

tā-men, "they" (give initial *t* a stronger puff of breath than in "tell").

dà, "big," "large" (pronounce like *ta* in "star").

kàn, "look at," "read" (strong puff after *k*).

gāu, "tall," "high" (like *cow* in "scowl"; no puff of breath).

chá, "tea" (strong puff of breath after *ch*).

Jūng-gwo, China *(j* pronounced as *ch*; no puff of breath).

tsúng, "from" (strong puff after *ts*).

dzǒu, "go" (*dz* as *ts,* but no puff of breath).

rén, "man" (*r* with tip of tongue curled up toward palate; *e* as in *the*).

syǎu, "little," "small" (hold tongue with tip against lower teeth as you pronounce; in another transcription system, this word appears as *hsiao*).

hěn, very (strongly aspirated *h; e* as in "the").

We may at this point begin with some expressions of greeting and politeness:

Dzǎu or *Nǐ hǎu ma* or *Nǐ hǎu bù hǎu* or *Hǎu bù hǎu.* "Good morning." (The first expression may be used only in the morning. The others may be used at any time. Literally, *nǐ hǎu ma* means "You well?"; *nǐ hǎu bù hǎu* is,

"You well, not well?" "Are you well or aren't you well?";
nĭ may be omitted in the latter expression.)

Dzěmmayàng? "How goes it?" (In word groups, all syllables without tone marks are unaccented, neutral syllables.)

Wŏ hău, or *hău.* "I'm well."

Dzài jyèn. "Good night," "Good-by." (Literally, "Again
see.")

Chĭng. "Please."

Syèsye. "Thank you." (In another transcription system,
this appears as *hsieh hsieh.*)

Bú syè or *byé kèchi* or *búkèchi.* "Don't mention it."

Dwèibuchĭ. "Pardon me."

Wŏ kéyi jìnlai ma? "May I come in?"

Chĭngjìn. "Come in" (more polite); *jìnlai* (less polite).

Dwèi. "Yes" (for "You are right"); *shr̀* (for "It is).

Búdwèi. "No" (for "You are wrong"); *búshr̀* (for "It is
not").

Hău. "Gladly" (for "All right"); *yídìng* (for "Certainly").

The old Chinese grammarians did not subdivide their words
into parts of speech, as we do. The same word may be used in
various grammatical functions, as often happens in English
("Mail this letter"; "Put this letter in the mail"; "Put this
letter in the mailbox"; or "Speak up"; "Up the river"; "I'll
up you five dollars"; "the ups and downs of life"). Thus, *dà*
may, in different contexts, mean "large," "to be large," "big-
ness." *Hău* means "good" or "well," according to context.
Chinese word order is for the most part fixed. The word
used as subject regularly comes before the word used as a
verb, and that in turn precedes the object. Modifiers generally
precede the word they modify, so that an adjective normally
precedes its noun, and an adverb its verb. The indirect object
precedes the direct. These rules, coinciding almost precisely
with those of English, make the initial steps in Chinese easy.
A few illustrations:

Wŏ kànjyen nĭ. "I see you" (I look-see you).

Nĭ kànjyen wŏ. "You see me" (You look-see I).

Wŏ gĕi nĭ shū. "I give you the book" (I give you book).

Nĭ gĕi wŏ shū. "You give me the book" (You give I book).

Nĭ gĕi wŏ jūnggwo shū. "You give me a Chinese book"
(You give I middle-country book).

Nĭ péngyou bù gĕi wŏ mĕigwo shū. "Your friend does not

give me an American book" (You friend not give I
America-country book).

Shopping terminology is of use:

Nín yǒu shémma shȓ ma or *Yǒu shémma shȓ wǒ kéyi bāng-
máng ma.* (*Nín* is a more polite form of *nǐ,* "you,"and may
be used more safely by the tourist; it is always used in
addressing an older person) "What can I do for you?"
Nǐ yàu shémma. "What do you want?" (You want what).
Méiyou shémma le ma. "Anything else?"
Méiyou shémma le. "Nothing else."
Wǒ yàu. "I want."
Chǐng gěi wǒ. "Please give me."
Chǐng gěi wǒ ná (object you want brought) *lai.* "Please
bring me."
Chǐng gěi wǒ kàn. "Please show me" (Please give I see;
Please let me see).
Jèige dwōshau chyén. "How much is it?" (This how much
money?)
Tài gwèi. "Too much."
Wǒ yàu . . . "I want . . ."
yìběn shū, "a book."
yìbāu syāngyēn, "a pack of cigarettes."
yíkwài féidzàu, "a cake of soap."
yìpíng píjyǒu, "a bottle of beer."
yìdyǎr chá, "some tea."
yìdyǎr jyǒu, "some wine."
yìdyǎr nyóunǎi, "some milk."

These last phrases illustrate the working of Chinese classifiers. Nouns used with numerals (and this includes "a" or
"an," which is the same as "one") call for a classifying word
added to the numeral. In English we often do something
similar (five head of cattle, two pairs of shoes, three pieces of
pie); in Chinese, the practice is more general, as can be seen
from the first example. The numeral "one" is *yī,* which
changes tone when joined to a classifier. English says "one
book", Chinese says "one-volume book"; with the other examples, the English "pack", "cake", "bottle" may be said to
be the equivalents of the Chinese classifiers, though German,
which omits "of", supplies an even closer parallel (*ein Stuck
Fleisch, ein Glas Wasser,* etc.). But Chinese classifiers appear
where no Western language would use a classifying word.

Here are some expressions of direction:

Ní néng bunéng gaùsung wǒ. "Can you tell me?"
Dzài shémma dìfang. "Where is?" "Where are?" (place
    you want goes at the beginning of Chinese phrase).
Dàu (place you want) *dzěmma dzǒu.* "Which is the way
    to —?"
Ní dàu shémma dìfang chyù. "Where are you going?"
Wǒmen dàu shémma dìfang chyù. "Where are we going?"
Jè shr̀. "Here is." "Here are."
Wàng yòu dzǒu. "To the right."
Wàng dzwǒ dzǒu. "To the left."
Yìjŕ wàng chyén dzǒu. "Straight ahead."
Gēn wǒ lái. "Come with me."
Dzài shémma dìfang. "Where can I find —?" (name of
    place or object comes at beginning of the Chinese phrase).
    Yínháng (*dzài shémma dìfang*). (Where is) "the bank?"
    Fàntīng, "the dining room"
    Lǐbàitáng or *jyàutáng,* "the church"
    Yàufáng, "the drugstore"
    Hwǒchē, "the train"
    Fànchē or *tsānchē,* "the dining car"
    Tsèswǒ, "the rest room"
    Yóujèngjyú, "the post office"
    Syìnsyāng, "the letter box"
    Fángjyān, "the room"
    Dyèntī, "the elevator"

As shown by the examples above, Chinese seldom indicates
the plural, though it may do so by various devices (the use of
numerals, or of words meaning "many," "several"). With
personal pronouns, however, the distinction between singular
and plural is regularly made:

wǒ, "I," "my," "me"	*wǒmen,* "we," "our," "us"
ní or *nín,* "you," "your"	*nǐmen,* "you," "your" (plural)
tā, "he," "she," "his," "her"	*tāmen,* "they," "their," "them"

The same personal pronoun form may be used as subject,
by placing it before the "verb"; as direct object by placing it
after the "verb"; as indirect object by placing it after the
"verb" and before the direct object; or as possessive by
placing it before a "noun."

Speaking about speaking is good practice:

Nǐ hwèi shwō Jūnggwo hwà ma.   "Do you speak Chinese?"
Yīngwén,   "English"
Déwén,   "German"
Fàwén,   "French"
Yìwén,   "Italian"
Syībānyáwén,   "Spanish"
Éwen,   "Russian"
Ŕwen,   "Japanese"
(While "Chinese language" is *Jūnggwo hwà,* the word *wén* usually does service for other tongues).

Nǐ dǔng bùdǔng.   "Do you understand?"
Yìdyǎr.   "A little."
Wǒ (bù)dǔng.   "I (don't) understand."
Nǐ jŕdau ma.   "Do you know?"
Wǒ (bù)jŕdau.   "I (don't) know."
Nín gwèisyìng.   "What is your name?" (last name only).
Jeìge, Jūnggwohwà jyàu shémma.   "What do you call this in Chinese?"
Jūnggwohwà dzěmma shwō.   "How do you say—in Chinese?" (Word desired goes at beginning of Chinese phrase.)
Shwō màn yìdyǎr.   "Speak more slowly."
Wài.   "Hello" (on the telephone).

The weather lends itself to conversation:

Tyēnchi hěn hǎu.   "It's fine weather."
Tyēnchi bùhǎu.   "It's bad weather."
Syà yǔ le.   "It's raining."
Syà sywě le.   "It's snowing."
Lěng (rè).   "It's cold" (hot).
Wǒ lěng (rè).   "I'm cold" (hot).
Yǒu tàiyang (fēng).   "It's sunny" (windy).

A few signs are more likely to appear in writing than in speech, and if they do, they will be in Chinese characters. But most requests and commands appear in spoken form primarily:

Chǐng wù syī yēn.   "No smoking."
Syén rén myěn jìn.   "No admittance."
Bùsyǔ.   "It is forbidden."

Bùgàu. "Notice."
Tíng. "Stop."
Jùyì. "Look!"
Syǎusyīn. "Look out!"
Tīng. "Listen!"
Děng yihwěr. "Just a second!"
Dàu jèr lái. "Come here."
Tyàubǎn. "Gangway!"
Jèi shr̀ shémma. "What is it?"
Wǒ shr̀ Měigworén. "I am an American."
Wǒ syūyàu. "I need."
Chǐng lyǔgwǎn jīnglǐ lái. "Please send for the hotel manager."
Chǐng yíge yīshēng lái. "Please send for a doctor."
Chǐng yíge jǐngchá lái. "Please send for a policeman."
Jyàu yíge jyǎuháng lái. "Please send for a porter."
Chǐng yíge fānyì lái. "Please send for an interpreter."
Jyàu yílyàng chìchē lái. "Please send for a taxi."
Chǐng Měigwo lǐngshr̀ lái. "Please send for the American consul."

(The phrases beginning with *chǐng yíge* and ending with *lái* literally mean "please one–come"; *yíge* is the numeral "one" compounded with *ge*, the commonest of classifiers, which has no special translation. *Jyàu*, used as a verb, means "call".)

Following is a list of words which normally translate the corresponding English adjectives. It must be understood, however, that many of them may be used as other parts of speech conveying similar basic meanings. The most frequent of such uses includes the verb "to be" understood with the predicate adjective. *Hǎu rén* is "good man"; *rén hǎu* is "the man (is) good"; *hǎu* may also be used in other functions, of which the chief is translated by the English adverb "well."

syǎu, "small"   *dà,* "large"
cháng, "long"   *dwǎn,* "short"
lyángkwai, "cool"   *nwǎnhwo,* "warm"
gānjing, "clean"   *dzāng,* "dirty"
hǎu, "good"   *hwài* or *bùhǎu,* "bad"
dìyī, "first"   *dzwèihòu,* "last"
chǎunàu, "noisy"   *ānjing,* "quiet"
lèi, "tired"   *dzwèile,* "drunk"
shūfu, "comfortable"   *bùshūfu,* "uncomfortable"
jìn, "near"   *ywǎn,* "far," "distant"
hǎukàn, "pretty"   *nánkàn,* "ugly"

kèchi, "polite"   *méilǐmau,* "rude"
hēi, "black"   *bái,* "white"
húng, "red"   *lyù,* "green"
lán, "blue"   *hwáng,* "yellow"

The Chinese "verb" (any word used in a verb function) is invariable, and distinctions of person, number, tense, etc., do not appear, save by the use of additional words, which include primarily subject nouns and pronouns and adverbial modifiers.

syě,   to write; writing (in general)
wǒ syě,   "I write"
tā syě,   "he writes"
tāmen syě, "they write"
wǒ syě le,   "I wrote" (I write finish)
wǒ míngtyēn syě,   "I shall write tomorrow" (I bright day write)

Following is a list of words generally used to translate English verbs. They are subject to the same caution as the adjectives above, and many of them may be used in other functions, depending on the context. *Kàn,* for example, which used as a verb means "to look," "look at," "read," "visit," in combination with *hǎu* becomes "pretty" or, to find a more exact English parallel, "good-looking."

shř, "be"   *yǒu,* "have" (in negative, use
                                         méiyǒu, not *bù yǒu*)
mǎi, "buy"   *mài,* "sell"
(These two verbs, combine into *mǎimai,* "buy-sell," mean "business.")
lái, "come"   *chyù,* "go"
ná, "take"   *jǎu,* "look for"
dzwò, "do," "make"   *jǎu,* "find"
dyōu, "lose"   *dzwò,* "work"
nyèn, "read"   *syě,* "write"
kànjyen, "see"   *shwō,* "speak"
chř, "eat"   *hē,* "drink"
mùyù, "bathe"   *syǐ,* "wash"
jù, "stay"   *kàn,* "look at"
gěi, "give," "pay" (for)   *yàu,* "want," "ask" (for)

Armed with this knowledge, we can now say:
Wǒmen yàu dàu Jūnggwo chyù; wǒmen hwèi shwō yìdyǎr Jūnggwo hwà.
("We are going to China; we can speak a little Chinese.")

chapter fifteen
japanese

If you travel to Japan, you may be able to get along with English, which millions of Japanese speak, more or less well. But you may also wish to reciprocate, to the extent of uttering a few phrases in the language of Nippon. Japanese is rich, rewarding, poetic, imaginative, strange, harmonious like the twang of the samisen, ceremonious like the Kabuki dance, complex like the Oriental soul, and as bafflingly mysterious as is the origin of the Japanese race.

Most anthropologists hold that the Japanese are a blend of the races of the Asiatic mainland (Manchu, Mongol, and Korean) with a brown-skinned Polynesian strain that came up to the Japanese islands from the southeast, with, perhaps, an admixture of the hairy, straight-featured Ainu who still live in limited numbers on the northern island of Yezo or Hokkaido.

If this were true, we might expect the Japanese language to be a similar blend of Manchu, Mongol, Korean, Polynesian, and Ainu. For this there is no evidence. The only similarity perceptible, and it is a rather remote one, based on structure rather than vocabulary, is to Korean.

There is a widespread notion that Japanese and Chinese are linked. But this is based on nothing more than the borrowing by the Japanese, in the first cenuuries of our era, of the Chinese system of ideographic writing. At the same time, they borrowed many Chinese words and incorporated them, with some change of form, into the Japanese language. That is as far as the similarity goes.

At the beginning of the nineteenth century, when the science of linguistics was still in its infancy, many linguists believed in the existence of a "Turanian" or "Scythian" family of languages, extending from Europe to Japan and including Finnish, Hungarian, Turkish, the languages of Siberia and Turkestan, Mongol, Manchu, Korean, and Japanese. More careful examination at a later period, however, showed that these languages did not have a common vocabulary, or even too much of a common structure. Today, cautious linguists are willing to accept only the relationship of the Uralic tongues (Lapp, Finnish, Estonian, Hungarian), with a separate Altaic classification for Turkish, Manchu, and Mongol, and a possible, but not too probable, link between Japanese and Korean.

The Japanese language is somewhat of a mongrel. It has a body of "native" words, from whatever source they may have been derived. These are generally words of more than one syllable and have a simple syllabic structure reminiscent on the one hand of Malay, Polynesian, and Hawaiian, on the other of Italian. The syllable usually consists of a consonant plus a vowel, and most Japanese words consist of a sequence of two or more such syllables. In addition, Japanese has freely borrowed Chinese roots, which are distinguished by the fact that they are monosyllabic. Some of these words came in earlier, others later; sometimes the same word was borrowed twice in different forms, so that Japanese synonyms often come in groups of three—a native Japanese word, an early Chinese borrowing, and a later Chinese loan-word. This is not unlike what happens in English, where we have *flimsy*, from Anglo-Saxon, *frail*, from Old French, and *fragile*, a later French borrowing, all with approximately the same meaning.

In Japanese there is a double series of numerals, one native and polysyllabic (*hitotsu, futatsu, mittsu, yottsu*), the other originally Chinese (*ichi, ni, san, shi*). Here a remote English comparison would be *one, two, three* and the Latin numerals contained in *unity, duality, trinity*. The native Japanese word for raw rice is *kome*, while cooked rice is *gohan;* but in addition, there is a Chinese-derived word, *bei*, which appears in the poetic name by which the Japanese designate the United States: *bei-koku*, literally, "rice-land." Another possible derivation for *bei-koku* is the Chinese name for our country, *Mei-*

gwo. This is even more complimentary, for it means "beautiful land."

English borrowed words not only from French, Latin, and Greek, but reached out to all the tongues with which it came in contact. Japanese did the same. It picked up words from the Portuguese of the earliest European navigators to reach the islands. Later, it borrowed heavily from the English of the British and Americans whom the Japanese strove to imitate.

The story of word borrowing is an ancient one. When one group does not possess an object, and another group does, the first group adopts not only the object, but also its name. The rice-eating Japanese did not know bread until the Portuguese brought it to them. The Portuguese word for bread is *pão* (derived from Latin *panis* and related to French *pain*, Spanish *pan*, Italian *pane*). The Japanese word for "bread" is therefore *pan*. The Portuguese, as good Catholics, rejected meat on Ember days, which they called by the Latin name of *Quattuor Tempora*, the "four times" of the year. They asked instead for sea food, usually shrimp. Eventually, the name *tempura* became attached to the fried shrimp the Portuguese favored on these occasions. Thus did the ancient Latin word for "times" turn into the Japanese word for "shrimp fried in batter."

People who note the large number of English words in Japanese imagine it was our army of occupation that contributed most of them. Actually, English linguistic penetration had begun much earlier. Western style foods, clothing, objects, institutions, including baseball, were popular in Japan long before World War II. Here is a partial list of Japanese food terms that require no translation: *bata* ("butter"), *sūpu* ("soup", side by side with the native *suimono* and *shiru*); *bifuteki, hamu, beikon, soseiji* ("sausage"; but you may also use a native *chōzume*), *sarada* ("salad"), *chiizu* ("cheese"), *remon* ("lemon"; there is no *l* in Japanese, so *r* takes its place). Compare these imported forms, for which the object did not exist prior to Western contacts, with such native terms as *yasai* ("vegetables"), *tori* ("chicken"), *niku* ("meat"), *tamago* ("egg"), *sakana* ("fish"), *sakurambō* ("cherries"), *momo* ("peach").

The Japanese use chopsticks, for which the term is *hashi*. The "teacup" (*chawan*) came from China. They have always had "spoons" (*saji*). But now notice what happens to the rest of the tableware. A "knife" is *naifu*, a "fork" is *fōku*, a "glass" or "cup" is *koppu*, a "napkin" is *nafukin*. "Water" is *mizu* and the native "rice wine" is *sake*, but the originally imported "beer" is *biiru*, "whisky" is *uisukii*, and "coffee" is *kōhii*.

Even more startling is what happens in the matter of clothing. A Western style "shirt" is *shatsu*, a "necktie" is *nekutai*, a "collar" is *karā*, a "pocket" is *poketto*, a "handkerchief" is *hankechi*, a "button" is *botan*, a "pin" is *pin* (*anzenpin* if it's a "safety pin"), "slippers" (Western style) are *surippa*. We, borrowing a Japanese article of attire, do the same, and "kimono" has become part of our language.

"Soap" must have come to the Japanese from the Portuguese, for its name is *shabon*. But English has contributed the Japanese words for "bus" (*basu*), "ink" (*inki*), "pen" (*pen*), "tobacco" (*tabako*), "match" (*matchi*), "baseball" (*beisubōru*). Often there is rivalry between an old Japanese word and an imported one. A "picnic" may be *ensoku* or *pikunikku;* a "hotel" may be *ryokan* (Japanese inn) or *hoteru* (Western style hostelry). Occasionally the rivalry is between a British and an American pronunciation: "dollar" may be *doru* or *darā*.

The Japanese writing system is taken from the Chinese, but there are subtle differences. In Chinese, every spoken, monosyllabic word is represented by a pictogram (originally the picture of the object named, if it was picturable), or by an ideogram (two or more pictograms ingeniously combined to represent a non-picturable concept, like the written symbol for "east," which is the picture of the sun placed over the picture for tree: the sun rising over the trees in the east).

The Japanese, falling under the spell of Chinese culture about 300 A.D., adopted the Chinese system of pictograms and ideograms. This was easy, since pictograms and ideograms have no connection with the sounds of spoken language, but symbolize objects and ideas, and can readily be used internationally, like our Western system of numerals. The same symbol for "man" is used by the Chinese, who pronounce it *ren*, and by the Japanese, who pronounce it *hito* (it sounds more like *shto* in the Tokyo dialect). But there were snags due to the fact that the two languages do not have the same structure.

In Chinese each word is an independent monosyllable; there are no endings, the nouns are not declined, the verbs are not conjugated. Hence, there is an ideal relationship of one symbol for each spoken word. But in Japanese, nouns and verbs have endings, and this means additional symbols and modified meanings. To take care of this, the Japanese set aside a certain number of symbols and gave them a purely phonetic, syllabic value. If they want to write the equivalent of the English "man's," they use the Chinese pictogram for man, but under it they write the syllabic character pronounced *no*, which means "of," and which spoken Japanese places after the noun, just as English places *'s* after *man*. The presence of these syllabic symbols, representing endings and interspersed with the Chinese ideograms and pictograms carrying basic meanings, distinguishes Japanese from Chinese writing. A Japanese trying to read a page of Chinese would be able to figure out the basic meanings, but would be stumped by the Chinese word order and lack of endings. A Chinese trying to read a page of Japanese would likewise be able to figure out basic meanings, but would be baffled both by Japanese word order and by the presence of these syllabic symbols, which to him would be meaningless.

There are two sets of syllabic characters, of forty-eight symbols each. One, more cursive, is called *hiragana*, and is used in ordinary writing. The other, called *katakana*, is in a square style and used primarily in writing words borrowed from Western languages. To become literate, the Japanese schoolboy must learn both syllabaries, plus a number of Chinese pictograms and ideograms ranging from one or two thousand to as many as twenty thousand, if he wants to be a real literary scholar. This imposes a terrific burden on the memory, even greater than the one endured by the English speaker in learning how to spell.

It has often been suggested that the Japanese discard this complicated writing system and go over to the Western alphabet, which could adequately portray all the sounds of their language. The dead hand of tradition prevents this, however, just as it halts every attempt to reform the complicated spelling of English. One major obstacle in both languages is that if spelling reform were adopted, all books and other printed material would have to be scrapped and reprinted in the new system, which would be a very slow and expensive process, and in the meanwhile everybody would have to learn both systems, old and new.

It is perfectly possible to learn spoken Japanese from a Roman alphabet transcription. This will not enable you to read Japanese signs and documents, but it will save you the half-dozen or more years of study which are normally required to produce a literate Japanese.

The transcription used here is the same as the one used by the various groups in Japan that favor Romanization, and it is thoroughly adequate to represent the rather simple sounds of the language.

Japanese vowels are long or short: $\bar{a}$ is the a of "father," a is the same sound shortened; e is the sound of e in "met," $\bar{e}$ is the same sound prolonged; i is as in "big," $\bar{i}$ or ii as in "machine"; o is as in "obey," $\bar{o}$ as in "hole"; u is as in "push," $\bar{u}$ as in "rude." Short i and u are frequently dropped from pronunciation inside a word, and short u at the end of a word: *gozaimashita*, for instance, is usually pronounced *gozaimash'ta; sukiyaki* comes out as *s'kiyaki*, and *desu* as *des'*.

The consonants are generally pronounced as in English. The Japanese f is pronounced by bringing the lower lip against the upper lip rather than against the upper teeth, just as wh⸱ ı you blow out a match; the Japanese g is often pronounced *ng;* the r is lightly trilled, as in British "very." Consonants that are written double are to be lengthened in pronunciation, exactly as in Italian.

Japanese does not have a heavy stress, but tends to stress all the syllables of a word equally. There is a tendency to put some extra stress on long vowels and on vowels followed by two consonants, as well as on the case endings of nouns.

Japanese grammar is strange to one brought up with Western grammatical concepts. In syntax and word order, Japanese is sometimes faintly reminiscent of Latin (the verb, for example, usually comes at the end of the sentence). In other respects, Japanese has points of contact with Uralic and Altaic tongues like Finnish and Turkish. Here and there, we get similarities to Chinese. But all these points are so vague and indefinite that they do not lend themselves to any clear-cut theory of relationship.

The tourist who wants a few spoken phrases need not be too concerned with the intricacies of Japanese grammar. During the occupation, many of our soldiers got to have a fairly good functional command of spoken Japanese without mastering either the system of writing or the involutions of grammar.

Still, a few grammatical comparisons will prove of interest, if only to show how the same idea may be conveyed by al-

together different devices. But first, a few formulas of greeting
and politeness:

Ohayō. "Good morning" (this sounds almost like the name
of one of our states).

Konnichi wa. "Good afternoon," "Good day."

Komban wa. "Good evening."

Oyasumi nasai. "Good night."

Sayonara. "Good-by."

(I)kaga des(u) ka? "How are you?" (We put in parentheses
the two short vowels, *i* and *u*, which are commonly
dropped in rapid speech.)

Dō des(u) ka? "How goes it?"

(Watak(u)shi wa) jōbu des(u). "I'm well." (The first part
is often omitted.)

Dōzo or *kudasai.* "Please." (If you use the latter, be sure
it follows a *-te* form of the verb.)

Arigatō. "Thank you."

Dō itashimash(i)ta. "Don't mention it."

Gomen nasai. "Pardon me."

Like many Oriental and a few European languages, Japanese makes no distinction of gender. This means, among other
things, that the same word is used indifferently for Mr., Mrs.,
and Miss. The word is *san,* and it is put after the name.
Suzuki San may therefore mean Mr. Suzuki, Mrs. Suzuki or
Miss Suzuki. If a special distinction must be made between
Mr. and Mrs. Suzuki, one may use for the latter *Suzuki san no
ok(u)sama,* literally, "Suzuki Mr. of (honorable) wife."
Sama has about the same force as *san,* and forms part of
many words of family relationship when it is implied that you
are speaking of the wife, father, mother, etc., of the person
you are addressing, or of a person you wish to honor. If you
are speaking of your own relatives, you will use instead "hum-
ble" words. These are sometimes the same as the polite words
minus the *sama* or *san,* sometimes entirely different. Thus, if
I speak of "father" implying that it is my father, I will use
the normal or noncommittal *chichi;* but if it is your father, the
word will be *otōsama;* my mother will be *haha,* but your mother
is *okāsama;* my son is *mus(u)ko,* your son is *mus(u)ko san.*
Before we decide that this is utterly strange and unwestern,
let us recall that French often says *Madame votre mère,* and
Spanish *su señor padre,* for what would in English be "your
mother," "your father."

The tourist is likely to hear phrases inquiring as to his wants:

Nani ka hoshii des(u) ka? "What do you want?"
Nan no go yō des(u) ka? "What can I do for you?"
Hoka ni nani ka iriyō des(u) ka? "Anything else?"
Sore kara? "What else?"
Mō arimasen. "Nothing else."

It is fairly obvious by this time that most Japanese questions end with *ka*, which is like a spoken question mark.

Various ways of expressing tourist wants are:

Motte kite kudasai. "Please bring me." (The object you want brought appears at the beginning of the phrase.)
Misete kudasai. "Please show me" (as above).
Kudasaimas(u) ka? "Will you give me?" (as above).
Ikura des(u) ka? "How much is it?"
Ammari takai des(u)! "It's too expensive!"

The object you want brought, shown, or given comes at the beginning of the phrase, and is regularly followed by the little word *o* (formerly spelled and pronounced *wo*), which may be likened to an accusative or objective case ending:

Mizu o motte kite kudasai. "Please bring water."
Hon o misete kudasai. "Please show me a book."
O cha o kudasai? "Will you give me some tea?"

It is a little confusing that in addition to the (*w*)*o* that follows a noun and acts as an accusative marker, there is another *o* which frequently comes before nouns and adjectives, and is used as a sign of respect. This is the word that our comic strips so often translate as "honorable" modifying the object mentioned, but this is a misconception. If *o* is used, the "honorable" connotation attaches to the person you are speaking to, not to the object you are speaking about; thus, *O mizu o kudasai* would mean not "Please (bring) the honorable water," but "You, honorable sir, please bring water." Since there is no compulsion to use this honorific *o*, it may be conveniently stored away for recognition purposes only.

Some of the things you might want shown, brought, or given to you:

niku (w)o, "some meat" (meat + object sign)

momo o hitokago, "a basket of peaches" (peach + object sign + basket)

hamaki o hitohako, "a box of cigars" (cigar + object sign + box)

sake o hitobin, "a bottle of wine" (wine + object sign + bottle)

A short cut in asking for what you want is simply the word *kudasai,* "Give me please," added to the name of the thing you want. This is equivalent to our "Water, please!"

Kondate o kudasai. "The menu, please."
Kanjō o kudasai. "The bill, please."
O cha o kudasai. "Some tea, please."
Gohan o kudasai. "Some rice, please."
Hi o kudasai. "A light, please."

A few directional expressions:
. . . wa, doko des(u) ka? "Where is?" "Where are?" (The place you are inquiring about comes at the beginning.)
. . . e iku michi wa dochira des(u) ka? "Which way to?" (as above).
Doko e ikimas(u) ka? "Where are you (we) going?"
Kochira e. "This way."
Achira e. "That way."

Since the verb regularly comes at the end of a Japanese sentence, if one wanted to ask "Where is the bridge?" the proper word order would be "Bridge + sentence-topic sign + where + is + question mark," or *Hashi wa doko des(u) ka?* "Which way to the mountain?" is *Yama e iku michi wa dochira des(u) ka?*
Here is a sampling of inquiries of this type:

Ginkō wa doko des(u) ka? "Where is the bank?"
Shokudō wa doko des(u) ka? "Where is the dining room?"
Kusuri-ya wa doko des(u) ka? "Where is a drugstore?"
Keisatsu wa doko des(u) ka? "Where is the police station?"
Shokudō-sha wa doko des(u) ka? "Where is the dining car?"
Yūbin-kyoku wa doko des(u) ka? "Where is the post office?"
Yūbin-bako wa doko des(u) ka? "Where is the letter-box?"
Benjo wa doko des(u) ka? "Where is the rest room?"
Haya wa doko des(u) ka? "Where is the room?"

A phrase like "Where are you (we) going?" brings out an important principle concerning Japanese verbs. The verbs change their endings for tense, mood, and degree of politeness toward the person you are addressing or the person talked about, but not for person or number. *Ikimas(u)* indicates present time and a polite frame of mind, but not "I," "you," "he," "we," "they." A good literal translation for it would be "There is a going," and the entire phrase *Doko e ikimas(u) ka?* really means "Where to is-there-a-going?" The Japanese mind figures that two intelligent people who are conversing are familiar with the situation, and that it is not necessary to indicate "who" is going. There are ways of specifically indicating "who" if there is danger of a misunderstanding, but they are normally avoided. If used without necessity, they sound awkward and foreign. Suppose you wished to reply: "*I* am going to Tokyo, *you* are going to Yokohama" (the sort of thing where in English we put stress of the voice on the subject pronouns), then you might say: *Watak(u)shi ga* (I + subject sign) *Tōkyō e ikimas(u)* ("Tokyo to there-is-a-going"); *anata ga* (you + subject sign) *Yokohama e ikimas(u)*. But this sort of thing is rare.

If you must use subject pronouns, they are as follows:

watak(u)shi, "I" (women more often use *watashi*).
anata, "you" (singular).
ano okata, "he," "she" (that honorable person) or *ano hito* (that person); you may also use *ano onna no kata* (that woman of honorable person) for "she"; *ano otoko no kata* (that man of honorable person) for "he."
watak(u)shi domo or *watashi domo*, "we."
anata gata, "you" (plural).
ano hito tachi, "they" (persons).
are, "it," "they" (referring to things).

Japanese, which does not care too much to indicate gender, has the same feeling about number. Nouns normally have the same form in the plural as in the singular. If there is a strong urge to indicate plurality, suffixes like *domo* and *gata* may be used for persons. For things, numerals or words like "many," "several" do the trick, as happens occasionally in English when we say "five deer," "many sheep."

Speaking activities are of importance:
Eigo ga dekimas(u) ka? "Do you speak English?" (Eng-

lish-language + subject sign + is-possible?)

S(u)koshi dake, "A little" (little only).

Wakarimas(u) ka? "Do you understand?" (Is-there-understanding?)

Wakarimasen. "I don't understand." (Usually, changing the ending from *-mas(u)* to *-masen* makes the verb negative.)

Anata no o namae wa? "What is your name?" (You of honorable name so-far-as-is-concerned?)

Kore wa nihon-go de nan to iimas(u) ka? "What do you call this in Japanese?" (This-thing so-far-as-is-concerned Japanese-language in what as call?)

Book wa nihon-go de nan to iimas(u) ka? "How do you say book in Japanese?" (Same construction as above.)

Nihon-go wa s(u)koshi dake dekimas(u). "I speak a little Japanese." (Japanese-language so-far-as-is-concerned little is-possible.)

Dōzo motto yukkuri hanash(i)te kudasai. "Speak more slowly." (Please slower speaking please.)

Moshi moshi! "Hello!" (on phone) (I-say I-say).

Japanese nouns are real nouns, and recognizable as such by their behavior. There is in Japanese a series of signs (postpositions is perhaps a better word; the preposition precedes the noun, the postposition follows it) which function somewhat like case endings in Latin, German, or Russian, or like the English possessive *'s.*

A noun or pronoun that in English would be the subject of the sentence will be usually followed in Japanese by one of two postpositions, *ga* or *wa. Ga* emphasizes the subject, *wa* isolates it:

Dare ga ikimas(u) ka? "Who is going?"

Watak(u)shi ga ikimas(u). "*I* am going." (For the ordinary "I am going," without emphasis on "I," *ikimas(u)* is all you need.)

Ano hito wa, dare des(u) ka? "That man, who is he?"

The postposition *no* expresses, among other things, possession, ownership, and the sort of relation that English shows by using "of": *Ano hito no hon,* "That man's book."

The postposition *ni* indicates, among other things, an indirect object, while *(w)o* shows the direct object: *Hon (w)o Suzuki San ni yarimas(u).* "I am giving the book to Mr.

Suzuki." (Book + object sign + Suzuki Mr. to there-is-a-giving.)

Ni also often denotes the place where a thing is: *Tokyō ni tak(u)san arimas(u)*, "In Tokyo there are many." (Tokyo in many are.)

Other common postpositions are *de* ("by," "with"); *kara* ("from," "after"); *e* ("toward," "to," "into") *made* ("up to," "as far as," "until"). There are many others.

The weather lends itself to conversational interchange:

Ii o-tenki des(u) or *yoi o-tenki des(u).*   "It's fine weather."
   (Good honorable-weather is.)
Warui o-tenki des(u). "It's bad weather."
Atsui, atatakai. "It's hot," "It's warm." (*Des(u)* may be added or omitted.)
Samui (des(u)). "It's cold."

The two above expressions can be personalized and made to mean "I'm warm," "I'm cold," by prefixing *watak(u)shi wa*, "so far as I am concerned."

Ame ga futte imas(u). "It's raining."
Yuki ga futte imas(u). "It's snowing."
Hi ga tette imas(u). "It's sunny."
Kaze ga fuite imas(u). "It's windy." (*Kaze*, "wind,"
   may be recalled as part of the expression *kamikaze*,
   "heavenly winds," that designated Japanese suicide
   planes during the war.)

Japanese adjectives, in their simplest form, end in *-ai*, *-ii*, *-oi*, or *-ui*, and are placed, as in English, before the noun: *takai uchi* ("an expensive house").

If they are used as predicate adjectives, they are handled as though they were verbs, and take on tense endings:

Uchi wa takai. "The house is expensive."
Uchi wa takakatta. "The house was expensive."
Uchi wa takakarō. "The house probably will be expensive."

A few high-frequency adjectives are:

chiisai, "small"	*ōkii,* "large"
suzushii, "cool"	*atatakai,* "warm"
chikai, "near"	*tōi,* "distant"
yoi or *ii,* "good"	*warui,* "bad"

shiroi, "white"　　　　　*kuroi,* "black"
utsukushii, "pretty"　　　*mazui,* "poorly done"
yakamashii, "noisy"　　　*kitanai,* "dirty"

The Japanese verb has a base form, generally ending in *-u,* which is used familiarly, if you are addressing a member of your family or a close friend. Usually, the final *-u* of the base or familiar form changes to *-imas(u)* to give the polite form, which the tourist is more likely to use. This gives you what may be described as a polite present tense. But there are many other tenses and forms.

Kaku is the base form of the verb meaning "to write"; it is also the form that would be used familiarly. The polite present is *kakimas(u).* The polite past is *kakimash(i)ta.* There is a future of probability, formed by ending *deshō* to the base form (*kaku deshō,* "will probably write"). There is a conditional ending in *-eba,* (*kakeba,* "if one writes"), and a past conditional in *-imash(i)tara* (*kakimash(i)tara,* "if or when one wrote"). There is a participle in *-ite,* which is used when one wants to say "please" (*kakite kudasai,* "writing please," or "please write"). There is a "let us" imperative in *-imashō* (*kakimashō,* "let us write"). There are additional familiar forms, passive forms, even desiderative forms, like *kakitai,* "want to write."

There are verbs which are honorific, and differ entirely from their familiar-polite counterparts, like *itadaku,* which replaces the customary *morau,* "to receive," if I wish to imply that I have received something from you, who are an extremely honorable person; or the *gozaimas(u)* which replaces *des(u)* in the sense of "to be" if you are speaking to a person you particularly wish to honor: "How are you? How are things?" *Ikaga de gozaimas(u) ka?,* instead of *ikaga des(u) ka?*

Here are a few regular high-frequency verbs. The base form is also the familiar present. To form the polite present, change *-u* to *-imas(u).* For the negative, drop *-u* and add *-imasen.* For the past, drop *-u* and add *-imash(i)ta.*

aruku, "walk"　　　　　*iku,* "go"
kau, "buy"　　　　　　*uru,* "sell"
yomu, "read"　　　　　*kaku,* "write"
sagasu, "look for"　　　*wakaru,* "understand"
shiru, "learn," "know"　*toru,* "take"
tsuku, "arrive"　　　　*tomaru,* "stay"

matsu, "wait"   *korobu,* "fall down"
hataraku, "work"   *oku,* "put"
nakusu, "lose"   *dekiru,* "can," "be able"

(In *dekiru,* drop *-ru* and add *-mas(u)* or *-mash(i)ta,* as also in *taberu,* eat; *miru,* look at, see; *ageru,* give.)

Directional signs would be of use, but they are far more likely to appear in Japanese characters, possibly with an English translation, than in transcription:

Migi e   "To the right."
Hidari e.   "To the left."
Massugu ni.   "Straight ahead."
Iru bekarazu.   "No admittance" (in writing only); *Haitte wa ikemasen.*
Tabako goenryo kudasai.   "No smoking."
Chūi.   "Notice."
Dekimasen.   "Forbidden."
Tomare! or *Māte!*   "Stop!"   wait

A few other expressions in very common use:

Goran nasai!   "Look!"
Abunai!   "Look out!" "Careful!"
Ano ne!   "Listen!" "Look here!" "Say!" (this is slightly vulgar); *Chotto! Moshi moshi!*
Chotto matte kudasai!   "Just a second!"
O hairi kudasai!   "Come in!"
Koko e oide nasai!   "Come here!"
Gomen nasai! Doite kudasai!   "Gangway!"
Dō shita n des(u) ka?   "What is the matter?"
Nan des(u) ka?   "What is it?"
Watak(u)shi wa Beikoku-jin des(u).   "I'm an American" (The word for "man" in an expression of nationality is the Chinese loan-word *jin* rather than the native Japanese *hito;* if the latter is used, it must be preceded by *no,* "of").
Tak(u)san.   "Much," "Many."
Taihen.   "Very much."
S(u)koshi.   "Little," "Not much."
Sugu ni.   "At once," "Soon."
Mō.   "Already."
Ima.   "Now."
Nao.   "Yet," "Still."

Mada. "Not yet."
Motto. "More."
Atokara. "Afterwards."
Ikura? "How much?"
Ikutsu? "How many?"
Ammari, or *Ōsugiru.* "Too much."
Ammari tak(u)san. "Too many."
Hayai. "Fast."
Osoku. "Slowly."
Koko ni. "Here."
Asoko ni. "There."
Hai. "Yes."
Iie. "No." ＊ＩＡ
Tash(i)ka ni. "Certainly."
Yorokonde. "Gladly."
Mata. "Again."
Tabun. "Perhaps."
Dōsh(i)te? "Why?"
Yoku. "Well."

The poetry and imagery of the Japanese language have long been recognized. There are some who object to literal translations of Japanese expressions on the ground that they tend to cast ridicule on the speakers. I have never been able to see it that way. It seems to me that the literal translation is the only way to get into the spirit of the foreign tongue.

Take, for example, the standard Japanese formula for "I'm sorry," *O ki no doku des(u)*. Literally, this means "Honorable spirit of poison is"; "This is poison to your honorable spirit." Is this not a monument to the delicacy of feeling and the capability of poetic expression of the Japanese?

"I shall see you tomorrow" and "I'm happy to meet you" both contain the same imagery. The first expression is *Myōnichi o me ni kakarimashō*, "Tomorrow I shall hang from your honorable eye"; the second is *O me ni kakarete saiwai des(u)*, "to be able to hang from your honorable eye is happy."

"I'm hungry" is *Hara ga hette iru*, "The stomach has grown small" (*hara* is the first part of the expression *hara-kiri*, "stomach-cutting," the ıcient Samurai way of committing ceremonial suicide). "I'm thirsty" is *Nodo ga kawakimash(i)ta*, "The throat has become dry." Can there be any doubt that this is the language of a race of poets?

There is no use denying the complexities of Japanese syntax from the standpoint of one who approaches it with a Western background. Yet it has often been remarked, particularly by those who lean toward the theory of monogenesis of language (all languages stemming from one common origin) that certain Japanese constructions resemble those of Latin and other early members of our own language family. Take, for example, the Japanese and the Latin way of saying "There are many books on top of the table":

Japanese: *Tsukue no   ue   ni hon ga tak(u)san arimas(u).*
Latin: *Mens- ae culm-ine libr-i   permulti sunt.*
Literally: Table of top on book-s   many   are.

Or take the impersonal Japanese verb. *Iku* or its polite variant, *ikimas(u)*, really means "There is a going." In archaic Latin, as well as in other ancient Italic languages, there is a similar impersonal use of the passive of verbs that would not ordinarily take a passive: *Itur in antiquam silvam,* "There is a going into the ancient forest," for "They go into the ancient forest."

But these are points more likely to interest the philologist than the tourist. At any rate, for our forthcoming tour of Japan, let us be able to say:

Watak(u)shi wa Tōkyō e ikimas(u); Nihon-go wa s(u)koshi dekimas(u)! which, as you know by this time, means: "I am going to Tokyo and I can speak a little Japanese."

chapter sixteen

arabic

The number of languages in spoken use throughout the world is large. One precise estimate puts it at 2,796. Other estimates vary between two and three thousand. But the overwhelming majority of these tongues are spoken by bodies of speakers small in size and insignificant from the standpoint of civilization. There are only a hundred or so languages that have over one million speakers. The truly big languages of the world, with over fifty million speakers, are barely thirteen in number.

Seven of these are the well-known important tongues of the West—English, French, Spanish, German, Russian, Portuguese, Italian. The other six are languages of those upcoming continents, Asia and Africa, that figure so largely in the news reports.

Chinese and Japanese need no introduction. The first is the world's largest language in terms of speaking population, far outstripping English, its closest competitor. The second is the tongue of a group that has shown high adaptability to modernization. Then we have Hindustani, composed of India's Hindi and Pakistan's Urdu; the Bengali of the region around Calcutta; the Indonesian of the big island republic that was built up out of the Dutch East Indies. Lastly, we have Arabic, in many ways the most dynamic and promising of the Afro-Asian languages.

In round numbers, the speakers of Arabic now approach the 100 million mark. In geographical distribution, Arabic

203

is by far the most widespead of the non-Western tongues, having expanded out of its original Arabian homeland in the seventh and eighth centuries of our era to cover all of North Africa, from Egypt on the east to Casablanca on the west, and from the Mediterranean coast to the southern edge of the Sahara and beyond. At the same time, it overspread the Near East from Syria, Lebanon and Jordan to the eastern borders of Iraq. The number of countries where Arabic is the popular and official language now rivals the number of those that speak Spanish.

But outside of the countries that actually use the language in daily intercourse, the influence of Arabic is felt in all those lands (and they are even more numerous) where there are Moslems. For Arabic is the sacred, liturgical language of Islam, the language in which the Koran is read and prayers to God (Allah) are voiced. The only parallel of this phenomenon that comes to mind is the influence exerted by Latin in all western Christian lands, both the ones that remained Roman Catholic and the ones that turned to Protestantism, for by the time of the Reformation most of the linguistic penetration of Latin had already been effected.

This means that the Arabic language has infiltrated to a remarkable degree the African Negro languages south of the Sahara, the tongues of central and southern Asia, from Turkey to western China, and from Iran and Afghanistan, across northern India, to Indonesia. It even came up through the Balkans, from Constantinople to the Danube. Moslem populations from Sarajevo in Yugoslavia and Tirana in Albania to Mombasa and Dar-es-Salaam ("the Abode of Peace") on the east African coast, and from Dakar to Jakarta listen reverently to the Arabic words of the muezzin intoned from the minaret tops.

There is a third form of penetration and infiltration effected by Arabic upon the rest of the world, and that appears in the many words and expressions, few of which are generally recognized as Arabic, that were spread by the Moors of Spain and the Saracens of Sicily, first to Spanish, Portuguese and Italian, later carried to French, German, English, to the point where many hundreds of originally Arabic words, including even slang expressions, are in common, everyday use among us.

Can a language as widespread as Arabic appear in a

single, unified, standardized form? Obviously not. Each
Arab country has its own vernacular. The popular tongue
of Morocco, that of Egypt, that of Saud's Arabia, differ to
approximately the same extent as Brooklynese, the Scots
Lowland dialect, and the popular language of Australia.
But Arabic enjoys one advantage that English does not
have. There is a standardized Classical Arabic (a modernized version of the Arabic of the Koran), which is generally
used in writing, in exalted speech, and in communications
between one part and another of the vast Arab world. Classical Arabic is the rallying point for Arab unity. Without it,
the Arab nations would have disintegrated, linguistically
and culturally, as did the Romance countries after the fall
of the Roman Empire.

There are other ways in which Arabic has displayed its
powers of penetration and adaptation. Malta, for many
years under Arab rule, has evolved a recognized language,
Maltese, which is a blend of Arabic and Italian, with Arabic
predominating. In the Middle Ages, the Mediterranean
world carried on its cultural and commercial activities in
Lingua Franca (the name is variously interpreted as meaning "free language" or "language of the Franks"; the Franks
or French were to the Arabs the epitome of the non-Islamic
world, which they knew collectively as "Feringhistan," "the
land of the Franks"). Lingua Franca was, like Maltese, a
hybrid consisting mainly of Arabic and Italian; but elements from other Mediterranean languages, French, Spanish, Greek, went into the melting-pot. It eventually died
away, but not until Molière had given samples of it in his
Bourgeois Gentilhomme.

It would be a fatal mistake to view Arabic as a "primitive," "undeveloped" language, or to place its speakers in
the same category with some of the other nations that are
now emerging out of the wreckage of nineteenth-century
colonialism. The speakers, though they may have lagged
somewhat behind in the technical civilization which, after
all, only began to evolve in the course of the last three centuries, are the proud heirs of a culture which in the Middle
Ages was more advanced, scientifically and in many other
respects, than that of medieval Europe. There is nothing
whatsoever to keep them, once they have taken a few giant

steps in some technical fields, from resuming their old and rightful place in the very forefront of world civilization. A group that has given the West most of its notions about mathematics, chemistry and astronomy can certainly get back into stride in the fields of medicine, engineering, even nuclear physics. The people who first introduced public street lighting to the West, and constructed such jewels of architecture as the Alhambra and the Mosque of Cordova need not live forever in tents and kasbahs. A trading people that brought to Europe the paper of China, the citrus fruits of India, the coffee of Abyssinia, can still be in the forefront of modern industry and business. The Arabs do not have to prove themselves, as do other fledgling nations. They have already shown their capacity to fit into a modern picture.

As for their language, it is one of the most venerable and well-developed on earth, with family ramifications that link it directly with the Hebrew and Aramaic of our own Scriptures, the tongues of the Assyrians, Babylonians, Phoenicians and Carthaginians, and indirectly with that of the ancient Egyptians.

Among modern spoken languages, Arabic's closest tie is with Hebrew, the reborn language of Israel. The words and structures of one language are as easily recognizable in the other as if one were comparing two Romance tongues, like Italian and Spanish. There is also a more remote link with the leading tongue of Ethiopia, Amharic, whose speakers apparently crossed the Red Sea from southern Arabia in distant times.

There is also a hint, from time to time, that there may be an ultimate kinship between Semitic languages like Hebrew and Arabic and the Indo-European tongues of the West, English and German and Romance and Slavic. Occasional vocabulary similarities appear in words not seemingly borrowed, like the English *earth* and the Arabic *arth* (Hebrew *erets*), or the Arabic *sitta* (Hebrew *shishsha*) that sounds like and means *six*. There is also similarity in the way both Semitic and Indo-European tongues divide up and handle their parts of speech (nouns, verbs, adjectives, etc.). The older Indo-European languages, like Sanskrit and Greek, share with the Semitic languages a dual number in addition to a singular and a plural. The Romance languages, like the Semitic, treat all their nouns as either masculine or feminine, with only remnants of ancient neuters. But we need more evidence than we already have before we can accept the link as established.

With or without the link, there is the vast contribution that the Semitic languages, and particularly Arabic, have made to our own. This contribution was made in historical times, and its details are clear and well-established.

Arabic, in its Classical form, was originally the language of southern Arabia. About the year A.D. 600, the prophet Mohammed began to preach his doctrine of a single God to a south Arabian population that worshiped many idols. The principle of a single God had been established long before by the Hebrews, another Semitic people. Appropriated now by the Arabs, who were in a mood for nationalistic expansion, it was quickly carried by force of arms into the lands of the Near East, then into Persia, Egypt and North Africa. North African Christianity was submerged, and the Berber populations of the Mediterranean's south shore merged with the Arab conquerors. In 711 a mixed force of Arabs and Berbers swept across the Straits of Gibraltar into Spain, where a Visigothic monarchy had held sway since the fall of the Roman Empire almost three hundred years before. In a few decades, the Moslem North African Moors had extended their power to the Cantabrian Mountains in the extreme north of the Iberian peninsula, where a long thin line of Christian Visigoths held them at bay. Baffled in their attempt to subjugate the entire Peninsula, the Moors swept on around the pockets of northern resistance, across the Pyrenees, and into France. Had they succeeded in overwhelming the Frankish kingdom as they had overwhelmed the Visigothic, they would have been masters of Europe. Rome, the Papacy and Christianity would have fallen, and we who today speak languages that stem wholly or partly from Latin would be speaking a variant of Arabic and worshipping God under the name of Allah.

But the Franks, led by Charles the Hammer, halted the Moors and drove them back across the Pyrenees. Now began that strange process of togetherness between Moors and Christians in the Spanish peninsula that the Spaniards have oversimplified by calling it the *Reconquista*. It lasted over seven centuries, and ended with the expulsion of the last Moors from Granada in 1492, the year of America's discovery.

In the portions of the peninsula held by them, the Moors, speaking Arabic and worshipping God under the name of Allah, proved generally tolerant of both the Christian populations they had conquered and the Jews who had accompanied them across the Straits from North Africa. Plenty of border warfare went on between them and the Christian principalities of the north that were eventually to evolve into the kingdoms of Castile, León and Aragón and the principality of Portugal, but it was a strange form of warfare, with the lines not clearly drawn, and frequent coalitions of Christians and Moors against other Christians and Moors.

During the entire seven hundred year period, the Moors of Spain poured out their treasure of scientific, architectural and commercial lore to the populations that were mingled with their own and to the French across the Pyrenees. At the same time, other Arabic-speaking Saracens, who had made themselves masters of Sicily in 829, gave out their culture to the Sicilians and Italians, while the Crusades to the Holy Land that began about the end of the eleventh century brought Europeans and Arabs more and more into contact. The total result of these activities was a raising of European standards of living, a broadening of European culture, an increase in trade, as well as in the spirit of curiosity and scientific research. The Arabs were the vehicle not merely for their own civilization, but for a good deal of the Greek culture that had been lost to western Europe in the stormy early Middle Ages, and for the culture of the Far East with which they were in contact. Words, symbolical of the objects they betokened, began to pour in great numbers into the languages of the West; first of all, the two languages of the great Iberian symbiosis, Spanish and Portuguese; secondly, the Sicilian dialect which was the first truly literary form of Italian; then, indirectly, and by a process of loan-words, the other great languages of western Europe, French and German and English.

If we examine one of the comprehensive etymological dictionaries, we shall find at least five hundred Arabic roots that appear in English everyday words; another five hundred, in round numbers, were carried by the Arabs from the tongues of the East to those of the West.

We can begin with those words which are felt to be Arabic because they deal with things Arabic: *Islam* ("submission" to the will of God), and *Moslem*, from the same root; *salaam* ("peace"; used as a form of greeting, and still from the same root: Semitic roots normally consist of three consonants, with the vowels playing a secondary role that fixes the meaning; SaLaMa, "submission," "surrender," "peace," is the common element in all three words; the initial *m* in *Moslem* is a collective prefix; the Hebrew *shalom* is from the identical Semitic root).

Kasbah (citadel), referring to the native quarter of Algiers, has been much in the news; but at an even earlier date it had been popularized by Charles Boyer's softly whispered: "Hedy, come weez me to ze Kasbah!"

Koran (more properly spelled *Qur'ān*, from a root QaRaA that means "to read," almost exactly like our Scriptures, "those things which are written"), and *Allah* (the same Semitic root for "God" that appears in the Hebrew *El* and the -*el* suffix of Babel, Daniel, Raphael, etc.) are two religious terms. Another is the Mohammedan month of *Ramadan*, "the hot month," when all true believers fast every day from sunrise to sunset, not permitting themselves even a swallow of water.

Various civil and religious dignitaries are represented by *caliph, muezzin, imam, sultan, emir, vizier.* The Caliph is the "successor" (of Mohammed), the spiritual and temporal leader of all the faithful. The muezzin is the "crier," who summons the faithful to prayer from the top of the minaret. An imam ("one who stands before the people") is a priest, though the title may also be bestowed upon the Caliph himself. *Sultan* comes from a root SaLaTa, meaning "dominion," and represents more properly the temporal power. An *emir* or *ameer* ("one who gives orders") is a military commander; special interest is attached to the word because in the form *amīr al gaish*, "commander of the army," it gives rise to *admiral*, whom we, along with other Western nations, have restricted to a purely naval function. A vizier, or *wazīr*, starts out by being a bearer of burdens, weight, sin, a porter, but then his function is transferred to that of a carrier of the burdens of state, and he becomes a high official indeed. Strangely, in both Spanish and Italian, he is lowered again in function to the point where he becomes the Spanish *alguacil*, "sheriff" or "marshal," and the Italian *aguzzino*, "hangman's assistant." *Mufti* ("he who solves problems") is in origin a court attendant, but he wears a special garb which is nonmilitary; the word is appropriated by the British to mean "civilian dress."

The ranks of Arab officialdom are rounded out by two more picturesque terms, *sheik* and *sherif*. The first, much to the disillusionment of Valentino fans, literally means "old man"; but then, so do the Spanish *señor*, the Italian *signore*, the French *seigneur* or *sieur* (*monsieur* is etymologically "my old man"), even English *sir* and *sire*. After all, the cult of youth is a modern phenomenon; at the time when these words and meanings were evolved, to call a man one's *senior* was an indication of respect.

There are two *sheriffs* in English. One is the Anglo-Saxon *scīr gerēfa*, "shire reeve," who turns into the strong arm of the law. The other, spelled with a single *f*, is the Arabic *sharīf*, "noble." The term was originally applied to descendants of Mohammed by Fatima, later extended to betoken high Moslem dignitaries.

Another sprinkling of words taken at random, of whose Arabic origin everyone is reasonably sure: *mosque* (the Arabic *masjid*, from the root of SaJaDa, "to adore"); *minaret* (*manārat;* the root word is *nār*, "light," and the *m*- or *ma*- prefix, which is collective in some words, is here indicative of a place (as also in *mosque*). *Houri* is a white-skinned, black-eyed woman; the Moslem paradise is peopled by such, to minister unto the faithful, particularly those who have died in battle. *Hegira*, which in New York newspaper slang used to mean "moving day" back in the days when apartments were abundant, cheap, and not tied down by three-year leases, means "flight," and is applied to the Prophet's quick departure from Mecca in 622. *Harem* comes from a word that means "forbidden," "sacred," "taboo." Then there is *Kismet*, the equivalent of our *fate* or *destiny*, from a root QaSaMa that means "portion," "lot." *Fez*, beloved headgear of our fraternal orders, is the name of the capital of Morocco, where it seems to have originated, replacing the older turban, which is a Turkish, not an Arabic, word.

Now we come to words which are not generally suspected of being Arabic in origin. Here are the names of plants and foods and drinks: *sumac* and *cotton* and *saffron* and *coffee* (this comes to us, along with the beverage, straight from the Arabs; but they may perhaps have taken their *qahwa* from the name of the Ethiopian province of Kaffa, where the coffee berry probably originated; the Ethiopians chewed it; the Arabs conceived the brilliant idea of roasting and grinding the bean, then preparing an infusion; whether your morning beverage is coffee, tea or cocoa, it is non-Western in origin; our medieval ancestors dunked their morning bread in either milk or wine; the Arabs brought us coffee, the Chinese tea, the Mexican Aztecs cocoa and chocolate).

Saffron, artichokes and *spinach* come to us from the Arabs, along with the words. *Candy* is the Arabic *qand,* "cane sugar." The *lemon* is Arabic; the *tangerine,* as its name implies, comes from Tangier in North Africa; the *tamarind* is the Arabic *tamr hindi,* or "Indian date." *Syrup* and *sherbet* are two English variants of the same Arabic word, *sharbah* or *sharab,* from a root that means "to drink." There are names of animals, like the *giraffe* and the *gazelle;* names of winds, like the *sirocco* (Arabic *sharq,* "east") and the *simoon* (Arabic *simūm,* "poisons"); a few mythological names, like *Shaitan* or *Satan* (the latter is the Hebrew form); *ghoul* (this comes from a root that means "to seize"); and the *jinni* of Aladdin's bottle, whom we have anglicized into *genie.*

Two strange words are *Bedouin* and *assassin.* Both show a typical Arabic *-in* plural (the Hebrew equivalent is the *-im* of *Elohim, cherubim, seraphim*), which we pluralize all over again when we say *Bedouins* and *assassins.* The *bedawi* is a "desert dweller," and the *hashishi* a hashish eater; the name was given to a fanatical sect that fought the Crusaders, using commando tactics while under the influence of a drug obtained from hemp. The *dragoman* who guides you around the Pyramids and the Sphinx is the Arabic *tarjuman,* from the root of TaRJaMa, "to interpret"; he got into the Western languages quite early, for we find *drogueman* already used in thirteenth-century French (Hebrew *targūm,* "interpretation," is from the same root).

The color *scarlet* comes from Arabic; so does *arsenal,* which in the original means "house of industry" (*dār as-sina'ah*). *Sofa* and *alcove* (whose original meaning is "arch"), *ream* (*rizma,* "bundle") and *mattress* (from *matrah,* "a place of laying") come from the Arabs. So do *lute* (originally *al-ūd,* "piece of wood"), *mohair, jar, carafe, mask* and *mascara* (both of these come from a word meaning "buffoon"), *hazard,* and *tariff* (originally a "notice").

The story of *magazine* is an interesting one. It starts with the Arabic *makhzan,* "warehouse," which Spanish takes with the article *al* and turns into *almacén.* But the plural of *makhzan* is *makhāzin,* and this is the form that gets into Italian, French and, eventually, English. The original meaning of "warehouse," "storehouse," "store" continues in all three languages (we even speak of the magazine of a rifle, and the French of the *grands magasins* of Paris). Then, in eighteenth-century England, there arose a periodical that called itself *The Gentleman's Magazine,* in the same way in which we might speak of a "storehouse of information." The term not only stuck, but spread, until it covered a variety of periodicals and became a generic name for them, a usage which appears only in English.

The truly startling contribution of Arabic to the Western languages consists of scientific terms, particularly in three fields, chemistry, mathematics and astronomy, which the medieval Arabs cultivated to a degree far outstripping anything known or done at that period in the Christian lands. Some of these terms had come into Arabic at an earlier period from Alexandrian Greek; but it was characteristic of the genius of the Arabs to appropriate elements of Western culture, then develop them far beyond the stage where they had picked them up, and lastly to return them gracefully, vastly improved, to the people from whom they had gotten them.

There is no doubt that *alchemy,* from which *chemistry* is derived, both in etymology and in fact, comes from the *al-kīmiyā'* of the Arabs; does the Arabic word itself go back to the Greek *chymos,* "juice"? On this point the experts are uncertain. In like manner, *amalgam* and *amalgamate* definitely come to us from an Arabic word; it is possible that this in turn goes back to Greek *malagma,* "poultice." *Alembic* is Arabic; does it contain the Greek *ambix,* "cap of a still"? No Greek seems to be involved in *alcohol* (the Arabic original means "fine powder"; it is the West that transfers the term to "fine spirits"; in accordance with the Koran's prohibition, Moslems are not supposed to

use liquor in any form, though some of the more progressive
modern ones among them justify an occasional sip of *raki*
or *'araq* on the ground that the Koran mentions only wine).
There is no Greek in *amber*, or in *soda* (the Arabic original
means "headache"), or in *alkali* ("ashes" in Arabic).

Algebra is *al-jabr*, from the root of *jabara*, "to put together." Both *cipher* and *zero* come from the same word,
sifr, "empty" (mathematicians will recall that it is the use
of the zero symbol that confers upon Arabic numerals their
enormous advantage over the Roman system). *Algorism*
comes from a proper name, that of al-Kuwarizmi, a ninth-
century Arab mathematician. *Caliper* and *caliber* both come
from *qālib*, "form" or "mold."

Half our astronomical terms are of Arabic origin. *Almanac*
represents the Arabic word for "climate." *Zenith* and *nadir*
are both Arabic. Then there are the names of constellations,
as often Arabic as Greek: Cepheus-al-Multahib, "the flaming one"; Zuben-al-Genubi and Zuben-al-Shamali, "the
north claw" and "the south claw"; Alkaid, "the chief";
Algol, "the ghoul"; Rigel, "the foot"; Aldebaran, "the fol-
lower" (it follows the Pleiades); Deneb, whose full Arabic
form is *Dhanab ad-Da-jājah*, "the tail of the hen." There
are Akrab and Betelgeuse and Vega, where we have taken
only the last part of the Arabic name, *an-Nasr al-Waqi*,
"the falling vulture." The Arabs viewed the Great Dipper
as a funeral procession, so the North Star is *Banāt an-
Na'ash*, "the coffin girls."

Strangely enough, the Western languages even have slang
words and expressions that come from Arabic. The slangy
British *bint* for "girl" is straight Arabic, brought in by those
colonial troops whose exploits Kipling describes so well. *So
long* is the Malay *salang*, but that in turn comes from
Arabic *salaam*. *Faker* is the Arabic *faqīr*, "poor man" (the
beggar who performs magic tricks, such as causing a rope
to stand on end, climbing up it, and vanishing); from *faker*,
American English, by the process known as back-formation,
has derived *fake*.

In French slang, there is the name for a hangover, or the
blues (*j'ai le cafard*), also used for a cockroach, and its
feminine *la cafarde*, applied to the moon; both are Arabic
for "infidel," the same word that moving in another direction

gives rise to Kaffir, the name of a South African tribe. A strange French slang expression, meaning "I don't give a damn about it," is *"je m'en moque comme de l'an quarante"*; on the face, this would seem to mean "I laugh at it as I do at the year forty," and makes no sense at all, until we are told that *l'an quarante* is a corruption of *l'Alcoran*, the Koran; a Christian infidel would quite naturally laugh at the Koran.

The Spanish slang term that corresponds to our *jalopy* is *matraca*, Arabic for "hammer." The Italian slang for "dope," "jerk," is *mammalucco*, which goes back to *Mamluk*, the bodyguards of the Egyptian Sultan, who were supposed to be long on brawn, but short on brains. *Salamelècco* is Italian half-slang for a lot of bowing and scraping; it is simply the Arabic greeting *salaam aleikum*, "peace to you," and has absolutely nothing to do with *salami*.

Second in importance only to the words that Arabic has given us directly are those words which Arabic has transmitted to us from other languages. We have seen this transmission process at work in the case of Greek words, often of a chemical nature. Here are a few more: *carat* is the Arabic *qīrāt*, but Arabic takes the word from the Greek *karation; elixir* is *al-iksīr*, but this goes back to Greek *xerion*, "dry"; *talisman* comes through Arabic from Greek *telesma*, "payment"; *natrium*, the scientific name for sodium, is Arabic *natrūn* and Greek *nitron*.

The Arabs were in touch with India during the Middle Ages, and the Westerners were not. Hence, many words from Sanskrit, the ancient tongue of India, were brought in by the Arabs: *sugar, orange, crimson, carmine*. The last has a curious Western parallel: the Arabic form is *qirmiz*, and the original Sanskrit has *krmi*, "worm" (worms are normally reddish in color); the Romans in the West had the same idea; their word for "worm" was *vermis*, and *vermiculum* was a "little worm"; its reddish color gives rise to *vermilion*.

Arabic contacts with the Persians gave us many Persian words in Arabic form: the *julep* of the South, the *tasse* of *demi-tasse, borax, lilac, azure, jasmine, divan*, and a few chess terms, notably *rook, check* and *mate*. *Check* goes on to bigger and better uses, notably in finance, whether you spell it *check* or *cheque* (and note the British *exchequer*);

the word is originally the Persian *shah*, "king," and *check-mate* (*shah mawt*) means "the king is dead." The word that gets to us only in the form *divan*, a "couch," but also a "council of state" where the participants sit on divans, has more extensive uses in the Romance languages, where it means "custom-house," "customs" as well (an extension of the power of the state council: French *douane*, Spanish *aduana*, Italian *dogana*).

Arabic, finally, brings us the Malay *camphor* and the Hindustani *nabob*, originally "governor" in plural form.

But it is difficult to place boundaries on Arabic infiltration and influence. They show up where you least expect them. The Swahili of East Africa is the Arabic *sāhil*, "coast," and simply means "the language of the coast." In Swahili we find such words as *simba*, "lion" and *safari*, "hunting expedition." Both are Arabic. *Simba*, in fact, appears everywhere through the Orient in the form of *singh;* Singapore is "lion-city," with an Arabic lion and a Sanskrit city; and the name of Ceylon was originally Sindhalawipa, "lion island"; the predominant language there is still Singhalese, the "tongue of lions."

Farther south in Africa we find not only the Kaffirs, who were dubbed "infidels" by the Arabs, but a Zulu weapon that will be remembered by those older generation readers who used to be entranced by the works of H. Rider Haggard, the *assegai*. This is the Portuguese *azagaia*, drawn from the Berber-Arabic. Italian has the word in the form *zagaglia*, a "throwing spear."

The Arabic *aljuba*, "garment," gives rise to French *jupe*, *jupon*, "skirt," and to Italian *giubba*, "coat" (the most famous air in *Pagliacci* is *Vesti la Giubba*, "Put on your coat"). The Arabic *kuffiyah* shows up in Italian *cuffia* and in French *coiffe*, *coiffeur* and *coiffure*, all of which we use in our better beauty salons, along with *coif* (here, however, there is an opposing theory to the effect that these words may be of Germanic origin). Arabic *sikkah*, "stamp," "die," goes into the Italian *zecca*, "mint" (for the coining of money), then into *zecchino*, which gives us *sequin*. Arabic *tunbur* gives us *tambour, tabor, tambourine*, even the Yugoslav *tamburitsa*, which is not a drum at all, but a stringed instrument.

All who have studied Spanish or Portuguese know to what extent these languages are infiltrated by Arabic. If you go through the *al-* section of a Spanish or Portuguese dictionary, you will find it tremendously lengthy and tremendously Arabic. Here are *alacrán*, "scorpion," *aldea*, "village," *alfiler*, "pin" (the original Arabic word means "thorn"), *alcazaba*, "fortress," *albañil*, "mason." There is *alcalde*, "mayor," with a variant *alcaide* (the root is *qāda*, "to judge, decide").

Sometimes the Arabic *al-* is disguised, as in *adobe*, which gets very much into the English of the Southwest, or *azulejo*, "tile" and *azotea*, "flat roof." The disguised *al-* gets also into *aceite*, "oil," *ataúd*, "winding-sheet," *ahorrar*, "to save." The Spaniards apparently got the idea of "saddlebags" from the Arabs (*alforja*), along with the waterwheel (*noria*). *Marrano*, a Moslem or Jew converted to Christianity, is the Arabic *muharram*. The word the Spaniards use for "so-and-so," "John Doe," is the Arabic *fulano*. Even the Spanish expression of wishful thinking, *ojalá*, is the Arabic *wa shā' Allah*.

Both Spanish and Portuguese take their words for "up to," "as far as," "until" (*hasta, até*) from Arabic *hatta*. When you cross the Spanish-Portuguese border, you get two customhouses with different Arabic names, *aduana* on the Spanish side (our old friend *divan*) and *alfândega* on the Portuguese (this is Arabic *fondak*, "storehouse"). A tailor is *sastre* on the Spanish side (Latin *sartor*), but on the Portuguese side he is *alfaiate*, from Arabic *al-haiate*. Medieval Spain gives us the names of coins like the *maravedí*, so called because it was originally put out by the Almoravid Moorish dynasty, and *Cid*, which is the Arabic *sayyid*, "lord" (they will still address you as *Sayyid, Said, Sidi* in Arabic countries if your behavior warrants it, and the *sahib* of India is the same word).

Then there are those strange words which Arabic took from Greek or Latin, modified to suit its own taste, then passed on to the Spaniards who were the direct descendants of Latin speakers, and the Spaniards in turn to us. *Apricot* starts out as the Latin *praecoquum*, "early-ripe" ("pre-cooked" would be even more etymological). The Arabs turn this into *al-barqūq*, the Spaniards take the word from them as *albaricoque*, the French as *abricot*, and you can guess the rest. The Spanish word for "rice," *arroz*, appears in the name of that delectable dish, *arroz con pollo;* it was taken by the Spaniards from the Arabs, but the Arabs had previously taken it from Greek *oryza.* One Spanish word that everyone assumes must be of Arabic origin is *alcázar* (please don't mispronounce it; put the stress on the *second a*). The Alcázar of Toledo became famous for its heroic resistance during the Spanish Civil War, but it is only one of many *alcázares* ("palace-fortresses") that dot the Spanish landscape. What happened was that the Arabs took the Latin *castrum* (the same word that gives us all our place-names in *-chester, -cester* and *-caster*), turned it into *qasr,* prefixed their article *al-,* and handed it back as *alcázar* to the unsuspecting Spaniards, who already had *Castro* directly from the Latin word. Incidentally, they did the same thing to the Sicilians, whose beautiful Palermo drive, the Cassaro, is the Arabic *qasr* taken from Latin *castrum.* On the other hand, the *palatium* of the Romans became the Arabic *balat,* restricted in meaning to "royal palace."

The place-names of Spain, Portugal, and the Latin countries of America have almost as much Arabic in them as they have Latin. To begin with, all those names that start with *Guad-* (Guadalajara, Guadalupe, Guadarrama, Guadalquivir) represent the Arabic *wad* or *wadi,* "river," "stream"; Guadalquivir, for instance, is *Wadi al-kibīr,* "the big river"; its literal translation from Arabic to Spanish is Río Grande. Andalusia is the *al-Andaluz* of the Arabs, though they may have taken it from the name of the Vandals, a Germanic tribe that invaded Spain before the Visigoths. Calatayud is *qal'at Ayyūb,* the "citadel of Job," and the same "citadel" root appears in Alcalá, of which there are at least half a dozen in Spain alone (Alcalá de Henares, "The city of haystacks," for instance). The old Arabian town of Medina finds its name repeated in almost as many Spanish town names (Medina del Campo, Medina Coeli). Alcántara is "the bridge." The Ramblas of Barcelona are the Arabic "sands," and the word appears again in Guadarrama, the mountain chain north of Madrid ("Sandy River"). Granada's lovely Alhambra is *al-hamrā',* "the red house," and the Generalife gardens that lie beside it are *Jannāt al-'Arif,* the "gardens of the scholar." Gibraltar is *Jebel Tarik,* the "Mountain of Tarik," the one-eyed Moorish leader who led the invasion into Visigothic Spain in 711. The entire south-ernmost province of Portugal is named Algarve, "the West" (interestingly, Morocco's Arabic name, *Maghreb,* is the same word, with the *ma-* prefix that denotes either collectiv-ity or place). *Arab* itself means "westerner," and *Europe* may be a Greek modification of the same Semitic "west" root.

Sicily, too, where the Saracens ruled for two centuries, has plenty of Arabic in its place-names: Caltanisetta, Calta-girone, Calatafiuri, all show the Arabic *qal'at.* Sometimes the names are curiously combined and repeated. Mongibello is "mountain-mountain" (first the Latin *mons,* then the Arabic *jebel*); Gibilrossa is "red mountain," but the moun-tain is Arabic, the red is Italian. The first part of Regalbuto may fool the Italians into thinking it means "royal," but it is the Arabic *rigl* or *rijl,* "foot." And the Sicilians have all sorts of widespread family names, like Mugavero and Morabito, that go back to the Arabs (the first is *mugawir,* "skirmisher," "warrior"; the second is *murābit,* "hermit," seemingly the same root that gives rise to the Almoravid dynasty of Spanish Moors).

Italian takes from Arabic its word for "eggplant" (*melan-zana*); "go-between" (*sensale*); "aplenty" (*bizzeffe*); "note-book" (*taccuino*); "burden" (*fardello*); and numerous meas-ures (*cantaro, quintale, tomolo, rotolo,* Sicilian *cafisu*). For "to look," continental Italy says *guardare,* using the same Germanic word that gives us *guard* and *ward;* but Sicily uses the Arabic *taliari.*

It is remarkable what different Western languages will do with the same Arabic word. Arabic *zebīb* means "raisin"; it gets into Italian as *zibibbo,* with the same meaning; Portu-guese, however, gives it the form *acepipes* and turns its meaning into "hors-d'oeuvres"; anyone who has had the good fortune to partake of Portuguese *acepipes* knows that they consist of far more than raisins.

What sort of a language is this Arabic that has traveled so far and wide over the earth? To a Western ear, it is a language of strange, unfamiliar, throaty sounds. Far more conservative than its sister tongue Hebrew, Arabic has re-tained all of the old, harsh Semitic consonants, including three varieties of *h* (h, ḥ, kh in transcription; the first is

more or less like the *h* of English, the second far more vigorous, but without rasping, the third practically the *ach*-sound of German). There is also the catch in the voice, or glottal stop ('), which in the Semitic scheme is a true consonant, in fact, the first letter of the alphabet (we get it in English between the two *o*'s of coordinate). Then there is a constriction of the pharynx accompanied by vibration of the vocal cords, somewhat like a retching sound, which must be heard to be properly reproduced (for this, there is a special symbol in the International Phonetic Alphabet; we may use *&* to transcribe it). There is a gargling sound (gh), which does not differ too much from a Parisian uvular *r*. There are "emphatic" consonants (*ṭ, ḍ, ṣ, ẓ*), pronounced with the blade of the tongue pressed firmly against the palate. There is a sh, and another consonant which in some parts of the Arab world is like the *j* of *jeer,* in others like the *g* of *get.* There is a firm distinction between k and q (the latter is to be pronounced far back in the throat, even farther back than the English *k* of *milk;* it is a standard joke among Arabs that Europeans are forever mixing "heart" and "dog": *qalb* and *kalb*). More or less as in English are b, t, z, r, s, d, f, l, m, n, y, w.

The vowels in the Semitic languages take a back seat. They are used as fill-ins for the consonants, which provide the true backbone of the word. Here, for example, is the Semitic root k-t-b, which has to do with writing: *kataba* is "he wrote," *kutiba* means "it has been written," *yaktubu* is "he will write," *'aktaba* is "he made someone write," *kitābun* is "writing" or "book," *kātibun* is "writer," *katbun* is "the act of writing." It is no wonder that the Semitic alphabets, such as Arabic or Hebrew, make no provision for vowels, which are supplied instinctively in speaking and appear in writing only occasionally (Hebrew has vowel-points, which appear only in late writings; Arabic has three vowel symbols, u, a, i, written above or below the line, which may or may not be used, as the writer sees fit). A typical bit of Arabic script, which runs, like Hebrew, from right to left, would be paralleled if we were to write an English sentence this way: "the mn wnt dwn th strt"; you would have to practice a while to figure that this reads "the man went down the street." The Arabs are used to it; still, some of them say that the reason why the reader sings

the Koran in a slow chant is because he is trying to figure out the proper vowels that go into the written text from which he is reading. Speed reading is definitely not indicated for Arabic. It may also be remarked that this indefiniteness about the vowels is reflected in the spoken varieties. The definite article should be *al;* but don't be surprised if it sounds like *il* or *el* or even just *l* in the mouth of an Arabic speaker. What we are giving in the phrases that follow is a transcription. You may even recognize from it the sounds of some utterances. But with Arabic, even more than with other languages, the only proper way to acquire the sounds is to listen to a native speaker or a recording of one.

Like English *the,* Arabic *al* does service for all numbers and genders. Of the latter there are only two in colloquial Arabic, masculine and feminine. Feminine nouns often, but by no means invariably, end in -*a,* and form the plural in -*āt* (sā&a, "watch," sā&āt, "watches"). Adjectives used as nouns have a plural in -*īn,* like the *hashishīn* that gives us "assassin," but most masculine nouns change the vowel pattern in the word: *kitāb,* "book," becomes *kutub* in the plural; *kalb,* "dog," becomes *kilāb.* Some feminine nouns do the same thing: *bint,* "girl," becomes *banāt,* "girls." This reminds us a bit of our *foot-feet, mouse-mice, brother-brethren.*

Adjectives follow their nouns, agree with them, and repeat the article (*al kitāb al kabīr,* "the big book"; *al kutub al kabīra,* "the big books"). If you omit the second article, the phrase means "the book is big." If two nouns are used in succession, the first without, the second with the article, the second indicates the possessor: *kitāb al bint,* "the book *of* the girl."

Arabic verbs, like English, have a strong and a weak conjugation. The former changes the vowel from present to past, like our *see-saw, write-wrote;* the latter does not change the vowel, but adds prefixes and suffixes, like our *love-loved.* Arabic makes special provision for a feminine as well as a masculine "you" (*katabta,* "you, a man, wrote," but *katabti,* "you, a woman, wrote"). *Ma* before the verb serves to make the sentence negative (*ma katab,* "he did not write").

The structure and imagery of Arabic may be gleaned from a few phrases that the tourist may feel tempted to try in

streets or restaurants: *Salām aleikum,* "peace to you," a general term of greeting; reply: *Aleikum salām,* "and to you, peace."

Lēltāk sa&īda is "good evening" (the literal meaning is "evening-your happy"; if you are speaking to a woman, the "your" becomes feminine, and the phrase is *lēltik sa&īda*).

"Thank you" is *kattar khērak* ("may He [Allah] multiply your prosperity").

"Please" is *min faḍlak,* "from your generosity."

"You are welcome," the favorite Arabic phrase of hospitality, is *'ahlan wa sahlan.* These are two adverbs connected by "and"; the first means "family-like," the second "like a plain or meadow." The general idea is "We consider you a member of our family, and we assure you that you will walk in our home as if it were a plain or meadow; no obstacles to stop you, no mountains to climb; every spot in it is smooth; go ahead in any direction."

"Where?", "Where is?", "Where are?" is *fēn?*

"Yes" is *na&am* or *aiwa.*

"No" is *la;* this may be repeated many times, leading to confusion with a similar French usage that does *not* have a negative meaning; also, it may be accompanied by a clucking of the tongue.

"How are you?" is *keefak* (but to a woman, *keefik;* and to more than one person, *keefkum*).

"Very well" is *kuwayyis.*

"How much is it?" – *bi kām da?*

"To the right" – *&al yimīn* (this is the same word as Yemen, which to an inhabitant of North Africa or the Near East is the country on your right as you face Mecca to pray).

"To the left" – *&ash shimāl.*

"Straight ahead" – *&ala ṭūl.*

"What is your name?" *'ismak ēh?* ("name-your what?"; speaking to a woman, the "your" will have to change: *'ismik ēh?*).

"My name is—" – *'ismi* ("name-my").

"Do you speak English (Arabic)?" – *'inta bititkallim al inglīz (al &arabi)?*"

"Very little" – *shuwayya.*

"Give me" – *'iṭīni.*
"Show me" – *warrīni,* or *rawwīni.*
"Tell me" – *'ulli.*
"Do you understand?" – *'inta fāhim?*
"I don't understand" – *ana mush fāhim.*
"Do you know?" – *'inta &arīf?*
"I don't know" – *ana mush &arīf.*
"Excuse me" – *wala mu'akhza.*
"What do you want?" – *'inta &āwiz ēh?*
"What is the matter?" – *gāra ēh?*
"Come in" – *khūsh!*
"Get out" – *imshi!*

To express sorrow or sympathy (English "What a pity!," "Too bad!") an Arab might use *ya khṣāra!* ("Oh, the pity!") ; he might also wax ironical and say *ya salām!* ("Oh! the peace!") ; and if you ask him how things are, and his reply is meant to be pessimistic, it might be *zayy iz zift,* "like tar," thus paralleling the popular Russian expression under the same circumstances, *kak sazhe byela,* "as soot is white."

"Excuse me," in the sense of "Gangway," "Let me through," is *rijlak,* literally, "Your foot!" (*rijlik* if you are addressing a woman, *rijlkum* if more than one person). This harks back to the days of camel-driving, when if a herd of camels passed through the street, bystanders had to be warned that their naked feet were in danger from the hoofs of the ponderous beasts.

There is humor in Arabic designations. The garbage collector, for instance, is called *abu l zibl,* "father of garbage." There is poetry in Arabic names. The name of Mohammed himself comes from the root *h-m-d,* "to praise," and might be translated as "the praiser"; variants of the same root are Hamid and Ahmed.

Many Arab first names are simple variants of familiar Hebrew ones: Yashaq (Isaac), "he laughs"; Yaqub (Jacob), "he holds heels"; Yashua (Joshua or Jesus), "he saves"; Yusuf (Joseph), "he increases." Note also Ibrahim and Musa, Arabic variants of Hebrew Abraham and Moses. More specifically Arabic is Gamāl (or Jamāl, or Gamīl), "beauty" or "handsome," the first name of the Egyptian leader, whose full second name is not simply Nasser (which would mean "victory-giver"), but Abd-el-Nasser, "servant of the Victory-Giver," who is Allah. *Abd-el,* "servant of the," is frequently combined with the innumerable attributes of Allah (Abd-el-Kassim, for instance, is "servant of the Destiny-Allotter"; *kassim* or *qassim* is from the same root as *qismet,* "fate").

The frequent ending *-din* in Arabic surnames means "faith," "religion." Saladin is "honoring the faith"; Nureddin is "light of religion." *Ibn* (or *ben,* or *bn*) is "son of," and introduces a patronymic, as does *ben* in Hebrew. Ibn Saud of Arabia has a name that means "son of happiness"; Beh Bella, the former Algerian leader, has a name which may mean "son of the beautiful woman," the second word being borrowed from Italian.

Among picturesque Arabic feminine names are, first and foremost, Fatima, "weaning mother," the name of Mohammed's daughter, whose descendants were indeed many, and at first were the only ones entitled to wear the green turban that later became characteristic of the *hadj,* or pilgrim to Mecca; Hoda, "guidance"; Najāh, "success"; Shamsa, "sun"; Laila, "night"; Badr, "moon"; Najma, "star"; Thurayya (one of the Pleiades, and the name of the former queen of Iran); Joza (Orion); and, of course, Jasmin or Jasmine. A woman is ceremoniously addressed as *Sayyida,* "lady," the feminine of *Sayyid,* "lord"; but this is colloquially shortened to *Sitt.* A young, unmarried woman may be addressed as *Ānisa,* "Miss," literally "one who makes your time pleasant," "enjoyable one," "entertainer" (the same root, apparently, gives rise to *anis* and *Tunis*). As with the French *fille,* the word *bint* does duty for both "daughter" and "girl." *Ya* is the sign of direct address (*Ya Sayyid,* "O Lord"; *ya bint,* "O maiden!").

A man may be addressed as *Sayyid* or *Effendi.* The latter, however, is Turkish and Greek in origin, and means "one who is literate." The Turks applied it to Westerners, who generally knew how to read and write, while the Persians used *Khodja* in the same fashion. Today, *Khodja Effendi* would be the equivalent of "Right Reverend," applied to a Christian priest or minister.

Among picturesque Arabic place names may be mentioned Iraq, "land of the sun," as opposed to Iran, "land of darkness"; Syria, "stony land"; Lebanon, "small milky one" (so called because of its snow-capped mountains). Algeria is *Al-Jazīr,* "land of the ebbing tide"; *al-Misr,* the modern name of the ancient land of Kem, or Egypt, means "border land," and comes from the same root as Hebrew *masor. Al-Maghreb,* or Morocco, like the Portuguese Algarve, is "the west."

Cities, too, have their stories. Damascus is "drinker of blood," for here Cain is supposed to have slain Abel. Cairo is *Al-Qāhirah,* "the victorious"; this is the poetic Arabic name for the planet Mars, which was in the ascendant when the city was founded. Interestingly, the Arab university of Al-Azhar bears the name of another planet, Venus or Zahra; but this was also the nickname of Mohammed's daughter Fatima.

The omens look bright for Arabic. As a great world tongue, with close to one hundred million speakers, now grouped into a dozen or more countries that have achieved full independence, Arabic is bound to succumb to the lure of standardization, which shows such powerful trends in the lands of the West. With the spreading of education and literacy, dialectal forms will tend to die out, and the language will once more become unified, as it was in the days of Mohammed. Its literature will again flourish, and it may easily become again a great tongue of science, as Arab universities spring up in the Arab countries.

There is one serious drawback to the spreading of literacy, and that is the complicated Arabic alphabet, where each letter has four possible forms, depending on whether it occurs in the initial, medial or final position, or alone. But powerful voices are already being raised on behalf of a simplification of the Arabic alphabet. A system with a single form for each letter has been devised and is being advocated by Dr. Alphonse Chaurize, editor of *Al-Isla'ah,* New York's Arabic-language weekly. It would safeguard Arab nationalism to the extent that it would retain a distinctive, though simplified, Arabic form. Others advocate romanization, a form of transcription such as the one we have used in this article. Turkish, which once used the Arabic alphabet, has done just that. Whichever way the reform goes, it is likely that a reform there will be. Even without such a reform, there is little doubt that the ancient Arab lands will flourish once more, and again offer their mighty contribution to the world's civilization, as they have done in the past.

chapter seventeen

the tongue of israel—hebrew

The language spoken in Israel today is an efficient implement for communicating. It is also a language of great literature. However, best-selling novelists in the American sense—works in the tradition of Norman Mailer, Henry Miller and James Jones—are unlikely to appear there. For, as not many people know, there are few curse words in the Hebrew language. Non-Israelis who know their Bible may challenge this on the ground that the Bible contains some picturesque and even blood-curdling curses. To those objectors I must quickly add that by curse words I refer to the equivalent of our four-letter words, which sometimes bring relief to a frustrated soul. Hebrew lacks these handy verbal lightning rods, so the angry Israeli finds relief by cursing in—of all languages—Arabic. The only explanation of this phenomenon lies in the similarity of the sounds of certain words in the two languages, both of which are Semitic. For example, mother: *emma* in Arabic, *íma* in Hebrew; father: *abu* in Arabic, *ába* in Hebrew; dog: *qalb* in Arabic, *qélev* in Hebrew. There are many other examples, but knowing just these three words equips a man for some very useful invective.

Parallel with the rapid development of their country, the Israelis are growing a healthy crop of slang. A pretty girl passing a gaggle (goggle?) of appreciative males would provoke such exclamations as *bómba!* (bomb) or *éizu hatihá!* (what a morsel). To have a good time is *laasót haím* (to make life). After getting a rough deal from someone, you say *hu dafák otí* (he knocked me).

Nor do many people know that the popular spoken tongue of Israel is called Ivrit, a language that is one of the oldest yet one of the most modern on earth. Basically, it is still the Hebrew of the Old Testament, the tongue that God is said to have conferred on man when He created him. The modern features are supplied by a superstructure of vocabulary and syntax added within the last 100 years, with the result that Ivrit is capable of serving the ultramodern civilization of the Israeli State today.

The linguistic history of the Jewish people is both fascinating and complicated. They started out around 4000 B.C. with a Semitic language of the same branch as the Akkadian spoken by the Babylonians and Assyrians and the Phoenician spoken in Tyre and Sidon, but during the Babylonian captivity they gave up their ancient tongue in favor of Aramaic also known as Chaldean or Syriac (another Semitic tongue very close to, but not identical with Hebrew), the common language of all the Semitic peoples of the Babylonian empire.

The Old Testament books of Ezra and Nehemiah, which deal with the post-captivity period, appear in Aramaic. So do most of the Talmuds. Aramaic was still the popular language of the Jews at the time of Christ, while Hebrew continued to be used as a liturgical and literary language. It was in this evolved Hebrew that the Mishna was written around 200 A.D., after the great dispersion, or Diaspora, that followed the fall of Jerusalem. With the Jews scattered over the shores of the Mediterranean, the more stable, traditional Hebrew endured in liturgical poetry, while the popular Aramaic was eventually lost as a regular language, surviving only, until this day, as a medium for Talmudic and Rabbinical writings. The smooth Mishnaic Hebrew prose, on the other hand, served as the basis for the renewal of modern Hebrew, some eighty years ago.

With the Moslem conquest of North Africa, the Jewish communities, which had been in close contact with the Greco-Latin civilization of the Roman Empire, found themselves almost engulfed in the huge Arabic wave that had issued from southern Arabia and overspread the former Roman provinces of Egypt, Libya, Numidia and Mauretania. Islam was perhaps closer to the Jewish tradition than any other faith, yet the Jews managed to retain their individuality, particularly in religion and language, even while mingling with the Arabs.

When the Arabic-speaking Moors crossed the Strait of Gibraltar and conquered most of Visigothic Spain early in the eighth century, many Jews accompanied them and made valid contributions to the Moorish civilization that flourished there until the end of the fifteenth century. They developed a richly varied Hebrew literature; their most brilliant poet, Juda Halévy, was described by Heine, seven hundred years later, as a "flaming pillar of song."

When the last Moors were driven from Spain by Ferdinand and Isabella, the Jews were expelled with them. By this time, the Spanish Jews had adopted as their popular tongue a form of medieval Spanish, though they wrote it with Hebrew characters. This Sephardic Jewish Spanish, known as Ladino, accompanied the Jews in their wanderings along the northern shores of the Mediterranean, to southern France, Italy, Greece and Turkey. Today the most numerous Ladino-speaking groups are in the Balkans, particularly around Salonika and Monastir, and in Istanbul, the former Constantinople. But though they spoke and even wrote in Ladino, their liturgical, intimate language continued to be Hebrew.

In the early Middle Ages, other Jewish groups had wandered off to northern Europe, especially France and Germany. In these countries, too, they adopted the languages of their Christian neighbors, and also wrote them with Hebrew characters. In their migrations from Germany to eastern Europe—Poland, Lithuania, Hungary, Rumania and Russia—they retained the medieval German dialects, later known as Yiddish. But they, too, kept their ancient Hebrew as a liturgical and intimate language.

The Ladino-speaking Sephardim and the Yiddish-speaking Ashkenazim formed the two predominant Jewish groups. As they continued to use their ancestral Hebrew and impart it to their children, interesting differences of pronunciation, vocabulary and syntactical usage appeared, which were later to be reconciled in the Ivrit of Israel. Many other minor varieties of Hebrew were and still are in existence: the Yemenite, the Moroccan, the Tunisian-Algerian, all of which have merged, with their speakers, into the unified tongue of Israel.

This was the background from which early Zionists, who believed in a return to the Promised Land and a reunification of all Jews, had to work. As practical men, they realized that a Jewish state without a unified language would quickly fall apart. So they began rebuilding Hebrew, the linguistic common denominator of all Jews, into a modern spoken tongue. Eliezer Ben Yehuda, one of the early Zionists, not only wrote a comprehensive dictionary of the Hebrew language, but made his wife learn Hebrew by speaking to her in no other tongue. Theodor Herzl, a Viennese journalist inspired by the Dreyfus case to seek a homeland where Jews would not be persecuted, was another apostle of Hebrew. Most instrumental, perhaps, in the Hebrew revival were the essayist Ahad Ha'am (Ascher Ginsburg) and the poet-novelist Hayim Nahman Bialik, whose writings in modern Hebrew showed what could be done with the ancient Biblical tongue in a contemporary setting.

Hebrew as a spoken tongue was therefore already clearly established when the Jews began to pour into Palestine in great numbers at the end of World War II, and the United Nations sanctioned the creation of a separate Jewish state in 1947. Actually, several Jewish communities had persisted throughout the centuries in various towns of Palestine. After a short expulsion, they returned to Jerusalem in 1267, never to leave it again. It is from Jerusalem's lively community that the first agricultural settlements went out in 1872. Since then, small groups of colonists kept on moving to Palestine, founding more and more agricultural settlements. In 1909, Jews from Jaffa founded Tel Aviv ("Hill of Spring"). The use of Ivrit as an all-purpose modern popular tongue is therefore not quite so recent as some would have it appear.

Despite the modern superstructure of Ivrit, its foundation is still the ancient language of the Bible. The alphabet, from which have stemmed the Greek, Roman and Cyrillic alphabets of the West, is still the same. The pronunciation leans to Sephardic rather than Ashkenazic standards, because the former are considered more in accord with the ancient (actually, the pronunciation of the Yemenite Jews may be even more traditional and conservative). The basic grammar and

vocabulary are still those of the Hebrew portions of the Old
Testament.

The Semitic languages, like the Indo-European, recognize
gender, number and verb conjugations. Nouns are either
masculine or feminine. The adjective follows the noun and
agrees with it in gender and number. There is a single form
of the definite article, *ha*, which corresponds to English "the."
We are familiar with it, even though unconsciously, because
we see it in words we know: *Habimáh*, "the stage," used as
the name of the Israeli national theater; *Hatikváh*, "The
Hope," the title of the Israeli national anthem; *Halévy*,
"the Levite," a Jewish family name. The use of this little
word *ha* covers several points of Hebrew syntax. *Séfer tov*
is "good book" or "a good book." If you want to say "the
good book," you must use *ha* before both noun and adjective:
haséfer hatóv. If you omit *ha* before the adjective (*haséfer
tov*), you get "the book is good." (Note that Hebrew has
three sounds resembling our *h*, and that they range from
throaty to light aspiration; for simplicity, only *h* is used
here.)

Masculine nouns and adjectives normally end in a consonant, and form the plural by adding *-im*. Feminine nouns
and adjectives normally end in *-ah*, with a shift to *-ot* in the
plural. "The good (male) student" is therefore *hatalmíd
hatóv*; "the good (male) students," *hatalmidím hatovím*.
"The good (girl) student" is *hatalmidáh hatováh;* "the good
(girl) students," *hatalmidót hatovót*.

The verb in the present tense is a mere participle, like our
"reading," and "to be" is understood with it. The Semitic
languages are very conscious of gender, and while they do
not distinguish between a masculine and a feminine "I" or
"we," they make a distinction between masculine and feminine "you," both in the singular and in the plural. "I" is
aní; "we" is *anáhnu*. "You," singular, is *atá* if masculine, *at*
if feminine. Plural "you" is *atém* if masculine, *atén* if feminine. "He" is *hu*, and "she" is *hi;* masculine "they" is *hem*,
feminine "they" is *hen*. A little word *et* is used as a sort of
accusative marker before a noun that has the definite article
and is the direct object of a verb. But both *et* and *ha* are
omitted if the meaning is "a" rather than "the."
Therefore:

"I am reading a book," *aní qoré séfer.*

"I am reading the book," *aní qoré et haséfer*.

"You (a man) are reading the book," *atá qoré et haséfer*.

"You (a woman) are reading the book," *at qorét et haséfer* (note the shift from *qoré* to *qorét* if the subject is feminine).

"You (men) are reading the book," *atém qorím et haséfer* (masculine plural verb).

"You (women) are reading the book," *atén qorót et haséfer* (feminine plural verb).

Like other Semitic languages, Hebrew works largely on roots consisting of three consonants, among which the vowels dart and play. Let us, for instance, take the concept of "writing." Its basic root is *K-T-V* (with the possibility that *K* may appear as *H*, and *V* as *B*). Observe: *KaTáV*, "he wrote"; *ekHTóV*, "I shall write"; *KaTuV*, "written"; *mikHTáV*, "letter"; *KeTóVet*, "address"; *hitKaTVút*, "correspondence"; *miHTaVá*, "writing desk."

The traditional Hebrew vocabulary is familiar to Bible readers. Such words as *Messiah, mammon; hosannah*, "save us"; *hallelujah*, "praise ye the Lord"; *sabbath, gehenna, sheol, Satan, Ba'al*, "Lord"; *Adonai, Elohim, Jahveh* or *Jehovah; shibboleth, shekel* (originally a measure of weight, later a coin); *rabbi* (*rab-i*, "master-my" or "lord-my"); the *abba* that gives us "abbey," and "abbot" (originally Aramaic, but used in modern Hebrew for "daddy"); and the mysterious *selah* of the Psalms, are all well known.

Those of us who live in contact with American Jewish communities have learned much more: *Yom Kippúr*, "Day of Atonement"; *Rosh Hashanáh*, "Head of the Year" (note that if two nouns appear in sequence, "of" is understood between them); *Yeshiváh* (literally "dwelling"; from the same *Y-SH-V* root as *yishúv*, "settlement"); *barúch*, "blessed"; *B'nai B'rith*, "Sons of Covenant"; *goy*, "gentile"; *mazal tov!*, "good luck," "congratulations," literally "good planet"; *lehayím!*, "to your health," literally "to life"; *Kol Nidre*, "All Vows"; *koshér*, ritually proper, along with the *shachét*, who is the ritual slaughterer; *matzáh*, unleavened bread, with its plural *matzóth* or *matzót; menoráh*, the seven-pronged candlestick; *Purím*, the Feast of Lots celebrating Esther's rescuing of the Jews from the holocaust decreed for them by the Persian prime minister, the date of which was being set by casting lots; *shofár*, the ram's horn; *yovél*, giving us "jubilee"; *Sukkót*, the Feast of Tabernacles; *Talmúd*, "learning," of which *talmid*, "student," is a variant; *Toráh*, "law, science"; *Pésach*, Passover, and *Séder*, its ritual meal (literally "order," "arrangement"; the foods are served in a given order).

Even a few of the familiar Jewish family names become clear with a little knowledge of Hebrew. *Cohén*, for example, is "priest." *Katz*, a common Jewish name that many assume to be German or Yiddish for "cat," is in reality the anagram of *Kohén Tzédek*, "priest of righteousness." *Levi* (or *Levy*), a member of one of the Twelve Tribes of Israel, appears in our *Levi's*, pants of a material made for tents, which a Jewish peddler named Levy was unable to dispose of for its original purpose. *Mizráhi* is literally "easterner" (from *mizráh*, "east").

Those who have gone a little deeper into Hebrew lore (or perhaps into the theater and literature) will recall that the *dibbúk*, the spirit that takes possession of a living body, is literally an "adherent"; that the *gólem*, "shapeless one," "dummy," is the legendary creation of the sixteenth century rabbi of Prague, Juda Loew; that the *Hasidím* are the "pious ones"; that *get*, "divorcement," may be the source of *ghetto* (the alternative etymology being the Italian *borghetto*, "little borough," "city ward").

News items have made most of us familiar with a number of Hebrew political expressions: *Knésset*, the Israeli parliament, means "assembly"; *Magén Davíd*, "Shield of David," the six-pointed star that serves as a symbol and appears on the Israeli flag; *sábra*, a native-born Palestinian Israeli (the word is originally Arabic and literally means "cactus"; the explanation is that it is spiny outside but sweet inside); *kibbútz*, the farming settlement, from the same root as *kvutzáh*, "group." The Hebrew greeting, *shalóm*, corresponding to the kindred Arabic *salaam*, means "peace"; to it may be appended *aléhem* (*aleikum* in Arabic), "to you."

Of special interest to the etymologist is the process whereby Hebrew has added and continues to add to its word stock so as to cover present-day conditions and activities. Here the same processes are operative that appear in all languages. Ancient meanings are transformed into new ones, as when *ótzer*, the old word for "restraint," gets to mean "curfew." *Séret*, once "ribbon," now also means "film." *Hashmál*, Ezekiel's Biblical "source of light," now is used for "electricity." Variants of ancient forms are used with new meanings for new concepts: *hug* is the word for "circle"; *hayég* is "to dial" the phone; *tsélem*, the ancient "image," gives rise to *tsalém*, "to photograph"; *shakáf*, "to watch attentively," produces *mishkafáim*, "eyeglasses"; *et*, "time," is modified into *ittón*, "newspaper."

There are curious word combinations. *Qatsér*, "short," gives rise to *qatsranút*, "shorthand." *Qol* is "voice" and *nóa* is "motion"; combined into *qolnóa*, they mean "movies"; *nóa* also combines with *qatán*, "small," to produce *qatnóa*, "moving object," the designation for "scooter." *Beth charosheth*, "house of craftsmanship," has been adopted for "factory." *Mechqár garini*, "nuclear research," is composed of the root CH-Q-R, "to search," plus the noun *garín*, "kernel."

But in addition, Hebrew being a Semitic language of three-consonant roots, it is easy to coin words out of them. The root of *B-R-Q*, "lightning" (with interchange of *B* and *V*) has been used to coin the word for "telegram," *mivráq*. The ancient root that means "to ride an animal," *R-K-V*, has given rise to *rakévet*, "train"; *L-V-H*, "to accompany," has given birth to *lavyán*, "satellite"; *R-M-Z*, "to hint" or "light," has produced *ramzór*, "traffic light"; *N-G-F*, "to strike," has gone on to *nagíf*, "virus"; *CH-B-L*, "to wreck," has produced *chabaláh*, "sabotage." *Gofríth* was "sulphur" in the ancient tongue; from its root comes the word for a modern match, *gafrúr*.

Then there are loan translations and loan words from the European tongues: *oféret*, "lead," gives rise to *iparón*, "pencil"; here perhaps the influence of German *Bleistift*, with its "leaden stick" idea, is at work. And Hebrew is not averse to taking words directly out of other languages: "to flirt" is *le-flartét*, "to bluff" is *le-baléf*, "to telephone" is *le-talfén*.

The influence of English on Hebrew slang is apparent when erratic driving is called "Chicago"; an aggressive woman is "bulldozer"; a wide-hipped girl has a large "tender" ("tender" also means pickup truck); a flat tire and an accidental pregnancy are both called "pancher,"

from the British "puncture"; hitchhiking is "tremp," from
the English "tramp"; and "picnic" is a bring-your-own-food
party.

In what was once Palestine, Ivrit lives side by side with
Arabic; in fact, both languages are official in Israel. What
of those two other widespread Jewish tongues, which most
of the settlers brought with them, Ladino and Yiddish? The
latter was, and still is, much used outside of Israel, to the
point where it gave rise to dialectal variants (Lithuanian,
Galician, Hungarian, Polish, Bessarabian); to a large body
of excellent literature (the names of Sholem Aleichem and
Sholem Asch are well known in America); and even to
separate departments of study in American universities
(Columbia has a Department of Yiddish Language and
Literature).

It was recognized from the very outset that the use of
Jewish popular languages in addition to Hebrew would prove
to be a highly disruptive influence in the new state, creating
cleavages and rivalries. The Israelis today are too civilized
to ban such languages by edict; indeed there are a Yiddish
daily, a Yiddish monthly and a Yiddish publishing house in
Israel, and Yiddish and Ladino programs are broadcast on
the official Israeli radio. At the same time, they give no
official or educational status to Ladino and Yiddish, as they
give to Arabic and even to English, which was until lately
co-official with the two great Semitic tongues.

Nevertheless, lifelong habits are difficult to eradicate.
Elderly Jews who moved to Israel from the ghettos of Poland and Rumania may still be heard using Yiddish among
themselves, though seldom in speaking to the younger generations. There are even a few Yiddish coinages that seem
to have arisen on Israeli soil: *kúmsitz*, "come sit," the
gathering that takes place in the cool of the evening when
the *kibbútz*'s labors are done, and *áyzin*, from German
Eisen, "iron," in the slangy meaning of "strength."

English, though no longer official, is still widely spoken
and understood, but a few phrases of spoken Ivrit will do
the tourist no harm if he chooses to use them. *Shalóm!* and
lehayím have already been presented.

Ma shlomhá (How are you? Literally, "What is your
peace?" To a woman, use *ma shloméh?*)

Tov meód, todá (Very well, thanks)

Umá shlomhá? (And how are you?)

Bóqer tov (Good morning)

Érev tov (Good evening)

Láila tov (Good night)

Todá rabbá (Many thanks)

Hashém shelí (My name is ——)

Naím meód (Pleased to meet you; literally, "Very pleas-
urable.")

Bevaqashá ten li (Please give me ——)

Atá medabér anglít? (Do you speak English?)

Atá mevín ivrít? (Do you understand Hebrew?)

Ken (Yes)

Lo (No; not)

Raq meát (Only a little)

Ma shaá? (What time is it?)

Lehitráot (See you again; good-by)

Mar (or *Adón*) (Mr.)

Gvéret (Mrs., Miss)

chapter seventeen
world pidgins

In one of his plays, George Bernard Shaw has Androcles addressing the Lion in this fashion: "Did um get um awful thorn in um's tootsums wootsums?"

This type of speech, called hypocorism by the scientists, baby talk by the layman, differs in degree but not in kind from the first impression of New York voiced by a Solomon Islands chieftain on a visit here: "Me lookum one big fella place. He high up too much. He alla same one fella mountain."

Hypocorism is what we perpetrate on our young children, who without it would grow up speaking as good English as the adults around them. Concerning it Noah Webster, earliest American authority on the subject, said:

"The silly language called baby talk, in which most persons are initiated in infancy, often breaks out in discourse at the age of forty, and makes a man appear very ridiculous. A boy of six years may be taught to speak as correctly as Cicero did before the Roman Senate."

Pidgin, the adult, international, and interracial version of hypocorism, is what we have done to those adult children who first began to be the "white man's burden" in the seventeenth century, the natives of the trade ports of China, the islands of the Pacific, the west coast of Africa, and many other far-flung localities.

In Shanghai and Hong Kong your ear will be caught by "Numba one first chop" (Chinese-English Pidgin for "superfine") and "Have got wata top side" ("crazy"). In the Solomons and New Guinea it is "Put clothes belong table"

("Set the table") and "Cut 'im grass belong head belong me" ("Cut my hair"). Among the Australian Blackfellows we hear "Sing 'im along dark fella" ("mosquito") and "Big fella talk talk watch 'im that one" ("salesman"). In Samoa it's "Apple belong stink" ("onion" and " 'Im fella coconut 'im bad" ("He has a headache"). In Hawaii a radio performer says to her announcer, "You regla popoki awaawa dis mornin'?" meaning he's a sourpuss. And in West Africa you hear "Who dat man?" for "Who goes there?" and "One-time" for "Hurry up." All this, outside of a few loan-words from native languages, like the Hawaiian *popoki awaawa* above, is English; quite different from the English spoken in New York or London, but English nevertheless, in much the same fashion that "Dadums," "Momsie," "Woofies" and "Bekus pudáy" are English.

The number of Pidgin English speakers throughout the world is estimated at between thirty and fifty million, which is greater than the number of speakers of Polish, Dutch, Swedish, or Hungarian; in fact, of all but a handful of the world's major tongues. Pidgin is neither a dead nor a dying language. The Hobart, Tasmania, *Mercury* some time ago stressed the fact that Pidgin is the only means of communication with the natives in certain quite extensive areas. The director of education in Lagos, on the West African coast, says: "In several polyglot areas Pidgin is the only possible medium in the lowest forms of our elementary schools."

The West Pacific high commissioner of Suva, in the Fiji Islands, says: "I am convinced it is a living language which is expanding rapidly and with increasing vitality." During the Second World War the Japanese found it not merely expedient, but necessary to issue millions of propaganda pamphlets in Pidgin, and the Americans, British, and Australians took up the practice as they reconquered the islands. In New Guinea, ever since 1935, a monthly magazine entitled *Frend Belong Mi* has been published by Catholic missionaries; it is completely composed in Pidgin, even to the fiction and crossword puzzles.

The history of Pidgin is a simple one. It began in the trade ports of South China, where some means of common intercourse had to be devised between the Chinese and the Western traders (the word "Pidgin" itself is the Cantonese corruption of the English "business," so that "Pidgin English" is really "business English"). The compromise lay along the line of least resistance, which consisted of using for the most part English words with Chinese word arrangement and syntax. This meant using such expressions as "cow-child" for "girl" and "bull-child" for "boy," disregarding factors of number and gender, making the verb timeless and invariable, and using translations of Chinese classifiers ("fella" in connection with any human being: "one fella Mary" for "a woman"; "piecee" in connection with inanimate objects: "two piecee shirt," for "two shirts"). It would have been almost equally easy to teach the Chinese straight English; but the traders thought the Chinese would learn faster if their pattern of thought and speech was respected in the translation of words. So Chinese-English Pidgin has many picturesque expressions: *all-same*, *blongey* ("belong"), *catchee* ("to have"), *chin-chin* ("worship"), *chop-chop* ("quickly"), *dlinkee* ("drink"), *flower-flag man* ("American"), *fo what?* ("why?"), *larn-pidgin* ("apprentice"), *longside* ("with"), *what side?* ("where?"), *top-side-piecee-Heaven-pidgin-man* ("bishop"), *ah say* ("Englishman"; derived from the English custom of interjecting "I say!" into the conversation), *ah kee* ("Portuguese"; from the Portuguese *aqui*, "here").

Spreading southward, the Pidgin habit progressed to the Pacific islands, where it turned into the Pidgin *par excellence*, Melanesian Pidgin English. This was taken up not only by the copra traders and growers, but also by missionaries, and religious instruction was soon imparted in the new medium. Then it moved on to Australia, New Guinea, Samoa, and Hawaii.

But the variety current in the Melanesian islands (Solomons, Fiji, New Hebrides, etc.) is the most widespread. This linguistic form, which in some localities has become fully standardized and has even been reduced to rules of grammar and syntax, has forms at least as picturesque as those of China. A few of them are: *Water he kai-kai him* ("The water ate him up," "He drowned"); *Man belong bullamacow him stop* ("The butcher is here"); *This fellow hat belong you?* ("Is this your hat?"); *What for you kinkenau knife belong me?* ("Why did you swipe my knife?").

It is uncertain whether the West African variety of Pidgin was derived from or influenced by the Pacific branch. The nature of Pidgin is such that it could well have arisen independently in separate parts of the globe. In fact, there are several forms of bastardized English which are definitely known to have no connection with the main Pidgin stock. There are, for instance, the American Indian forms used upon our own aborigines in the days of colonization. "How?" "paleface," "heap big chief," "firewater," "plentum," interspersed with authentic native terms like "squaw," "papoose," "wampum," "wigwam," "moccasin," are fair samples of this pidgin language which died a-borning.

The Ningre-Tongo, or "Talkie-Talkie" of Dutch Guiana, the Kitchen Kaffir of South Africa, the Anglo-Indian, or "Hobson-Jobson" of India, from which we have gotten such words as "bungalow," "curry," and "tiffin," the Chinook jargon of the Pacific Northwest, the Afro-American Gullah of South Carolina, are all cases in point, proving that English can be pidginiz d in separate and unrelated corners of the globe. *Pochismo*, a queer dialect spoken along the Mexican border and extensively used by our border patrols in their dealing with Mexican migrants, makes use of such English loan-words as *bebi* ("baby"), *yaque* ("jack"), *lonche* ("lunch"), *pene* ("penitentiary"), *traque* ("track"), and *huachar* ("to watch").

There are not only numerous varieties of Pidgin English, but also Pidgins of other tongues. The most important of these is Pidgin Malay, called by the Dutch *pasar* (or *bazaar*) *Malay*, a compromise form of various Malayo-Polynesian dialects, which extends throughout the Malay Peninsula, the Republic of Indonesia, and is spoken as far as the Philippines; it is this Malay which forms the backbone of the world's most recent national language, Indonesian.

A *Petit-Nègre* (French Pidgin) appears in French West Africa, side by side with West African English Pidgin. Several forms of Portuguese Pidgin are in existence, both on the West African coast and in many cities of India. A Tagalog-Spanish Pidgin appears in the Philippines. *Papiamento* is a picturesque Spanish Pidgin used by the native population of Curaçao, in the Dutch West Indies. The French Creole of Haiti and Louisiana, the Dutch Creole of Georgetown and the Virgin Islands, the Portuguese Creole of the Cape Verde Islands, are also forms of Pidgin. The Afrikaans spoken by the South African Boers is a debased form of Dutch, pidginized by contact with the natives, but it has finally achieved the status of an official language.

Earlier in history we have the *Lingua Franca* of the Mediterranean, a pidginized form of Italian combined with elements taken from French, Greek, and Arabic, which was widely used by medieval and Renaissance traders and sailors. Before that came the literary Franco-Venetian of the thirteenth century *jongleurs,* who devised a linguistic compromise between French and Italian so that they could bring the rich tradition of the French *chansons de geste* to the avid ears of Italian audiences.

But Pidgin English surpasses them all, both in number of speakers and in territorial extent. It possesses a certain picturesque quality, even a majestic rhythm, which make it impossible to forget once you have heard it. Consider, for instance, the terse directness that transpires from this address, made to the natives by a physician sent by the Rockefeller Foundation to the Melanesian Islands to eradicate the hookworm:

"Master belong me, 'im make 'im altogether kerosene, 'im make 'im altogether benzene. Now he old fella. He got 'im plenty too much belong money. Money belong 'im allasame dirt. Now he old fella, close up 'im he die finish. He look about. 'Im he think, 'Me like make 'im one fella something, he good fella belong altogether boy he buy 'im kerosene belong me.' Now gubment he talk along master belong me. Master belong me 'im he talk, 'You, you go kill 'im altogether snake belong belly belong boy belong island.' "

Or, to take another sample, here is the account of the wedding of Princess Elizabeth (now Queen Elizabeth) that appeared at Lae, in New Guinea:

"Good news 'e come up long England. Long Friday twentieth November, number one piccininni belong king belong you and me, King George VI long England, 'e marry. Now number one piccininni belong 'e marry. 'Im 'e got two piccininni, Misses Princess Elizabeth now Princess Margaret Rose. Now Princess Elizabeth 'im 'e got marry long one fella man name belong Duke Edinburgh. All 'e hurrah much long this fella princess."

Other interesting samples come from New Guinea: *Capsize 'im coffee along cup* ("Pour the coffee"); *New fella moon 'e come up* ("It's the first of the month"); *Skin belong you 'im stink* ("You need a bath"); *Make 'im die machine* ("Stop the machine"); *Two clock he go finish, three clock 'e no come up yet* ("It's half past two"); *Shoot 'im kaikai* ("Serve the dinner"); *Me cross too much along you* ("I'm very angry at you").

Among quaint and suggestive individual expressions, we find: *Time belong limbu-limbu* ("holiday"); *kiranki* ("irritable"); *dim-dim* ("white man"); *lap-lap* ("calico waistcloth"); *make 'im paper* ("contract"); *clothes-sleep* ("pajama"); *long long along drink* ("drunk"); *machine belong talk* ("typewriter"); *cow oil* ("butter"); *turn 'im neck belong 'im* ("change one's mind"); *pants belong letter* ("envelope"); *screw belong leg* ("knee"); *pull-pull* ("flower").

Pidgin is spoken slowly, emphatically, even majestically, and in a very loud voice. Also, regrettably, it is chock full of profanity and obscenity. This, of course, is the heritage of the traders and soldiers, not at all of the missionaries, who steadfastly but vainly strive to eradicate it. An American officer stationed in the Solomons reported that on one occasion a native chieftain observed with growing astonishment the vast amount of supplies that came off the American ships. Finally he could stand it no longer. "Mission fella man," he remarked to the officer, " 'im 'e say God make everything. Bull —! America make everything!" But most Pidgin speakers, proud of their recently won Christianity, aver: "Me belong Big Fella along top!"

Imagery, both profane and poetic, abounds in Pidgin. A piano is "Hit 'im in teeth, out come squeal allasame pig." A violin is "Scratch 'im in belly, out come squeak allasame pussycat." An intellectual is "think fella too much." An automobile is "eat 'im wind cart," and a train "big fella firesnake."

A characteristic process of Pidgin is that of repetition to express intensity or thoroughness. *You go go go* ("keep on going"); *bamboo belong look-look* ("spyglass"); *wash wash* ("to bathe," in contradistinction to mere "wash"); *talk-talk* ("long palaver," as against mere "talk"). This is reminiscent of what goes on in many more cultured tongues, like Italian *piano piano* ("very softly").

Other curious parallels appear: *me-fella, you-fella, 'em-all* (respectively for "we," plural "you," "they," like southern "you-all"). *How much clock* for "What time is it?" reminds you of German, from which it may well have been borrowed (Germany had extensive Pacific possessions before the First World War). The Pidgin use of "belly" to denote the seat of the emotions corresponds to the ancient Greek belief that the stomach was the place where the emotions were born and bred. The use of "bone" to denote "courage" (*'Im got plenty bone*), or the lack of courage (*Bone belong 'im allasame water*, meaning "He's scared to death") has a curious similarity to our own use of "backbone" and "spineless," and perhaps even to our "tough."

The Islands have received contributions to their pidgin English from non-English sources. A Frenchman is variously described as *man-a-wi-wi* ("man of *oui, oui*"), *montour* (*bonjour*), *montwar* (*bonsoir*); in Java, he is known as *orang deedong* (*orang* is Malay for "man," while *deedong* is the French *dites donc*). Local variations of pidgin include such different forms as *kai-kai, chow-chow, kau-kau, fu-fu*, used on different islands in the sense of "to eat."

The Australian Blackfellows use a variety of Pidgin that largely coincides with the Melanesian and New Guinea brands, but sometimes contributes its own special expressions: *paper-yabber along big fella hawk* ("airmail"); *kill 'im stink fella* ("disinfectant").

Bèche la Mer, or Sandalwood English, is the form taken by Pidgin in the southern islands of Polynesia (Samoa, Tahiti, etc.). The addition of *-um* to verbs is characteristic (*eatum, callum, catchum*). So are *water belong stink* ("perfume") and *Belly belong me walk about too much* ("I have a stomachache").

Hawaii supplies us with what may be described as our own American variety of Pidgin. The Hawaiian language does not permit two consonants to follow each other or a consonant to appear at the end of a word. Furthermore, many consonants, including *b, d, f, g, j, r, s, t, v*, do not appear in the language. The result is that when a Hawaiian attempts to say "Merry Christmas!" he comes out with *"Mele Kalikimaka!"* The names of the months, which are all borrowed from English, run as follows: *Ianuali, Pepeluali, Malaki, Apelila, Mei, Iune, Iulae, Aukake, Kemakemapa, Okakopa, Nowemapa, Kekemapa*. Among native words and expressions that have crept into the English of residents from the American continent and thence back to the Continent are: *wahini* ("woman"), *lei* ("wreath"), *no* ("yes") and the famed *aloha oe* ("hello," "good-by").

A measure of topical interest attaches to the Pidgin of India by reason of the fact that India claims to be the third greatest English-speaking nation on earth, with perhaps twenty-five million speakers of English in a country of over four hundred million. Now that Hindi has been made the official language of India, these English speakers will continue to flourish in their evil ways, typified by the *babu*, or "scribe," who wrote to his former employer to bewail the fact that he had found himself "suddenly disemployed," although he had to support a family consisting of "four adults and three adulteresses."

Anglo-Indian Pidgin is also known as Hobson-Jobson. The latter name comes from the Moslem rallying-cry "Ya Hassan! Ya Hussein!" frequently heard in the old communal wars between Moslems and Hindus (Hassan and Hussein are two Moslem saints).

"He's an awful *bahadur*, but he keeps a good *bobachu*" is an Anglo-Indian remark which means that the person being discussed is a terrible "stuffed shirt," but keeps a "good kitchen." Among the local expressions of Hobson-Jobson are *to dumb-cow*, meaning "to browbeat" (derived from Hindustani *dum-khānā*, "to eat one's breath" or "be silent"); *to foozilow* ("flatter"); *to puckerow* ("lay hold of"); *summer heat*, meaning "hat" (but this is derived from Spanish *sombrero*, with a little imaginative crossing); *goddess* for "girl" (from Malay *gādīs*); and the graphic expression for cholera, *mort-de-chien*, which looks like French for "dog's death," but is actually an adaptation of Marathi *modwashī*.

Many words have entered standard English from Hobson-Jobson: "betel," "mango," "cheroot," "bungalow," "pariah," "gym-khana," "curry," "tiffin," and "griffin" (the last used in the sense of "newcomer"). A colloquialism like "grass widow" is said to have arisen in India, where British officers' wives went off to the cool, grassy hills while their husbands sweltered in the dusty plains below. The slangy "cheese" of "big cheese," "whole cheese," etc., is no cheese at all, but the Hindustani *chīz* ("thing"), and the "dam" of "I don't give a dam" is the Hindustani *dām*, a small coin of India. Among recent additions to English from this source are the British *coggage* ("papers," "documents") and *tiggerty-boo*, the British rival of "O.K.," which comes from Hindustani *tīga* and is said to have been first introduced to England by Lord Louis Mountbatten.

While speaking of Pidgins we ought not to forget our own immigrant dialects, which generally appear in double form, an English one distorted by foreign sounds and syntax, and a foreign-language one crammed full of American words adapted to the foreign sound pattern. It is the former that is of particular interest to us in this discussion, but the potentialities of the latter are not to be disregarded.

Foreign-language newspapers published in America were in former years composed in hybrid tongues which often could not be understood by European readers of the same languages. Advertisements used to appear in Italian-language papers for *lotti* and *plotti* ("lots" and "plots"; the correct Italian equivalent would have been *appezzamenti di terreno*), *grosserie* ("grocery stores"; *pizzicherie* in real Italian), *sciabolatori* ("shovelers," instead of the legitimate *sterratori*). The spoken Italian of the immigrants sported such forms as *ghenga di loffari* ("gang of loafers," instead of *banda di fannulloni*), *sanamagogna* ("son of a gun"), and *Broccolino* ("Brooklyn"). The Spanish of Mexican and Puerto Rican immigrants teems with expressions like *jatqueque* ("hot cake"), *te y ponque* ("tea and pound cake"), *lleñeral* ("ginger ale") *coctel* ("cocktail"), *champú* ("shampoo"), *fanfurria* ("frankfurter"), even *jamachi* ("How much?"). *Girabague* and *Anca Same* are the Portuguese immigrant versions of "jitterbug" and "Uncle Sam." *Papier nouvelles* is the literal translation of "newspaper," sometimes used in Louisiana French in the place of the legitimate *journal*. A Czech-language film produced in Hollywood with Czech-American actors was rejected in Prague on the ground that it was incomprehensible to people who knew only "Czech Czech," and had to be redubbed.

When the foreign immigrant attempts to speak English, which he must do with native Americans, immigrants from other countries than his own, and even his fellow nationals who come from a different dialect area, a form of Pidgin generally results. This is primarily a matter of sound substitutions. The foreigner uses, in the place of English sounds to which he is not accustomed, sounds from his own language which are close, but not identical. These substitutions, which occur in 99 per cent of cases where a person attempts to speak a language other than his own, are so distinctive that even the uninitiated can generally tell whether the speaker is accustomed to Italian, Yiddish, German, French, or Spanish. This, in fact, is the basis of our immigrant dialect comedy on the vaudeville stage.

In addition to erroneous sounds, there is confusion in both grammar and vocabulary. The cutting down of long words is common, and some linguists hold that forms like "delish" and "ambish" are due to Italian immigrant influence.

One of our most typical Pidgin languages is Pennsylvania Dutch, which is as perfect a blend of English and German (not

Dutch!) as one could imagine. Pennsylvania German speakers originally came from the Palatinate, and the error in naming their group goes back to our own misuse of the word "Dutch," which comes from *Deutsch*, but which we apply to Hollanders, who never use the term with reference to themselves. *Outen the light* for "Put out the light," *The milk is all* for "There is no more milk," and *The paper wants rain* for "The paper predicts rain" are typical of this dialect in its more Americanized version.

Immigrant languages have been a not inconsiderable source of accretion to the vocabulary of American English, which has to that extent become slightly pidginized. "Pickaninny" is either the Spanish *pequeño niño* or the Portuguese *pequenino* ("small child"); "calaboose" and "hoosegow" are, respectively, *calabozo* and *juzgado*, two Mexican Spanish terms for "jail." "Hamburger" and "frankfurter" come from the names of the German cities where the foods seemingly originated. American slang owes much to German immigrant contacts: "fresh" in the sense of "impudent" is the German *frech;* "crank" and "cranky" come from the German *krank* ("ill"); "spiel" is the German word for "game"; "loafer" may be connected with German *Läufer* ("runner," "footman"); "hoodlum," which first appeared in San Francisco in 1872, is said to stem from a Bavarian dialect *hodalump*. From Yiddish we have gotten such expressions as "fooey," "kibitzer," "What's with you?" and "It shouldn't happen to a dog." Immigrant Italian has contributed such food names as "spaghetti," "ravioli" (which are sometimes horribly pidginized, from the Italian standpoint, by being used with a singular verb, or being repluralized into "spaghettis" and "raviolis"), "zucchini," "broccoli" and "finocchi."

But these loan-words seem to be the only permanent effect that our immigrant Pidgins have upon our national language. Within two or three generations the immigrant dialect disappears, and speakers of pure American English replace the sound-substituting, vocabulary-mixing foreigners.

Two facts stand out significantly in connection with Pidgin. The first is that, far from dying out, it seems to be expanding with abundant vitality. The other is that English seems to lend itself to pidginization more than any other tongue. This causes one to wonder whether there may not be a projection of Pidgin into the future.

Shorn of its picturesque and humorous features, what does Pidgin portend? Does it perhaps point to the shape of things to come, an international language of the future that may eventually do service for universal linguistic exchange, if the world's governments do not forestall it in time by selecting an official world tongue?

Pidgin is indeed a symbol of man's erroneous and inefficient thinking. But it is also a monument to human ingenuity. It displays the multiplicity of wrong roads which the human mind can take, but also the relentless will of man to create understanding under the most difficult of circumstances. When Argentina creates a common tongue of intercourse like Cocoliche out of two related tongues like Spanish and Italian, one need not wonder. But when the faraway corners of the earth produce a meeting ground of understanding out of languages with no common origin or base, like Chinese and English, Melanesian and English, West African and English, there is occasion to marvel. Does the phenomenon perhaps indicate that human beings, left to their own devices and freed from artificial, government-inspired propaganda (even if the latter is disguised as a plea for linguistic and cultural purity), would seek and find comprehension and, eventually, tolerance? The implications are best left to the sociologist.

It remains for the linguist to explain why English, more than any other language, has developed Pidgin forms. The reason lies in part, but only in part, in the greater aggressiveness in navigation and colonization of the English-speaking peoples. Actually, one must remember that seafaring and colonization were far from being the exclusive prerogative of English speakers in the sixteenth, seventeenth, and eighteenth centuries. French, Dutch, Portuguese, and Spaniards did as much as the English in the way of discovery, exploration, navigation, and trading. Yet the Pidgin forms to which their languages gave rise are scanty in number and geographical extent as compared with the imposing mass of Pidgin English.

The real fact of the matter seems to be that among all Western languages, English most readily lends itself to pidginization—that is, to simplification and distortion which make the language accessible to foreign groups without at the same time removing it from the comprehension of its own native speakers.

In part, this is due to the fact that English has already reduced flectional endings, verb forms, and complications of gender, number and case almost to a minimum. If one is compelled by reason of ignorance to forego grammatical and syntactical correctness and literary expression, he can nevertheless make himself understood in English by a mere use of vocabulary. This is hardly true of the other great Western languages. A comparison between Pidgin English and the Pidgin French of Louisiana or Haiti makes this quite evident. An English speaker can get the gist of a Pidgin English passage, but a French speaker needs special instruction to understand Pidgin French, where the abolition of endings results in practical lack of understanding.

The willingness of English to grant naturalization to foreign words also plays a part. All languages accept borrowed words from other tongues, but no other great Western language does so to the same astounding degree as our own. This means that the primitive group that chooses, in a Pidgin English pattern, to insert its own distinctive words, like the *kai-kai* and *kinkenau* of the Melanesians, may do so, and have its choice respected and quietly accepted by the English speakers with whom it comes in contact. English has adhered to this process of linguistic liberalism since its very inception, when Anglo-Saxon borrowed words like "street", "cheese", "kiln" and "minster" from Latin; "bishop", "church" and "angel" from Greek; "they", "knife", "husband" and "ugly" from Scandinavian; "bald", "crag", "crock" and "bard" from Celtic.

Much has been said in recent times of Basic English and its paraphrasing process, whereby a limited number of words, by a method of constant repetition and ingenious combination, is made to do the work of a much larger vocabulary. The analogy with Pidgin is striking. In Pidgin, too, a word like "belong" does service for "of," the possessive case, and a vast number of other intricate constructions.

Basic, however, goes no farther than to attempt to simplify the process of vocabulary learning so as to insure acceptance of English by foreign speakers. Pidgin, on the other hand, points to what is possibly an additional, though unspoken, desire on the part of foreign speakers—a desire for further simplification of English grammar and syntax, something that will remove the stumbling block presented by such verb forms as "see," "saw," "seen," irregular plurals like "oxen," "mice," "children," complex subordinate clauses and prepositional phrases. Perhaps what is needed is some system of "model English" offering an invariable present tense always in the

infinite form ("I be," "he be," instead of "I am," "he is")
a past tense invariably formed with "did" ("I did see" for
"I saw"), and plurals that are always regular ("childs" and
"deers" for "children" and "deer").

Whether such deliberate pidginization of English would be
worthwhile, whether it would prove acceptable, whether it
would not arouse competition of a similar nature from other
languages, is something that would have to be carefully
studied. In the meanwhile, Pidgin English stands as a marker
of man's linguistic frailty and linguistic ambition, a living
tribute to those forces within man which impel him to seek the
understanding of his fellow man, at any cost, and by any
method available.

A few Pidgin expressions may come in handy for the
tourist:

"What do you want?" *You look out 'im wuh name someting?*

"I want." *Me like.*

"Bring me." *"Kiss 'im, ee come."*

"Bring me some milk." *Kiss 'im soo-soo, ee come.*

"Bring me some eggs." *Kiss 'im kee-au, ee come.*

"Bring me some vegetables." *Kiss 'im sah-yoo, ee come.*

"Bring me some water." *Kiss 'im water belong drink, ee
come.*

"How much?" *By 'n' by me buy 'im long how mas mark?*

"Too much!" *Dis fella someting, ee no eenup along (five
fella mark).*

"Yes." *Ee got.*

"No." *No got.*

"Do you understand?" *You savvy?*

"I don't understand." *Me long-long,* or *Me no har 'im good,*
or *Me no har 'im savvy.*

"Speak more slowly." *You no can talk hurry up,* or *Talk
easy.*

"Come here." *You come* (add *hurry up* if you want quick
action).

"What do you call this in Pidgin?" *Wuh name someting
'ere,* or *Dis fella someting belong wuh name?*

"How do you say — in Pidgin?" *Dis fella someting white
man ee call 'im wuh name?*

"What is your name?" *Call 'im name belong you.*

"Never mind." *Mahs kee.*

"I'm an American"   *Me man belong 'Merica.*
"Where is (are)?"   *Where stop—? or, —ee stop where?*
"It's very far."   *Man, ee go go go go go.*
"Where is the hotel?"   *House drink, ee stop where?*
    the rest room?   *House peck peck, ee stop where?*
    the church?   *House loh-too, ee stop where?*
    the village?   *Place belong kanaka, ee stop where?*
"Where is the dwelling house?"   *House married, ee stop where?*
"This way."   *'Im, ee stop along hap* (with a gesture).
"When did he come?"   *By 'n' by, sun, ee stop where; now man, ee come up.*

(The answer is a gesture pointing to the point in the sky where the sun is, was, or will be at the time of the occurrence, accompanied by the words: *Sun, ee stop allasame*).

"I" is *me,* "we" is *me fella* if the person addressed is excluded, *you-me* if he is included; "you" is *you, you two fella,* or *you fella,* according to whether you want a singular, dual or plural; "he" or "she" is *'im,* but "they" is *all.* For the possessive ("my," "mine," "your," "his," etc.), put *belong* before the personal pronouns above.

A few picturesque expressions that have not already appeared:

"sea," *soda water*
"swamp," *gi-roun ee no strong*
(*Gi-roun* is "ground," and *dee-wigh* is "tree.")
"boy," *monkey*
"with," *one time along*

"good," *good fella*
"large," *big fella*
"right," *shoot*
"high," *too mas* (*mas* is "much")
"clean," *clean fella*
"full," *full-up*

"year," *Christmas*
"fruit," *pickaninny belong dee-wigh*

"girl," *monkey mary*
"in front of," *along eye belong*

"bad," *no good*
"small," *liklik*
"left," *arm no good*
"low," *ee down*

"dirty," *ee got dirty*
"empty," *noting* ("nothing")

Armed with all this, we can proceed to the Solomons, and say: *Me fella go go go along island; now me fella savvy talk belong island.*

71 72 73 10 9 8 7 6 5 4 3 2 1